YVONNE-AIMÉE OF MALESTROIT: AN EXTRAORDINARY LOVE

RENÉ LAURENTIN

Yvonne-Aimée of Malestroit

An Extraordinary Love

TRANSLATED BY JIM GALLAGHER

Angelico Press

For information, address:
Angelico Press, Ltd.
169 Monitor St.
Brooklyn, NY 11222
www.angelicopress.com

ppr 979-8-89280-063-1
cloth 979-8-89280-064-8
ebook 979-8-89280-065-5

Book and cover design
by Michael Schrauzer

CONTENTS

BY HIS LETTER OF DECEMBER 10, 1984 Cardinal Ratzinger, Prefect of the Congregation for the Doctrine of the Faith, lifted the ban on giving an imprimatur "to any possible future publication about Mother Yvonne-Aimée" that had been imposed by his predecessor Cardinal Ottaviani on June 16, 1960. So, having examined it, I deemed that I could authorize this work by Canon René Laurentin. The approval granted by Cardinal Ratzinger is only for this book. It may not be assumed that this decision extends to other publications. On the other hand, nothing has changed regarding the Cause for Beatification which the Prefect of the Holy Office declared in 1960 to be "stopped definitively." The personality of this religious and the circumstances that brought out her exceptional qualities cannot be excluded from historical research. That is why the positive judgment of the Cardinal Prefect of the Congregation for the Doctrine of the Faith is welcomed with pleasure and gratitude.

Imprimatur
February 3, 1985
✠ P. A. Boussard
Bishop of Vannes

LETTER FROM THE AUTHOR
TO THE CONGREGATION FOR
THE DOCTRINE OF THE FAITH

THIS SHORT BOOK AIMS TO RESPOND TO the needs of Christians, both lay and religious, who owe much to Mother Yvonne-Aimée—conversions, vocations, interior or physical healings—and who are deprived of being able to get to know her better since all works about her have been withdrawn from sale since 1960.

This biography was written with the goal of not neglecting anything nor hiding anything important, while also keeping it short.

It is based on a dossier of 30,000 documents, meticulously filed in chronological order.

In light of the decree of the Congregation for the Doctrine of the Faith of June 1, 1960 (Prot. N 336/55/1)[1] this work was carried out *sub secreto*, in the hope of obtaining permission to publish it, which Cardinal Seper envisaged in his letter of April 29, 1980 in reply to the request of Sister Nicole Legars, Prioress of Malestroit (Prot. N 336/55):

"I am pleased to inform you that after consideration our dicastery willingly agrees to your request. To write such a biography, it seems to us that you could approach Canon René Laurentin, whose qualities in this field are well known. Our Congregation asks, nevertheless, that the manuscript of the planned book be submitted to it before its publication" (1980, no. 14).

Cardinal Ratzinger gave even more reason to hope, examination of the file having revealed the unforeseen and short-lived circumstances that had led to the publishing ban which was intended to avoid all danger of illuminism.

The clearing of Sister Faustina Kowalska,[2] whose exceptional life had led to similar restrictions, encour-

---

[1] Every item produced by a Vatican office has a protocol number.
[2] Maria Winowska, *Droit a la miséricorde, Vie de sœur Faustine* (Paris: Saint-Paul, 1958). Maria Winowska, *L'icône du Christ miséricordieux, Message de sœur Faustine* (Paris: Saint-Paul Religious Editions, 2006).

aged us in our task. God does not abandon his true servants and it is a joy to bring that to light, when it is so obvious.

It is in this spirit and this hope that this book is submitted to the examination of the Congregation for the Doctrine of the Faith.

R. Laurentin, September 8, 1984

Following this request, on December 10, 1984 the Congregation for the Doctrine of the Faith lifted the above-mentioned decree for this book (and this book alone). It authorized Bishop Boussard of Vannes to give the Imprimatur. The author expresses his thanks to Cardinal Ratzinger, to the Congregation for the Doctrine of the Faith and to Bishop Boussard, who was keen to oversee and advise with a stimulating demand for excellence and detail throughout all the stages of this work.

ACKNOWLEDGMENTS

WE WISH TO THANK THOSE WHO GRANTED permission for this book and those who helped it see the light of day.

H. E. Cardinal Joseph Ratzinger and the Congregation for the Doctrine of the Faith who examined the text and who, for this book, lifted the ban on publishing anything about Sister Yvonne-Aimée.

H. E. Cardinal Paolo Bertoli, Prefect Emeritus of the Congregation for the Causes of Saints, who was prefect May 1969 to March 1973. He was Cardinal-Bishop of Frascati from 1979 until his death in 2001.

Rt. Rev. Pierre Auguste Boussard, Bishop of Vannes, who assisted us with wise advice and gave the imprimatur.

The foundational convent of Dieppe and all the convents of the Augustinian Hospitallers of the Mercy of Jesus.

Sister Nicole, Prioress of Malestroit, who long desired this book and supported its undertaking from the start.

Rt. Rev. Guy-Marie Lamy de la Chapelle, Abbot of Notre Dame abbey in Tournay, who supported the project in various ways.

Miss Yvonne Bato, Miss Andrée Labéraudrie and the contemporaries, relatives and friends of Sister Yvonne-Aimée, whose living memory of her was always illuminative.

Rev. Fr. Paul Labutte, who shared generously his personal knowledge of Sister Yvonne-Aimée, his own research, archives and writings.

Dr. Suzanne Loth-Guéry, Yvonne-Aimée's friend and physician.

Dr. Patrick Mahéo, who contributed his medical expertise.

Sister Marie of Christ, who compiled the dossier of all the medical aspects of this book.

Mr Pierre Jeanneau for his graphological expertise, Francoise Courtin-Dutroux for her input on the morphopsychology, and Dr. Roger Ermiane for the prosopology of Sister Yvonne-Aimée.

Mr Victor Rajalu, photo editor.

Bernadette Lutrat, who conducted the genealogical research.

Sister Marie-Bernard, Sister Marie-Colette and Miss Marie-Thérèse Olivard, who typed up all our notes and the text of this book.

Rev. Fr. Jean Rolland for his incisive revision.

To the memory of:

Rt. Rev. François Kervéadou (†1983), Bishop emeritus of Saint-Brieuc et Tréguier, who supported the beginnings of this project.

H. E. Cardinal Franjo Seper (†1981) who granted me permission to write this book. Cardinal Seper was Prefect of Congregation for the Doctrine of the Faith from January 1968 until John Paul II accepted his resignation on November 25, 1981. He died in the Gemelli Hospital on December 30, 1981. ☙

WHY THIS BOOK?

YVONNE BEAUVAIS (1901–1951), WHO IN 1927 became Sister Yvonne-Aimée de Jésus, Augustinian Hospitaller of Mercy, founded and was the first Superior General of the federation of monasteries of her order. In doing so she created a model which Pope Pius XII adopted and spread throughout the Church. He saw it as one of the successes of his pontificate.

In France Mother Yvonne-Aimée is known as a national heroine—not as a combatant but because the hospital where she tended the wounded of both sides was open to everyone in need, even beyond what was possible! She saved the lives of many members of the French Resistance who were in danger, thereby risking her own life and that of her sisters. She was decorated with the highest honors—both French and foreign—of the Second World War. General de Gaulle himself presented her with the Legion of Honor.

That is only the visible part of a life inspired throughout by a total gift of self to God alone.

At the age of ten, Yvonne based her young life upon the singular love of Jesus Christ. Irresistibly inspired by the desire to "love him more than everyone," to give him not less than everything and to unite herself unreservedly to the Cross of Christ, she never separated love of God from love of neighbor—especially the poor, her first friends, the first served—right from her youngest childhood. She combined her burning search for Christ with a truly effective human and apostolic attention to everyone, in a constant and almost excessive renunciation of herself. Her successes appeared audacious to those who knew not the price she paid for them. She bore fruit in the long term. Since I've begun studying her I meet people daily who tell me that they owe their vocation, their conversion, their healing, or quite simply their escape from death to her and the risks she took.

Why have so many paradoxes on the surface hidden the clarity of these deep waters?

Her exceptional quality was misunderstood. Even from childhood, misunderstandings, failures, accusations, and calumnies were often her lot and they came back again, ever more seriously up until 1943 and the approach of her death in 1951. But her accusers, in varying degrees, recanted their objections or illusions about her. One has to wonder how, in those oppressive and negative conditions, her works and the very stability of her own life did not suffer but in fact bore such admirable fruit, which continues to our day. And how the amazing tally of physical, emotional, and supernatural sufferings that she was subjected to never changed her infectious joy and her radiance. And how the extraordinary respect that she had for each individual led not to anarchy but to an interior, harmonious, and spontaneous communion.

Why was it that this exemplary life had to be subjected to extraordinary and disconcerting supernatural phenomena? We find in her almost the entire collection of charisms and extraordinary gifts recounted in the annals of sanctity. And let us not forget the vengeance of the infernally supernatural, as if God had given the Prince of Darkness free reign over her as with Job in the Bible. These remarkable tangible supernatural phenomena took place despite her aversion to them. She saw them as a burden, often an overwhelming one. She asked to be freed from them, to return to a normal situation. She managed to keep knowledge of them confined to just a few close intimates, necessary to help her in her commitments and exceptional difficulties.

But after her death, people began to talk. The press latched onto the most sensational aspects, which were also the most superficial. The Congregation for the Doctrine of the Faith, keen to stamp out any outbreak of illuminism, which the tragic circumstances of the war had favored, judged it prudent to cut short any such risk, so that nothing unhealthy or misleading should arise after the departure of Mother Yvonne-Aimée. It stopped the cause for her beatification and forbade any publication about her.

That momentary measure was in no way aimed against her, and the reasons for it are no longer relevant.

And so Cardinal Seper, shortly before his death, granted permission to Sister Nicole for a "biography" to be written by Father Laurentin and submitted to the Congregation for the Doctrine of the Faith before publication. After four years of work along with Dom Bernard Billet, the former Superior General Sister Marie Emmanuel, Sister Odile, Sister Marie Bernard, and other helpers in the community, the biography was completed and brought to Rome by Father Laurentin on October 3, 1984. The ban previously communicated to the Bishop of Vannes and the French episcopate was lifted for this book.

This authorization only makes sense on condition that it avoid all the dangers or errors that the said ban wanted to prevent. Mother Yvonne-Aimée herself deserves that. Her life was centered on Christ alone, according to love alone, at the service of others, for whom she sacrificed—like Saint Paul before her—her desire to leave this world in order to be with Christ. Everything else, for her, was superfluous.

This brief life, based on a chronological dossier of 30,000 documents, aims only to present briefly the evidence demanded by historical honesty and the evaluation of facts, according to the traditional norms of theology and of mysticism.

1. Mother Yvonne-Aimée's life gives the lie to the too-widespread supposition that mysticism is akin to a dream world. Architects, doctors, military men, bishops, and priests who had dealings with her were struck by her exemplary pragmatism.

2. This pragmatism was proven in difficult and sometimes impossible conditions (at least during the war) spanning three continents. It combined, without fail, God's reality and human reality—which are inseparable according to the lived model of the Incarnation (1 Jn 4:10–11, 19–21; 5:1–3).

3. The Cross and the Passion have their place there, right at the forefront.

4. Love and giving were everything for her, in the forgetting of self. Everything else was extra.

xviii   Yvonne-Aimée of Malestroit

The love story between God and Yvonne-Aimée was the single axis of her life. It will be the axis of this short biography, which does not claim to cover all her work, writings, words, multiple activities, and countless fruits.

It has not erased the unusual and the marvelous, which are a fact in the life of Yvonne-Aimée. This fact was imposed on her, despite herself, and it never deviated from or disturbed the essential.

But this "unusual" or out-of-the-ordinary should not dominate the story. And it must above all not obscure the essential, as happened in the press in the 1950s. To this end, this short biography endeavors to discern the functional role of these exceptional phenomena in the life and work of Yvonne Beauvais.

Our ongoing critical studies[1] have begun to assess these extraordinary supernatural aspects with an open mind which excludes no hypothesis. Theoretically these wonders can be attributed to different causes:

—traps of the devil, as some adversaries thought;

—subjectiveness: deception or "feminine hysteria," as Father Rouquette suggested without ever having had access to a single file;

—unknown natural causes: along the lines of parapsychology and "clairvoyant abilities" as they're sometimes called for lack of a better definition.

—finally, has God once again been able to confound "the wisdom of the wise"? Could he have wanted to teach the strict (and often corrosive) rationalism of our day some extraordinary lessons to do with childhood (as in the gospel) and human love which flourishes in the language of mystics?

In their current stage these works exclude the possibility of self-deception. Mother Yvonne-Aimée was subjected to the most violent temptations from the devil, overcame his most

---

[1] Father Laurentin went on to write other books on Mother Yvonne-Aimée, particularly a study of her bilocations and one about her stigmata.

troublesome traps with strength, and unmasked them. When accused, when somehow compared to possessed abbesses of the Middle Ages, she called herself into question and clearly examined herself in all openness and humility. And finally, her life and her works have borne so many sustained and unquestionable spiritual fruits that the hypothesis of the demonic is unsustainable. Likewise deception, hysteria, or pretense, which are so contrary to her psychological profile which was pragmatic and completely forgetful of herself, opposed to all vanity or ostentation.

There remains therefore the difficult choice between the causes termed "unknown" about which we can say precisely nothing, in so far as they are unknown, and the work of God. This work is of itself mysterious. The Lord manifests his power only in a sort of chiaroscuro where our technical and rational instruments are put to the test and finally fail.

What our primary methical studies on particularly well-documented points establish is that many unforeseeable predictions are verified in a rigorous and irrefutable manner.

Perhaps we have never had in the annals of mysticism in such a precise and certain manner so many predictions *prior to the event, dated with certainty, incomprehensible to Sister Yvonne-Aimée herself as she formulated them, truly unforeseeable, and yet verified.* That well-established certainty invites us to consider with caution other accounts which, in varying degrees, lack such proof. Here we meet the difficult choices faced daily by those who study the miracles of Lourdes, or the processes of canonization. When God manifests his power in our world it is never in a restricting or geometric way but with a discretion that is always open to challenge by rationalism or even by pure reason.

The Lord who sometimes gives signs of his love and his power, gives them freely and has no interest in satisfying curiosity or scientific requests for verification. He certainly did not answer the scribes or the pharisees when they, as experts, asked him for signs from heaven. (Mt 12:39; Mk 8:12; Lk 11:16)

The real signs from heaven are given to the poor, not to experts. They can only be discerned and welcomed in the sure light of faith.

This "life" duly established, we will let it speak, on verifiable references but without commentary or superstructure. It aims to show, not to argue.

This story has not stopped challenging the author. May it also challenge its readers. It constantly reveals the quality of a love which inspires everything, guides everything, and overcomes everything because it is God's gift. And that is what is important. Why do we have so little love before Christ who loves us so much and wants to give us so much?

A NOTE ABOUT SOURCES

THIS BRIEF BIOGRAPHY RELIED ON A DOS-
sier of approximately 30,000 items, filed in chronological
order. We refer to each, first by year, then followed by the
number of the document within that year. Each year has its
own numbering—from 1 to 927 in the year 1924, for example.
Along with the 30,000 items of this chronological dossier
there are various other items, notably the daily correspondence, amounting to tens of thousands of letters, which has
not ceased since Mother Yvonne-Aimée's death, and the pho-
tographic dossier which contains over 1,000 photos, films, and
a recording of her voice.

We were most reliant on five principal sources.

Yvonne began an autobiographical journal in 1924 and
added to it in 1927. We identify excerpts from this with the
term *Autobiographical Notebook*.

Throughout her life Mother Yvonne-Aimée accumulated
some twenty notebooks and 102 diaries at the rate of two
or three per year. She recorded events as they happened
and made spiritual observations. Passages from these will
simply be indicated by *Notebook*, with the page number or
day, appropriate year, and number.

Abundant information has been gleaned from the above-
mentioned correspondence.

Many of Mother Yvonne-Aimée's contemporaries were
inspired to keep notes of their own observations of her
extraordinary life.

Finally, we have drawn on testimony provided during the
Ordinary Process, that is, the inquiry undertaken with a view
to the eventual beatification of Mother Yvonne-Aimée. This
was carried out from 1957 until 1960 at which point the cause
was halted by decree of the Congregation for the Doctrine
of the Faith.

Other sources that have contributed to a smaller extent
include:

Louis Barral. As postulator of Mother Yvonne-Aimée's cause, Father Barral brought together pertinent information in a collection titled *Articles* (1956), which will be referred to a few times in the following chapters. In 1955, Father Barral also published anonymously *Au service de Jésus, Roi d'amour: Mère Marie Yvonne-Aimée de Jésus.*

René de la Chevasnerie, SJ. Father Chevasnerie was so impressed by the young Yvonne's work with the poor that he insisted on writing three books based on her activities: *Monette et ses pauvres, Monette petite fille,* and *Monette en pension.* In these popular books "Monette" was the discreet alias used to protect Yvonne's identity.

Paul Labutte. Father Labutte painstakingly produced a very complete biography *Yvonne-Aimée, 1901–1951,* in five typed volumes, the result of thorough research in all the places where Yvonne had lived. When we refer to "Labutte," we mean the fifth version, that of 1974.

Henri Monier-Vinard, SJ. Father Monier-Vinard authored the small volume *Le Monastère de Malestroit et la mère Marie Yvonne-Aimée de Jésus.*

And, lastly, Mother Marie-Anne de Jesús Saillour. It was Mother Marie-Anne who composed the report "Très révérende mère Marie Yvonne-Aimée de Jésus: 1901–1951," which we refer to in our citations as *Obituary Notice.* ◉

I

Secrets of Childhood

I

Death of Her Father

J ULY 16, 1901. 6:45 P.M. YVONNE BEAUVAIS
was born at Cossé-en-Champagne (borough of Mayenne,
not Champagne in the district of Laval).

Lucie, the mother, twenty-six years old, valiantly gave birth
at home, as one did in those heroic times. It took place
on the second floor of an old provincial house situated on
the corner of two twisting roads. But the bedroom window opened onto a garden which adjoined fields and open
countryside.

All went well. Yvonne was a bonny baby. Grandma Brulé
brought her down to the kitchen to show the staff: the maid,
Hubert the handyman, and René Buchot, the gardener.

The father, Alfred Beauvais, thirty-four years old, was disappointed. The firstborn was a girl—Suzanne, now two years
old. This time he had wanted a boy. He had no intention of
kissing little Yvonne. He only did it so as not to upset his
wife. But he was an affectionate man—from then on there
would be hugs and kisses aplenty.

October 5, 1901, the Baptism feast (three months after
the sacrament given on July 18) was magnificent. Alfred had
the menu printed in color, Japanese style, with an illustra-
tion of the Mikado. The lavish meal, which was testament
to his oenological and gastronomic competence, included
Potage Crécy aux croutons arrosé de Madère,[1] Marennes
Oysters, with Barsac (1894), three dishes consisting of game
Alfred hunted himself, and a Turban of pineapple flowing
with Champagne (1901, no. 11).

---

[1] A creamy carrot soup garnished with Madeira-infused croutons.

Alfred was a keen huntsman and the best shot in the region. He enjoyed being a sportsman. He had abridged his secondary education to live off his private income, on his lands, close to his roots which he loved.

He was sensitive to the vitality of his second daughter, exuberant and round like him. "My little bubble," he called her tenderly.

Because of his height he did not appear overweight at 220 pounds. He was energetic and vigorous. Warm, generous, obliging, and open-hearted, he was loved by everyone. The domestic staff and the neighbors preferred him to his wife, a dutiful woman, demanding, and strict. One Sunday, lunch for the little maid, Marie, had been overlooked. When she asked for her meal, Mr Beauvais gave her a pot of rillettes[2] but "Madame took it back," she still remembered at the age of ninety-five in 1984.

To bring up his growing little family, Mr Beauvais' private income was not enough. He started a wine business. But alas, in the Spring of 1904 his health declined. His sight diminished. Then it failed completely. It was a blind man that the "little bubble," soon to be three years old, met when coming to play on his bed.

"Dear Daddy, do you see me?"

Reduced to powerlessness, he learned that the surety generously given to a friend had completed his bankruptcy.

"Sorry! Sorry for the situation I'm leaving you in with our two girls," he said to Lucie.

He died on October 17, 1904 at 10:00 P.M. Thirty-eight years old. He was mourned by everyone.

He had lived the high life. His wife would now work to pay for it. That was her temperament. The debts were there. They had to be honored. She put the house up for sale, and all its contents, and finally the carriage and the purebred horse which only she and her husband had dared to drive. This means of transport was needed by her in order to see

---

[2] A type of potted meat.

to things quickly. The house was sold by an auctioneer to debtors for 3,515.40 Francs. The widow, maintaining the style from the days of wealth, generously hosted a dinner for the creditors who were encircling her. She was merely the cook and never even appeared at table.

She no longer had a home. Where to go with her two daughters? Her father, Aldric Brulé, opened his house to her at Le Mans. He came to collect her and her little girls from the house with no furniture.

They let Yvonne keep her big furry rabbit. Lucie drove the carriage to the nearest railway station at Sablé, some twelve miles away. The grandfather, who had come to collect the little girls, took them to dinner at the hotel beside the station. The waitress only had eyes for Yvonne, who was smiling and attractive like her father.

"I love this little one here!" said the waitress.

"Well," replied Yvonne, "hurry up with your loving me; I'm leaving on the seven o'clock train!" (1953, no. 6 and 1956, no. 56) ✿

2

At Grandma's Knee

LE MANS, 1905–1907

LUCIE BEAUVAIS, NOW WITH NO HOME and no furniture, moved in with her parents, Mr and Mrs. Brulé, at Le Mans. Their house was situated in the new quarter of the lower town, 78 rue Montoise, so named because it was on the pilgrimage route to Mont-Saint-Michel.

WORKING MOTHER

Having liquidated all their previous financial assets, Lucie looked for a way to earn a living. For a lady "of society" at that time, this just was not done. Her pragmatic outlook, though, overcame the conventions of the time. She thought first of becoming an Inspector of Works. The social commitments and involvement of her father, a very active city councilor, drew her in that direction. But the urgent needs of imperiled Catholic education, and the advice of her uncle, the Jesuit Father Trégard, pointed her in another direction. Thanks to the Law of Separation, nuns were no longer allowed to teach in schools. Available lay people were needed to take up the baton and carry on this work. Lucie was to do a term at Boulogne-on-Sea.[1] She was hired for the school year starting in October 1905. She would be allowed to bring Suzanne who was now aged six.

AGONIZING WRENCH

But Vonnette, as they called Yvonne, at age four was too young. She would remain at Le Mans.

She begged, "Bring me with you Mommy, bring me!" But her pleas were in vain. It was a heart-wrenching separation. She cried her heart out every night. Grandma did her best to console her.

---

[1] Boulogne-on-Sea is approximately 225 miles from Le Mans.

SHOULD WE IMITATE THE SAINTS?

Grandma walked Yvonne to school, and she "got," or understood, her granddaughter's love of animals. Yvonne knew every cat in the neighborhood.

Grandma loved animals, but people even more so. Especially the poor. And God, of course! It's one and the same thing. Every evening she would read to Vonnette the life of that day's saint. They were printed in a popular publication, adapted by the Bollandists. Grandma's had a green cover.

"I listened really attentively, and it was my heart's desire to become a saint too. Except I didn't know how to go about it. I used to say to myself that as I wasn't rich (we were no longer so since Daddy's death) I couldn't offer up my wealth to God, nor give to the poor. And not being pretty, I couldn't give him beauty. I was still too little to go and live in the desert. I saw somewhere that saints would eat the great big maggots which were sometimes found in rotten fruit and so on. So I resolved to do the same. But my first attempt was disastrous" (*Autobiographical Notebook*, p. 4, 1924, no. 859).

She swallowed with all her might but the stomach, having more sense, rejected the foreign body. "What is to be admired is not always to be imitated," advised Grandma.

MAGGOTS AND CREAM CAKES

The story reveals a great zeal in Yvonne, who enjoyed the finest things.

"I was greedy and proud," she recognized (Ibid.). Yes, Yvonne was avid and desirous. She wanted not less than everything. Her uncle Labéraudrie told her, "I promise to buy you a cream cake for every prize that you win at school."

"At the end of the year I had eight prizes," recounted Yvonne. "I was taken to the cake shop—but after my sixth cake I stopped. That night I was ill!" (Ibid. p. 9)

ONLY JESUS

Neither maggoty fruits nor beguiling cream cakes were her way.

Yvonne learned to choose. And her choice was already Jesus. As they were leaving a visit to the Blessed Sacrament one day she asked her grandma, "Why can't little children receive Communion like the big people?"

"Well, they wouldn't really understand fully," replied Grandma. "You have to wait until the intelligence and will are more developed. In some dioceses First Holy Communion is made at the age of eleven, in others it is at the age of twelve."

"I didn't say anything, but I was sad about having to wait another five years before receiving Jesus into my heart. It seemed to me that despite being only six years old I would perfectly understand the great act I was making in receiving my Jesus. I felt sure that I loved him with all my heart, and that I proved this to him by offering many sacrifices and by mortifying my sinful nature."

READY TO GIVE EVERYTHING FOR JESUS ALONE

"Since that day, every time I passed a church, I would say to him, 'Dear Jesus, come out from your tabernacle and come into my heart!'

"But as I didn't feel anything, I thought that Jesus didn't listen to me because I hadn't been good enough; and I would work at becoming better" (Ibid.).

BETWEEN A VOLTAIREAN AND A FRIEND OF THE SAINTS

Grandpa and Grandma made a good couple, but they were very different. Grandpa's saints were Voltaire and Rousseau. Their portraits had pride of place on the staircase wall. To Grandma, they were "those ugly mugs." But Grandpa never complained about the Christmas Crib.

FRIEND OF THE POOR

Both of them were as one in "a great love for the poor," stressed Yvonne. In this she wasn't content just to follow them; she outdid them.

"Even while I was still very young, Jesus put into my heart a great love for the poor. I couldn't pass by them without my heart being moved with pity. When I didn't have anything on me to give to them, I'd say to them, 'I love you.' And I kissed them. Then I told them how to reach our house. For I knew that they would receive a warm welcome there" (Ibid., p. 5).

Every evening Grandpa and Grandma played a game of backgammon. The stakes of two cents was placed by the winner into the "Poor's prize fund."

One day both grandparents were out. Maria the housemaid dismissed an untimely beggar at the door. "No cents this morning. Come back later!"

But Vonnette ran after the old man. "I know where some pennies are." And she produced the backgammon "prize fund." It was for the poor. Therefore it was his.

"You stole the cents," said Grandpa that evening, chiding "the naughtiest girl in the world." But he was just calling her that to tease her. In fact, he was quite happy. For he saw in her instincts a reflection of his own heart.

As for Maria, she never held any grudge. Forty years later when Yvonne-Aimée was elected Superior General, she wrote her a letter full of affection and memories:

"Children would come to sing Carols at the door. The poor beggars would play tunes to please you. You were so amiable with everyone.

"My neighbor told me about your great conduct during the War. It's beautiful but it doesn't surprise me about you. You were afraid of nothing.... You climbed up trees like a cat. And the tightrope walking at the bottom of the garden!" (Letter from Maria Hamon, January 11, 1949, no. 49)

A little performing acrobat that she had become friends with taught her to walk on a cable suspended between two trees in the garden. Vonnette, who was good at climbing, took to it with ease. So much so that one evening when her little friend was sick and couldn't do her usual evening performance, Vonnette stood in for her, recounts Father René de la Chevasnerie. It might have sounded crazy, but the elderly housemaid was not mistaken when she recalled Vonnette's exploits as a tightrope walker "at the bottom of the garden."

CONNIVANCE WITH THE ANIMALS

There was great joy when Mommy came home for vacation. She saw how Yvonne was progressing—and also her mastery of animals! "One day," she recounted,

> the door of the chicken coop got opened and the hens scattered here, there and everywhere throughout the garden. I tried to round them up to get them back in. To no avail. Grandma came to help. Still no success. I called Yvonne. She came immediately and spoke to the fugitives in an authoritative voice:
>
> "Get back in there this instant! Aren't you ashamed to have made my poor dear Grandma run to and fro?"
>
> And the hens immediately formed into a line, nose to tail, and filed back into their enclosure. At the time I thought it was just that they knew Yvonne better, as she so often looked after them. It was only later I came to understand her power over the animals. She understood them and they understood her. (Lucie Beauvais, January 1953, no. 7) ☙

3
Frustration and Penitence

ARGENTAN, 1907–1909

SAVING CATHOLIC EDUCATION

In 1907 the pressure from Emile Combes[1] tightened its grip around Catholic education. Mrs. Beauvais, a laywoman who was both competent and confident, was a precious asset. The Sisters of Christian Education at Argentan in Lower Normandy had just set up from scratch the Joan of Arc Institute as a replacement for their boarding school that had been closed down by the Government. They needed a headmistress and appointed Mrs. Beauvais to the post.

This time Yvonne was allowed to come along too, as a boarder. She was happy to be back with her Mommy.

BACK WITH MOMMY—BUT...

On November 8, 1907 Grandma Brulé brought the child to Argentan. Her own heart was breaking but she covered it up and put on a happy face so as not to sadden her granddaughter. With no fanfare and no recorded trace, she had given Yvonne the building-blocks of her spiritual path. History never records the secret impact of grandmothers on the achievements of heroes and saints.

Yvonne's free-spirited nature and behavior was soon put to the test by the structured and disciplined life of school boarders in those times. How to hold her tongue in class?

[1] Emile Combes had studied for the priesthood but quit before ordination. His anti-clericalism would later lead him to become a Freemason. He qualified as a medical doctor and set up in practice. He later entered politics and was elected to the Senate, eventually becoming Minister for Education, and briefly Prime Minister. Through his efforts nearly 10,000 Catholic and other religious schools were closed. Thousands of priests and nuns left France rather than be persecuted. On December 9, 1905 a new law on separation of the Church and the State was passed.

How could she not run up to Mommy for the big hugs she had so long been deprived of? It did not come easy to her bubbly and outgoing nature to suppress her spontaneity.

But she forced herself to do so. And she was pleased with the results of her efforts.

"Dearest Mommy, we've been in class a whole hour and I've managed not to be sent to the 'naughty corner'" (Lucie Beauvais to Father Paul Labutte, January 14, 1954, no. 6).

Mommy was the headmistress of the whole school. Her numerous responsibilities meant she was rarely available to her little daughter who was so longing for affection.

It pained Yvonne:

"Mommy is so busy that she doesn't have any time for me. Even though we live under the same roof I only see her to say Good Morning and Goodnight" (*Autobiographical Notebook*, p. 10, 1924, no. 859).

The one little private moment together that Mrs. Beauvais sometimes managed to snatch with Yvonne was after lunch. But it was short. And soon interrupted by "the bell." "The bell again. The bell, the bell, always the bell," sighed an exasperated Yvonne one day.

> Mommy kept on her desk a very expressive little bust of Jesus crowned with thorns. The sight of it always made me want to weep.
> "You see these big thorns, dear Vonnette," said Mommy. "By your sacrifices you can remove them from Jesus's head."
> We heard the bell ring. (Always the bell!) So I left Mommy quickly so as to make a sacrifice. And when I was halfway up the stairs I called down to her, "Mommy, has that big thorn gone away?" Alas, in the evening the big thorn had come back—through my laziness, or my chatting in class—and Jesus's crown of thorns was as big as ever! (Ibid., p. 11)

FROM TOP OF THE CLASS TO THE BOTTOM

Yvonne was in the "infant class." She was the youngest, two years younger than her classmates. It was difficult for her. At Le

Mans, with other little ones of her own age, she had been top of the class. Now she was at the bottom—not always the very last perhaps but often second-to-last, recounted her teacher Marie-Ange Gautry.

"I'm fourth out of four again," she announced with candor and disappointment to Mommy.

Mrs. Beauvais was not pleased. Suzanne was a brilliant pupil; why wasn't Vonnette following in her sister's footsteps? Mrs. Gautry was asking herself the same question.

"It annoyed me that she wasn't getting there, wasn't succeeding. I'd tell her that she was lazy. I didn't find her an interesting pupil. It seemed that she wasn't interested in the lessons. She was often absorbed in her own thoughts. You got the impression that she couldn't be bothered with life. With the hindsight of sixty years, I wonder if it wasn't the secret hold of God upon her that prevented her from working to the degree that I wanted" (Testimony of Marie-Ange Gautry, October 4, 1968, no. 26).

FIRST CONFESSION

Yvonne made her first Confession on July 16, 1908, to Father Gaston Moiteaux, in the Institute's chapel.

"I prepared really carefully and my first confession brought me many graces. I made much more of an effort with regard to my conduct," wrote Yvonne. (*Autobiographical Notebook*, 1924, no. 859)

The effort continued the following winter:

"I was prone to chilblains," she recounted, "and to treat them Granny sent me an ointment which really did lessen the pain. In order to suffer a bit, I didn't put on any ointment. The chilblains flared up, became inflamed and burst open. An abscess formed. At first I wanted to bear it without saying anything. But the suffering became too much, so I told Mommy, who took care of me.

"'If I'm not braver than this,' I said to myself, 'I'll never become a saint.'"

She shifted her penitence to her relationships with others. During the vacations of 1909 she managed not to fall out with her older sister Suzanne. She managed to conquer her willful nature. She gave way at every opportunity. She agreed to play the favorite games of her cousin Andrea Labéraudrie.

"I wanted to love dear Andrea with all my heart. It seemed to me that the more I mortified myself for her, the more I'd be loving her" (Ibid., p. 13).

Andrea confirmed (in her testimony of January 1954, no. 2) that "I remember how kindly my cousins welcomed me during the vacations."

These vacations at Le Mans brought together a large band of cousins and friends. However young she may have been, Yvonne soon became the center, the very life and soul of it. ∗

4

A Decisive and Secret Step

TOUL, 1909–1913

ZEAL AND PENITENCE

The start of the new school year in 1909 brought a change of scene. Mrs. Beauvais and her two daughters set off to Toul in the harsh and militarized east of the country, next to Alsace-Lorraine which had been lost[1] since 1871. The Minister of War, General André, used to send officers "on report" to this somewhat stark garrison. It was like a "Go to jail" card!

Nowhere "would you find a finer troop," wrote Marshall Foche in his memoirs.

On the advice of her uncle, the Jesuit priest Father Trégard, Lucie Beauvais had just accepted the headship of the Mercy Boarding School at 6 rue de Rigny, in the shadow of Saint Stephen's cathedral. This post was less taxing and more favorable to family life. Here, Yvonne was no longer in a dormitory but shared a bedroom with her sister. She was thrilled to be left in peace in the evenings with her dolls, for whom she had a strong maternal instinct. "The little chatterbox" as Grandpa called her (1907, no. 32) now had mastery over her quick tongue.

"LET THE LITTLE CHILDREN COME UNTO ME"

In 1910, Pope Saint Pius X opened up Holy Communion to young children who had reached the age of reason (seven years old in principle but earlier if the child was obviously ready). Yvonne was happy at this prospect, which was being applied gradually. She meditated for five minutes every

---

[1] To Germany.

morning before starting her day's work. In all areas of her
life she mastered her fiery temperament. She had a horror
of idle chatter and malicious gossip.

"DO YOU LOVE ME MORE THAN YOUR DOLLIES?"
This is where a decisive choice was made:

> Among our group of friends we often made exchanges,
> bartered things. My dear little friend Reine de Mal-
> glaive had two beautiful little dolls—one dressed in
> blue silk and the other in pink silk. I wanted them
> more than anything in the world! I would have given
> everything I owned to get hold of them. And so,
> with this in mind I began to put aside pencils, silks,
> ribbons, little games and candies that I could use
> to "buy" the dolls. But I found Reine to be quite
> demanding! However, finally a day arrived when she
> said that she would soon be able to accept my col-
> lection of bric-a-brac in return for the famous dollies.
> I was beside myself with joy!
>
> Two days later they became my daughters and I
> settled them tenderly into their new home, inside
> my desk.

As well as being beautiful, these dolls had the added advantage of being small in size. Yvonne could keep them close to
her. But—this happiness was about to be challenged:

> A few days later, as my little friend was leafing through
> a book a little holy picture card fell out. It was nei-
> ther pretty nor artistic. Yet the expression on Christ's
> face struck me. At the same moment it seemed to
> me that in my heart Jesus was saying to me,
> "Do you love me more than your dollies?"
> I answered him,
> "Yes. Much more!"
> And to prove that it was true I immediately asked
> my friend to let me have her holy picture card in
> return for the dollies.
>
> Reine looked at me as if I were crazy—but she
> hastily agreed to the deal! I gave her back the dolls
> and I kept Jesus. He took the place of the two dollies

> inside my desk. And every time I opened up my desk
> I kissed the picture and said to him, "See how I love
> you? How we love one another?" (*Autobiographical
> Notebook*, pp. 26–27, 1924, no. 859)

At around the same age a crucifix played a similar role
in the life of Thérèse of Lisieux. In both cases a simple sign
(a holy image), transfigured by an interior light, prompted a
complete adhesion to Christ forever.

Yvonne had grasped that "dolls didn't have souls" (Ibid.,
p. 28).

SCHOLARLY FAILURE

At school her failures continued. This was perplexing, in
light of Yvonne's capabilities. The cause of it was her health.

> I often suffered headaches and pain in my right side
> (this lasted until the day I was operated on for appen-
> dicitis) but I didn't want to complain. I wanted to
> suffer for my Jesus. When I was really really hurting
> I would tell Mommy. She would put me to bed. As
> I would be better again the next day they thought
> that I must be a shirker and that I preferred my
> bed to my work.
>   At schoolwork I really applied myself but after
> an hour of work my head would become heavy and
> painful. I couldn't study any more but I didn't want
> to complain. The outcome couldn't be a very prom-
> ising one! (Ibid., p. 21)

This only served to reinforce the distinction that Mommy
made between Yvonne and her big sister. Suzanne was always
first. The headmistress was proud of her but often moved
her down to second place in the official lists, so as not to
be suspected of favoritism.

In any case, her eldest filled Mommy with pride. The
younger one, though, disappointed and irritated her. Vonnette
really felt Mommy's frustration but without any jealousy
toward Suzanne. What she was lacking was the affection of
her mother.

ACCUSED

A suspicion arose which only aggravated the wound. One day some candies went missing. Yvonne was suspected. She had access to move freely throughout the house and she was rumored to be bulimic, so much did she love all the nice things! And so Mrs. Beauvais suspected her. She tried to elicit an admission of guilt. She said publicly, in front of all the pupils:

"I ask the guilty person to own up." Yvonne didn't bat an eye. Her mother interrogated her but she continued to deny all guilt in the matter. Mrs. Beauvais did not believe her. She stopped giving her any hugs and kisses or even speaking to her at all.

> For four days I remained deprived of Mommy's kisses.
> When I did catch her looking at me it was with sad-
> ness in her eyes and a look of reproach. My heart was
> sore and ready to break, so much was I suffering. My
> only consolation was to tell myself that at the Last
> Judgment everything will be known and everyone will
> see that I was not guilty. And yet, I couldn't stand it
> anymore. On the evening of the fourth day, weeping
> copious tears and flushed red with embarrassment, I
> went to tell Mommy that I took the candies. (I told
> her) so that she would kiss and hug me again. But
> her tender loving caused me pain. I burst into tears.
> Mommy thought they were tears of repentance for
> my supposed "theft" but in fact they were tears of
> repentance over my first lie. I asked to go to Con-
> fession. I believed that I had committed a mortal sin.
> (Notebook, p. 16, 1924, no. 859)

Father Gérard of the cathedral, who she called upon out-side of his usual hours of attendance, reassured her and she made a firm resolution never to repeat this lie, the only one of her life.

Shortly afterward, Mrs. Beauvais discovered the real culprit: the daughter of the school cook.

"But being afraid of upsetting the mother who would prob-ably have caused a scene and even handed in her resignation,

I couldn't make known the result of my investigation and clear Yvonne of guilt," concluded Mrs. Beauvais. (Notes of April 1957, p. 28, no. 125)

Was the Lord preparing Yvonne to suffer accusations and calumnies? Her life would contain an extraordinary amount of them.

FIRST HOLY COMMUNION

December 1910. The day of First Holy Communion was nearing. On the advice of Father Trégard, Yvonne prepared for it with a four-day retreat in Paris at the convent of religious sisters known as Auxiliaries.

"Father Questel came to give me Instruction several times a day and the rest of the time Mother Saint Albert looked after me," recounted Yvonne.

She made her preparation using a little book with floral illustrations, similar to the one used by Thérèse of Lisieux, *Two Months and Nine Days of Preparation for My First Communion.*

"Every evening I wrote down the number of sacrifices I had made and I did my best to make more and more each day."

Also, every evening she prayed to Jesus to take away her pride, and she added this prayer to Our Lady:

"O my Queen, O my Mother, I offer myself completely to you...."

December 29. On the eve of the great day, the Auxiliaries offered Yvonne a visit to the poor. She chose from among several families.

"First, to the home of a Mommy who has many children!"

"And what will you bring them?"

"A big casserole, with lots of leeks." (Testimony of Mother Saint Albert, March 1939, no. 186)

That family was impressed by the politeness and evident respect of the child.

"The great day had arrived," recounts Yvonne, "and my heart was pounding. I was very moved but so completely happy!"

> In the Auxiliaries' beautiful chapel the Baby Jesus in
> his crib seemed to smile at me. It was December 30.

"Baby Jesus, Holy Innocents, do not let me commit a single mortal sin. Rather let me die. I want to remain white and pure; I want to be a saint."

I recited this prayer several times before approaching the holy table. Yes, I firmly wished, cost whatever it may cost, to become a saint. After receiving Jesus my happiness was so great that I thought I might die. I couldn't speak. I could only say to the Guest of my heart, "I love you, even unto death. I love you with all my strength, all my soul. I belong completely to you."

And I felt that he took possession of me entirely.

The next day I received my Beloved anew, from the hands of my uncle, Father Trégard, in the little chapel on rue Raynouard. It was once again a delightful meeting. I was in Heaven! I told him that I wanted to be like little Thérèse of the Child Jesus, a martyr of love, and to save many souls.

Jesus spoke to me a lot during my thanksgiving. Here's what he led me to understand. It's that all my faults stem from me being too satisfied with myself; pride in my appearance, bad mood, disobedience, vanity, etc. Doesn't all that arise from the fact that I'm happy with everything I do? And that I persist in doing whatever I want? I prefer my will to that of others, even Mommy's, and my teachers'. I'm unhappy when I'm obliged to do one thing when I had decided to do another. I believe myself capable of directing myself! What pride! I would cut out three-quarters of my sins if I would consent to do the will of others. That, I said to myself, is what I must now set myself to doing. (*Autobiographical Notebook*, pp. 18–21, 1924, no. 859)

THE GIFT AND THE PACT. JANUARY 1, 1911

Back at Toul, Yvonne puts this fundamental grace into action. On January 1, 1911, while the house was empty because of the holiday, she wrote—in her blood[2]—a pact with Jesus.

She kept it strictly to herself in a private drawer, where it was found after her death by Mother Marie-Anne.

---

[2] Examined under a microscope (enlarged 1,000 times).

Oh my little Jesus,
I give myself completely to you, and for always.
I will always want what you want.
I will do everything that you tell me to do.
I will live only for you.
I will work in silence
and, if you wish, I will suffer much in silence.
I entreat you to make me become a saint,
a very great saint, a martyr.
Make me be faithful always.
I want to save many souls
and to love you more than everybody else,
but I also want to be very small,
so as to give you greater glory.
I wish to possess you, my little Jesus,
and to radiate you.
I wish only to be yours
but above all I want your will.
Your little Yvonne

> January 1, 1911 (no. 54). Papers found
> after Mother Yvonne's death.

This crazy desire—"to love you more than everybody else"—was in no way comparative. It denoted the desire to accept no limit. It clearly arose from a profound inspiration. The desire "to save many souls" was inseparable from it. It came first in her expression of love.

Yvonne seemed to have already embarked upon the "passive ways" as they say in mystical theology. She was totally given, led by God more than she led, and yet more clear, free, and active than ever because she was living by love alone.

She rooted and radicalized her total dependence on Christ. He alone had inspired her desire. He alone would "make her become a saint." She knew it. But this abandonment to the transcendent God was in no way the passivity of a sculpture.

It was a surge, a boost of her whole being, a sort of circumincession wherein the movement of God responded to the hope that it inspired, where the grace given returned to God in the act of thanksgiving according to the beautiful model

given to us in the Magnificat. In this synergy everything
was of God, but everything was of the freely and actively
receptive Yvonne.

She expressed a limitless availability, even the desire to
suffer. She did not want to back away from the Passion, and
its Cross. Nothing stopped her. Everything engaged her on
this way, this path, with a will that had no weakness.

Her simple, childlike grammar expressed it with a singular
maturity. The "I will want" (future) was first of all hooked
onto "all that you will want." Then, in the wake of "if you wish"
it became a free act, a personal choice. The "I want" repeated
five times culminated, as at the start, in the will of Christ: "I
want above all your will." But it was not voluntarism.[3]

We should perhaps translate this text into Spanish, where
one and the same word—"quiero"—means both "to want"
and "to love."

"I will love what you will love."

The text is plain and unadorned. Not a word was useless,
sentimental, or superfluous. It was indeed the writing of a
child, but the act revealed a maturity attained by few adults.
The profound inner freedom evidenced in this gift of self
to God was a trait that would characterize her personality
throughout her life. Nothing would prevent her from giving.
The very blood of her veins gave expression to this irreversible
donation of her heart and soul.

The abandonment to the will of Christ prolonged and ori-
ented her resolve to renounce her own will so as daily to do
"the will of others." Such was the inspiration of her second
Communion, which she made the next day, December 31. It
was a total reversal of voluntarism in favor of love alone, an
absolute immolation of her own will in favor of welcoming
that of others—which can only find meaning and fulfilment
in the will of the Other par excellence, who is not really an
"other" but rather the principle, the fulfilment, and the interior
unity of all things.

---

[3] The philosophy that one's will is the supreme factor in one's life.

THIRD COMMUNION, FEBRUARY 2

Back at Toul, Yvonne had to wait over a month to make her third Communion, on February 2. Not a single time during the month of January! The archpriest of the cathedral wanted to wait for the private First Holy Communion of the children of the parish. They would be the first that the will of Pius X allowed to approach the altar at a younger age.

SPIRITUAL COMBAT AND MONASTIC LIFE

Yvonne continued her daily fight against her faults: her sweet tooth, which she called "greed," and her determination, which she called "pride." Her alert penitential self-sacrifice was guided by love alone.

Life at the boarding school in Toul was almost monastic. Very early, Mrs. Beauvais would read out a text for meditation. At supper, where there were just a few teachers and the boarders, she would read a passage from *The Story of a Soul*. Yvonne was delighted with that. It was with Saint Thérèse that she had prepared for her First Holy Communion.

"Mommy, that's my saint!" she said.

(Memories of Lucie Beauvais, collected by Father Paul Labutte)

NIGHT AND FOG

In 1912 she was plunged into a spiritual dark night, which added to the trial of her chronic poor health. Later, she summarized this new stage thus:

"At every trouble, every suffering, I would go to the church so that he might console me. I wanted only him. He was my only confidant, and often I left the church with my heart just as sad as when I had gone in. So many times I was tempted to leave him. He wasn't answering me. But I was faithful, yes, very faithful.... I am a poor soul with neither courage nor virtue but I was always true to him and never deceived him. I lived on trust."

(Letter to Father Théodore Crété, January 16, 1925, no. 31)

SOLEMN COMMUNION AND CONFIRMATION

It was still in this dark night that she made her Solemn Communion on May 11, 1913, in the cathedral.

"Jesus kept quiet. On that day there were more tears than joys. I believed in Jesus's love for me, but I no longer felt it. No consolation whatsoever... no joy at all, neither in praying, nor in going to Mass, nor in holy communion. I didn't know what to say anymore in my post-communion thanksgiving. Yet, nevertheless, without me feeling it, Jesus was enlightening and teaching my soul" (*Autobiographical Notebook*, pp. 28–29, no. 859).

Nobody knew what was developing within this little girl. She herself did not yet know. But she progressed in leaps and bounds toward the horizons of him whom she loved. It was the crossing of the desert.

On May 18 she received the sacrament of Confirmation, still in that same spiritual dark night.

Having frequented quite a number of schools and boarding schools, for Yvonne the stay at Toul was the longest of her young life—four years from 1909 to 1913. It was a formative and foundational period. It is often said that every life is based or founded on a single free act—from which everything else proceeds. For Yvonne, the act of January 1, 1911, signed with her blood, had this significance. It expressed and would inspire her whole life.

FAREWELL TOUL

In July 1913 a complex coincidence of circumstances brought Mrs. Beauvais back to Paris. Madeleine Daniélou had just opened the Saint Mary's Institute at Neuilly. It was to provide an educational, cultural, and spiritual formation.

Mrs. Beauvais was invited to take charge of the accounts. This she did after a short internship at the bursar's office of the Jesuit school on rue Franklin, where her uncle Father Trégard lived. It was her apprenticeship for this new responsibility. ❧

5
The Dark Night Continues

I N THE HEADY HEIGHTS OF SAINT MARY'S, where her sister was making a good impression, Yvonne would remain misunderstood. Perhaps her gifts and qualities remained somewhat foreign to the shining intellectualism of this environment. But, above all, headaches wore her down and sometimes overwhelmed her.

"It's to get attention, and so as not to have to work," they said. (*Notebook*, p. 35, 1914, no. 7)

Her energy was unappreciated by her companions. Her heroic silence came across as indifference. They demoted her from the fifth class to the sixth, a humiliation.

Finally, in November 1913 she fainted in the office of the school matron. A doctor examined her. She needed surgery, urgently.

"This chronic appendicitis which she had suffered for four years was the cause of violent headaches which so often prevented her from studying."

And so they now understood "that far from being lazy, she had been heroic in so bearing her illness" (*Obituary Notice* by Mother Marie-Anne, December 25, 1951, no. 154).

Her work returned to normal. She was reinstated to the fifth class.

One day, in the spring of 1914, she broke away from her companions who were engaging in "bad conversation." Her life lay elsewhere. So as not to draw attention to the culprits, she snuck off to the attic. Fatigue overcame her and she fell asleep. It was only in the evening that she was discovered up there. Mrs. Daniélou thought she had been playing hooky and reprimanded her severely in front of the whole Institute.

"I took my humiliation in silence but at heart I didn't regret my action; I remained pure," she wrote. (*Autobiographical Notebook*, p. 37, 1924, no. 859)

In July 1914 she began keeping a private journal, with no romanticism or floweriness. It was addressed to Jesus alone, on a new level of intimacy.

"By writing things down one can understand better, and that will help me to rise up toward you," she began. "In my instructions I addressed you as 'Vous' but if you like, in my journal I'll call you 'tu.' It will be more cozy" (*Notebook*, p. 27, 1914, no. 7).[1]

The new notebook was soon interrupted. Yvonne explained:

"I shan't write in my notebook anymore because every day all I have to write is that *I am suffering*. And it is pointless, when one has suffered, to think about it again by writing it down" (Ibid., p. 38).

---

[1] In French "vous" is the formal mode of address. "Tu" is informal.

6

The English Oasis

HAPPY PUNISHMENT

On July 13, 1914, realizing that war was nearing, Mrs. Beauvais took her two daughters to England. Suzanne had spent the school year of 1910–1911 there. She was returning now just for three months to help her sister settle in. Mrs. Beauvais had previously sent Suzanne across the channel because she had been so brilliantly ahead of her peers. It was a reward for her. For Yvonne, though, it was "a punishment" after her mediocre year at Mrs. Daniélou's Institute: the so-so schoolwork, the escapade in the attic, et cetera.

It was a happy penance for Yvonne. Her free and independent nature blossomed in the English system of education, which was stimulating and varied. Room was made for piano, for dance, for sport—for the body. The freedom given for personal development revealed her capabilities. British empiricism suited her better than the French university-style intelligence, born of the "meagre Sorbonne."

She did well in learning English and did better than ever before, both in studies and at sports. She became captain of the field hockey team. She enjoyed some rowdy escapades, stemming from her great vitality. There were some hilarious (and audacious) climbs on the rocks, and up trees.

The boarding school was run by the Daughters of Jesus of Kermaria, who had been driven out of France in 1905 by Emile Combes. His persecuting anticlericalism had unwittingly been the main reason for the worldwide spread of French missionaries.

The Sisters never forgot their roots. They still wore their great Breton headdress but their congregation, which attracted numerous vocations in Great Britain, became English in both language and culture.

"Right off, I loved them," recounted Yvonne who was so sensitive and receptive to any affection which her mother had so often frustrated.

THIEF

A shadow darkened this stay, which reinforced the suspicions undergone at Toul. Some candies disappeared from a cupboard in the classroom. Sister Hilda called on the guilty party to own up. Nobody budged. Three days later, another call to own up. With no result. After a heavy silence, Sister declared:

> "Alright, it seems that I'm going to have to say it...."
> She looked at Yvonne, who was stunned to hear her say,
> "It's you! You were seen."
> Gosh! Now she understood. Several times a young nun, Sister Teresa, had sent her to fetch candies from the cupboard and bring them to her. Yvonne obeyed, having no idea that the nun was using her.
> But not wanting to accuse a consecrated soul, nor cast a shadow on the Sister's life, she did not justify or excuse herself and shouldered the blame for the misdemeanor. (Letter from Sister Maria Mathilde of the Cross, Yvonne Bamélis to Father Paul Labutte, December 18, 1967, no. 34)

The incident aroused widespread dismay, for Yvonne was well-liked. Fortunately, Mother Saint Ignatius discovered the true culprit and without revealing that a mischievous nun had been the cause of this business, she rehabilitated Yvonne. As for the guilty Sister, having lost her way in the congregation, she did not remain.

For the first time, justice was done to Yvonne, after false accusation and calumny. Everyone understood:

> "She preferred to be taken for a thief rather than denounce the one who had given her the key to the cupboard with an instruction to bring the candies to her," wrote Sister Mary of Calvary. (February 9, 1954, no. 13)

SECOND YEAR (1915–1916)

The year had been so good that Yvonne asked to spend "another year in this good convent." A return required a visa. It was difficult because of the war. But Yvonne was determined. Nothing would stop her. She got her visa. And once again took the boat, somewhat dangerously, from occupied France to England under threat.

"It was during this second year that I heard a divine call, that of a religious vocation," she noted. "My dear mothers believed in it. I developed the habit of going to recite Vespers and Compline with them, and often...Matins and Lauds.

"A month later I made a resolution to recite the Little Office of Our Lady every day and since then I've only missed it when I've been ill" (*Autobiographical Notebook*, 1924, p. 40, no. 859).

She was only fourteen years old. On November 30, 1915 she wrote to her mother:

"When I come back to France, I've got something to tell you, dear Mom, which will surprise you a bit, I think. But you'll be so happy to know what I tell you that you'll jump for joy, I'm sure of it!" (no. 11)

However, she couldn't wait! Her next letter asked for permission to enter the convent. The reply was negative.

Yvonne persisted:

> I was pleased with your letter but...you haven't really grasped what I was saying to you in my last letter about responding to God's call as soon as possible. You tell me I'm too young. Not at all! You know that it's allowed to enter as a postulant at 16, and thus to be a junior[1] at 15. If I'm a junior at 16, I'll be a postulant only when I'm 17 and I want to be so before then. And also, do you think the idea just came to me on the same day I wrote to you? Oh no, dear Mommy, I waited and took my time before telling you.... Would you want me to delay even longer this grace which was given to me so long ago now? I suffer from only being 14. But when I'm 15 I hope that you won't

---

[1] Carry out junior studies.

oppose my taking the black veil. Oh, how sad I'll be
if you say the same thing again in your next letter.
(Letter to her mother, June 10, 1916, no. 8)

Already totally given to the Lord, in England Yvonne had
discovered a concrete way to live her vocation. She threw
herself right into it. But her repeated pleas were unsuccessful.
As far as her mother was concerned, and also Father Trégard,
it was Suzanne, the older, pious, and intelligent one who was
made for religious life. Yvonne (though still too young) was
meant for marriage.

On August 5, 1916 Yvonne left England for good, to return
to France.

AN EVENTFUL JOURNEY[2]

Between Southampton and Le Havre there was a submarine
alert. The ship sat still for thirty-six hours. There were only
provisions on board for a simple tea. Yvonne shared her bar
of chocolate with the other travelers in her cabin, a woman
and her child. To occupy and amuse the child she unpacked
her dance pumps and ballet dress. She danced "on point" as
she had learned to do in England. The other passengers gathered all around her in a circle. The display eased the general
air of anxiety. During the final applause the siren sounded
again. But this time it was not a danger signal. A telegram
had arrived. An officer read it out over the loudspeaker:

"Attention. Attention. Submarine captured. Crew taken pris-
oner. The route is now clear. Vive la France. Long live France!"

Yvonne was famished. Before the ship had set sail she
had managed, with the help of an umbrella, to throw some

---

[2] Mother Marie-Anne places this incident in the return of July 1915
(*Obituary Notice*). But the letter from Yvonne, dated August 8, 1916,
assures us that it is the following year: "Long and tiring crossing (of
the English Channel) which took more than 36 hours, and a total
journey time of 48 hours. We aim to leave for Le Mans on Thursday
or Friday morning" (Letter from Yvonne, August 8, 1916, no. 22). The
"three or four days" that Mrs. Favrot speaks about (Deposition of May
28, 1956) are an exaggeration. The stamps in the passport (August 5 at
Southampton and August 6 at Le Havre) confirm this. (nos. 20 and 21)

coins onto the quay so as to buy some bread rolls. These she shared and ate with gusto.

It was a new Yvonne who disembarked the ship. She was bedecked with diplomas from respected institutions: the London Conservatory for piano with a teaching diploma, the School of Arts for painting, and even a qualification in cartography!

She had just turned fifteen, on July 16. Her life was already given to Jesus alone.

The gracious ballerina who knew how to dance joyfully for the famished passengers came back to France only out of obedience. She would have preferred to stay in England—in the Juvenate, in order to effect immediately the gift of her whole life. ✒

7
At the
Lair-Lamotte Institute

1916–1917

A T THE START OF AUGUST 1916, WHILE the Battle of Verdun was raging, Yvonne took up the usual summer vacation at Saint-Jamme-sur-Sarthe on the outskirts of Le Mans, at the home of the local country doctor, Doctor Chaudet and his family.

THE HOLIDAY GANG

Yvonne was at the forefront of the hale and hearty gang. It comprised the doctor's six children, her cousin Andrea Labéraudrie, her sister Suzanne, and Marguerite Barrier, the daughter of a hunting friend of her late father.

The days were action-packed. There were bicycle expeditions in the Perseigne Forest, boating and fishing parties, picnics, climbs, country-dancing, games and sing-alongs.

By nightfall everyone was exhausted. But Yvonne was always the last one to sleep, after kneeling at the end of her bed and praying the Rosary in English. She had adopted the habit in England. She would add in French, the prayer "Oh my Queen, Oh my Mother."

It was during this summer vacation that she confided to Robert, one of the gang: "You know, later on I'll be a nun."

A MISUNDERSTOOD MATURITY

The start of the new school year in October found her back at the very first boarding school of her childhood. The Lair-Lamotte Institute was singularly antiquated. Miss Sophie Lair-Lamotte, faithful to her post, was still dressed as in

1906—a long dress and black stovepipe bonnet. She was now eighty years old.

Yvonne who was now, at age fifteen, in the third class, was sufficiently master of herself as to adapt to the discipline of a boarding school that had no sport or outdoor life, the opposite of the healthy freedom she had enjoyed in England.

But the outmoded style astonished her and she found it somewhat overbearing.

She had matured. Open and straightforward, she was somewhat ahead of her classmates. They admired her talents in dance and piano-playing. But some teachers were not so keen on this, notably her form teacher. Miss Nathalie Schoenberger was the school treasurer and a teacher of English (which she spoke with a German accent). She took an immediate dislike to Yvonne.

SUSPICIONS AND SUCCESS

The friendship and affection that she showed to certain classmates in difficulty would lead to her being suspected of "particular friendship." Yvonne retained an astonished memory of it:

> One day the headmistress summoned me to her study and told me that I must never again speak to my friend Lucienne. This was because I had held indecent conversations with her. And, we had been seen in the corridor of the dormitory hugging each other. And every particular friendship was forbidden. Et cetera.
>
> "Never have I had any bad conversation with Lucienne," I said to the headmistress. "I hugged her the other day because she was sad. Anybody who had a heart would do what I did."
>
> That poor Lucienne no longer had her father nor her mother. Her days off were spent at the boarding school and she was crying that she couldn't go home to a family like the rest of us. But I was not listened to. (*Autobiographical Notebook*, 1924, p. 99, no. 859)

She finished the school year with three prizes and three certificates of merit. Her maturity, her enthusiasm and

commitments, the dances that they asked her to perform—
all left a positive and happy memory. The jealousy of one
of her teachers toward Yvonne aroused such indignation
among her fellow-students that several of them quit the
boarding school. That teacher herself left soon afterward,
scarcely missed. (*Obituary Notice*)

During the summer vacation of 1917 Yvonne's influence
over the open and happy band of her cousins and friends
was confirmed.

8
End of School

FINAL YEARS OF STUDY

At the start of the school year in 1917, Yvonne rejoined her mother and her sister Suzanne in Paris. They had been living since July 17 at 69 avenue des Ternes. (Letter of Lucie Beauvais to Yvonne, July 16, 1917, no. 27)

Yvonne, now sixteen years old, was going to complete her studies at her sixth and final boarding school. It was run by Dominican sisters and situated in Neuilly, outside Paris. She joined the second class, then the "certificate class" (1917, no. 29). And with some success! She came in first out of eighteen girls and received the prize for overall excellence.

The following year (the first and baccalaureate class) was disrupted by an attack of scarlet fever (of which we have the temperature chart: February 3–March 8) followed by a long convalescence.

And here we come to the mystery of her baccalaureate. Did she take the exam? Or did she decline to take it, and for what reason? Detailed research by Father Labutte found no trace of the diploma. But Yvonne had told him that she had presented herself at the official exam hall, alone, without telling anybody, and had taken this first part but had never spoken about it.[1]

She resumed her studies in a Paris which was at war. Between March 23 and August 9 "the Paris Guns," a group

---

[1] Note by Fr Labutte, January 3, 1955, no. 2; cf. Letter of Mother Yvonne-Aimée to Suzanne Loth, August 14, 1950, no. 280, "It's not what I learned for my baccalaureate that has been most useful up to now." She never took her philosophy class; we don't know why.

of German long-range siege guns, had launched 367 shells, causing 264 deaths, and wounding 620. One of these shells landed on Good Friday, 1918, on the church of Saint Gervais in the middle of the Holy Week liturgy. Among the twenty-five dead were three teachers from Neuilly.

FAMILY MISUNDERSTANDING

Having rejoined her family, Yvonne felt a bit like a surplus unit, or an outsider. Mrs. Beauvais and Suzanne were extremely close. They shared the same intellectual interests, to which Yvonne was felt to be alien. Suzanne was pursuing her studies at the Sorbonne and was also doing a stint as a teacher at Saint Mary's school in Neuilly. The mother and daughter had begun their time of probation with the group Daughters of Saint Francis de Sales. They shared lots of things together, including spiritual matters. If by chance Yvonne should spontaneously venture to speak during one of these conversations she saw that they were astonished. Her business, it was deemed, was practical matters.

"Mommy was busy with her works. My sister was always at her studies and I at mine, so much so that we only came together at mealtimes. I found it hard. I barely spoke to Mommy and Mommy didn't know me. Having been apart from me since I was 13, she thought I had remained the same as before; the little girl who—supposedly—didn't like work" (*Autobiographical Notebook*, p. 106, 1924, no. 859).

And yet, Yvonne wasn't totally neglected. Mrs. Beauvais didn't judge her mature enough for the Daughters of Saint Francis de Sales. She sent her instead to Miss Yvonne Bato who ran, at 15 rue Monsieur, the group Children of Mary (in French, the Young Girls of Mary Immaculate).

"My little Yvonne is not very pious. I place her in your hands" (Interview of Miss Bato, May 3, 1956, no. 220).

NEW SPIRITUAL DEVELOPMENT

Mrs. Beauvais had no idea of the scale of Yvonne's spiritual progress since she was ten years old. Nor of the immense interior development which was occurring during these years of 1917–1920.

"I applied myself seriously to loving the Good Lord, and working for him," wrote Yvonne. (*Autobiographical Notebook*, p. 101, 1924, no. 859) ✎

9

Discovery of the Red Zone and Service of the Poor

1919–1922

A T THE WORKSHOP, YVONNE CAME across as friendly and jolly. But why did this unemployed young woman always arrive in a rush, and leave again in a hurry? She wasn't nervous, so why was she always in a flurry, wondered the manager, Miss Bato.

She finally learned the secret. Yvonne had got to know the poor people in the "red zone": the ring of huts and of rubbish which had grown like a gangrene on the No Man's Land of the old war-time fortifications and barriers circling the city and which had spread outward to the exterior.

SIX YEARS BEFORE FATHER LHANDE

This new "mission territory" at the gates of Paris would be revealed in 1925 by Father Pierre Lhande's articles in *Les Etudes* and grabbed the headlines on the emerging radio programs and in the newspapers. A popular play called *Our Lady of the Mouise* was a realistic portrayal of this pioneering mission. It became a great success and helped renew popular theater.

Six years previously, from 1919 onward, Yvonne had penetrated deeper and deeper into this zone of desolation, beginning with the first addresses of poor families given to her by a Daughter of Charity. It was still unknown territory that people just did not risk going into. Yvonne was the precursor, the pioneer, at eighteen years of age.

She went into districts and neighborhoods that Miss Bato judged it imprudent to venture into alone—because "even the police will only go there in pairs." (Notes of Mrs. Beauvais, p. 15, April 15, 1955, no. 58)

MOM

In 1919 she came upon a baby dying alongside its mother who was on her deathbed.

> I baptized that little girl myself.... The mother lived for another few months. She begged me to look after her little one as she had no family and had never had any contact with the family of her late husband.... When Mrs. L. died, I took Denise into my care. She was eight months old. A lovely little fair-haired baby whose big eyes already shone with intelligence. I already loved her dearly. But when she became mine I loved her as a mother loves her child. And yet, I didn't dare tell Mommy about my adoption. I was eighteen, I was just out of boarding school.... Obviously I couldn't take the little child with me. (*Notebook*, December 4, 1925, no. 756, which recounted this story, on the death of the child.)

So, she had the child adopted by a "fairly young family, who already had two children." But for the little one, right up to her death in 1925, Yvonne would remain her "Mommy."

MAID OF ALL WORK

How to find the means to provide for these innumerable and incalculable needs?

Yvonne had her pocket money. Mrs. Beauvais had set her allowance quite generously. But it was used up very quickly. She resorted to subsidies or handouts from her grandmother and other generous persons. But it was still not enough. She would have to find other resources.

In 1920 Mrs. Beauvais' housemaid handed in her week's notice to quit. "Let me take her place, for the same wage," Yvonne proposed.

She ended up getting the plan accepted. She became the household's maid-of-all-work. (Notes of Mrs. Beauvais, April 1957, p. 13, no. 125)

REVULSION AND FRIENDSHIP

There is no vacation from service of the poor and needy. At Le Mans every year, Yvonne would meet up again with the little girl to whom she had given her shoes and pinafore when she was six.

The girl's father had died. She tried to earn her keep. But her legs were "covered in horrible sores, which often forced her to remain in bed."

Yvonne took care of her with an outpouring of friendship which managed to overcome an extreme natural revulsion. "The sight and smell of the sores were quite something. Sometimes when I was tending her I would have to run out of the room quickly before being totally overcome."

She couldn't understand this revulsion which so undermined her unhesitating friendship with the girl. She could not allow this lack of cohesion in herself. Love is normally stronger than everything. She must quash "this foolish squeamishness."

"To overcome my repugnance and to punish myself," she continued, "I applied my lips to the weeping sore" (*Autobiographical Notebook*, p. 99, 1924, no. 859).

Father Trégard forbade her this unhealthy and dangerous excess. To love the sick is not to love their disease; it is to overcome it and not to contract it.

RISKS AND ATTACKS

Yvonne's adventurous peregrinations put her into situations that weren't always easy to get out of, despite her aplomb and her quick-wittedness. At Les Halles a big guy mocked this Little Miss from the smart side of town and threw a great big cabbage at her. She didn't miss a beat and threw it straight back at him, right on his head! (*Monette et ses pauvres*, p. 32)

But the attacks by men seriously tested both her nerve and her agility. There are not many details left about this dangerous part of her life. But she did suffer attacks, sometimes brutal. She was spared nothing.

UBIQUITY

The geography of her field of activities remains incomplete to us: Porte de Champerret, near Les Ternes (her home), Porte de Vannes and Porte de la Chapelle to the south-west and north-east of Paris are those that we know of. But it is not everything, and we quickly lose track. For, to "Yvonne's Poor," i.e., those she had found by herself or those who had been recommended to her, there were soon added those to whom she felt "sent" by an interior inspiration, in diverse and odd places—*Jesus's Poor* added to *Yvonne's Poor*. And to every one of these "friends" she gave the impression of a completely free and unending availability.

PERFECT JOY

One of these, Gisele Malauvé-Lebon, testified to this during the process of beatification.

> I was at the time about eight years old, the eldest of a family of five children. We were very poor and our parents were in poor health. (They died a day apart, in 1937.) Miss Beauvais went to great efforts every week, all of a long half-day. And she would come back, if necessary, to take us to the public baths, all five of us. I can still see her. She was strong, sweating, ruddy-cheeked, the sleeves of her dress rolled up, on her knees so as to be level with us little ones.
>
> She climbed the four flights of stairs, her arms laden, out of breath...always greeting us with a great big smile. You could really feel that she was full of joy. Not allowing her time to catch her breath, we would climb up all over her to sit on her lap. She kissed and hugged all of us.
>
> She would put on her apron to do the washing-up, the laundry, the ironing, the cooking, when our Mommy was ill in bed.... Then she would go do the shopping to fetch in provisions. I've seen her come back up all the stairs, a shopping bag in her hands and two eleven-pound sacks of coal, one under each arm....

She never missed a visit on holidays either, and she would always do something "extra." Apart from the usual casserole there would be a chicken, a bottle of fine wine, cigarettes for our Dad, lovely cakes, etc.... There was nothing lacking.

"For once," Mommy would say, "we can forget poverty and worries."

Her greatest reward was to see our Mommy happy.

Christmas at our place was always a holiday, thanks to Miss Beauvais. From a fancy store she would have delivered to us electric train sets, a rocking horse, lovely dollies. And every year I got a subscription to La Semaine de Suzette (Suzette's Week).

She could just as well have bought us secondhand clothes.... But no; she bought brand new.... And if we were silly enough to complain to her about this, she would say, "My dear little ones, nothing is too beautiful for you. I don't do anything. It is the good Lord who loves you."

I remember well a beautiful red straw hat and a dress in red wool (with daisies embroidered on the right-hand side) which she came with me herself to choose and buy. She supervised the fitting, wanting to avoid me being badly dressed.

"Not too long, Miss," she would say to the dressmaker. "Too short is not nice, but neither is too long."

After the purchase she was so happy and said to me, "What will Mommy and Daddy say? They're going to find you so pretty!"

She did crazy and wonderful things for her poor people; she who was happy with so little for herself. (Testimony submitted to the Process, May 20, 1958, no. 242)

10

Engagement

"WE HAVE TO GET YVONNE MARRIED!"
Mrs. Beauvais decided. A dutiful woman, she set
about the task. While Suzanne, the elder, had
all the qualities to be a nun, the younger one, well-meaning
and practical, was surely the housewife.

Yvonne had given everything to Jesus alone, and had found
her happiness among the poor. She was somewhat surprised
to find herself caught up in the conventional machinations
of the bourgeoisie of the day. To marry off one's daughter
was *the* great duty of parents. Mrs. Beauvais was adept at
finding candidates. She presented them to Yvonne, but with
no success.

Yvonne would soon sum it up thus:

"Young men, each more smug than the other, apart from
the railway engineer, the lawyer, and the Count of B. The first
I would marry in order to galivant around; the second ... is
too rich and seems too important. And as for the handsome
Count, he has too many titles!" (Musings collated by Robert
Chaudet, May 21, 1921, no. 25)

The problem was that Father Trégard, SJ, relative and spiritual adviser of Mrs. Beauvais, backed up the mother's point
of view with his priestly authority. In April 1921 he concluded
a meeting with Yvonne by saying, "But you ... you are made
for marriage!"

For Yvonne, it was more than a disappointment. She was
bulldozed, completely disconcerted. She tried to obey, in this
as in everything, with "submission of will." Father had spoken!
And so? God doesn't want me? No doubt I am unworthy of
it, just as unsuited to a vocation as I was to studies.

She forced herself to obey. The plans of authority were nothing other than the design of God, however much she did not see them as such.

During the Easter vacation, it seems, she met up again with her best friend from childhood—Robert, a medical student. Their two grandfathers had studied together at the Faculty of Medicine in Strasbourg (one in pharmacy, the other in medicine) and their two families had remained close. Robert was also born in 1901. They were the same age. She respected him. She trusted him. As she had to marry, and the others were stupid, then why not him? She began to think of wedding plans.

At Easter 1921, in Le Mans, on the lawn where they had played as children, she said to him:

"As I must marry, it is you I choose. Do you want me, later on?" (Letter of Robert, May 21, 1921, no. 25)

Robert could hardly believe his ears. He had admired and secretly loved this marvelous young lady throughout all their summer vacations together. In those days the gang of friends and cousins had voted her "the most lively," "the sweetest," "the kindest." (Barral, p. 62, and Letter of Robert, May 1921, no. 27)

A few weeks later, he reminded her,

> I was blown away... speechless with astonishment and happiness and I said a heartfelt Yes and kissed you, heedless to the fact that we were out there on the lawn, near the sitting room. My display of affection toward you could, rightly, have shocked the family! We set off, the two of us, to the end of the garden and I asked you:
>
> "Is it true, what you've just said to me? You want to become my wife?"
>
> Then you burst into tears and it was the first time I had ever seen you weep so. I was upset, and you said to me: "Robert, it's been decided. I am at the age to get married. I'm at my wits' end. I've had it up to here.... Out of everyone, I prefer you. And, if you like, we could be happy together. At least we know each other!" (Letter of Robert, May 21, 1921, no. 25)

And if Robert was reminding his fiancée of the scene, it was because a question had soon formed in his mind: "Am I perhaps just a last resort? Reassure me!" (Ibid.)

The response from Yvonne (who kept a copy of this crucial correspondence) was only partially reassuring.

"I've always loved you, since you were little. Be calm, my dear Robert, I love you sincerely. I admire you. I trust you. And as they tell me that my path in life is to marry, I will always be for you, I promise, the most faithful, the most loving of wives" (First Letter of Yvonne to Robert, May 1921, no. 26).

It was to be a marriage of duty. Sometimes they work. Love grows there, in heart and body, on the bases of respect and friendship. Yet Robert asked: "Will you be able to love me other than, and more than, a brother?" (Second Letter of Robert, May 1921, no. 23).

The admiration of his mother had long ago fired him up. In a letter of May 1921 he confided to Yvonne:

> One day—you were 14—and you were home from England. Mother asked you to perform for us—the Greek and Spanish dances that you had learned in England.... You went upstairs to a bedroom to dress the part (the blue bedroom) and put on your dress and satin slippers.
>
> Mother joined you a few moments later, to give you a yellow ribbon that you needed to tie your hair. When she came back downstairs to the sitting room, Mother said to your Mom: "Yvonne was already undressed when I went in. I must have disturbed her. She has such a fine figure. She is upright and elegant, she is gracious and her skin is fine and as white as satin."
>
> Your Mom, quietly proud, added, "Doctor Chaillon said to me just recently that in his career as a doctor treating young people he has never seen a young woman so well formed and in such perfect proportion as my Vonnette."
>
> I heard everything (I had cocked my ear when they began speaking about you) and without thinking

anything of it, or with any other motive, a mad desire
to see you overcame me. I ran up the stairs and
opened the door just slightly. You were almost ready
and you were putting on your dress. Your arms were
still bare and your long hair made a long and lush
coat reaching to the hem of your skirt.

Oh, how pretty you were Vonnette, so pretty!

But then I was afraid of doing something wrong,
of displeasing you. I pulled away from the door. Oh!
Rest assured, you were most decent. I was still by the
door when I heard you speaking. I put my head back
to the door. Standing on a chair, you were kissing
the picture of the Madonna and Child above the bed,
saying, "It's for you that I'm going to dance." (Letter
from Robert to Yvonne May 1921, no. 27)

His love was genuine and deep but Yvonne, who had offered
herself beyond all hope, remained inaccessible, wrapped in a
secret as transparent as it was impregnable. He worried, without knowing why. He hoped. He waited with gentle delicacy
and sought a way in, without upsetting her. He overcame
his natural reserve in order to give her the time to open
up. Hadn't she said "Later"? She wasn't yet twenty years old.
He suggested:

"Let's not disturb our Moms. They would create fears and
scruples and would no doubt adopt and impose a code of
conduct according to the old conventions. Let's wait. Let's
keep our secret. Let's not tell anyone" (before May 21, 1921;
Second Letter of Robert, no. 23).

She admitted to her fiancé that her mother had not taught
her "the facts of life" (which was often the case at that time).
"Yes, I am still an innocent young thing" (Letter of May 1921,
no. 29).

That he pulled her to him on his lap like a fiancée moved
her but worried her. For her life remained deeply committed
in another direction, which still involved obedience. Robert
wrote to her:

"It is time, I assure you, for you to be instructed about
certain things. It's your duty now. You will be no less pure, no

less good. Knowledge is not a sin. We'll speak about all that during the next vacation" (6 Letter of Robert, 1921, no. 30).

She displayed no sign of eagerness. It was in a tone of some distress that she spoke to the Lord:

"I can't pull out now; I'm promised. And anyway, you don't want me, Lord, as they didn't recognize my religious vocation! I really thought I had one. I thought that I would love and serve you faithfully. Jesus, have pity on my distress! Simplify my mind, enlighten my understanding. I know that I'm not worthy of belonging to you. No doubt I don't have the necessary qualities to be a good nun. And then, I'm told to obey. So I have to get married, I have to accept the common path" (Notebook, June 1921, no. 32).

After the chat that he had suggested about the realities of marriage, she wrote: "Oh my God, I've never felt so distressed. Marriage frightens me since I've learned certain things, and I'm even more scared of what I don't know. And yet, I try to reason with myself. It is you who have desired this.... You who instituted this great sacrament. There are saints among married people! Ah! How it all addles my brain!" (Ibid.)

She called upon her own pragmatism: "I never heard anyone complain. None of my married friends seemed sad to me. Oh Lord, I don't know what to think... But you, who can do all things, you'll keep me for yourself all the same!" (Ibid.)

And then Robert was struck down with tuberculosis—a bane which still left medicine at a loss. Deeply honorable, he returned his "troth," his word, to Yvonne:

"You know how serious and dangerous this disease is...what I would expose you to, what I would expose our children to. I do not have the right and so, with a broken heart, I give you back your freedom" (June 1921, no. 37).

And it is here that Yvonne's love was roused and proclaimed itself. No, she was not going to abandon, because he is ill, the one that she had chosen! She loved him even more. Compassion extinguished her interior doubts and love began to grow in her. And so she wrote him her warmest-ever letter:

"I love you and want only you, Robert. I will never marry anyone else" (Letter of June 1921, no. 38).

Perhaps she was reassuring herself with this "never" which joined the "later on" of her marriage proposal. The betrothal remained secret. Mrs. Beauvais continued to present candidates to Yvonne. It was her duty...

December 9, 1921, Yvonne fell sick of a serious paratyphoid. She used the occasion to beg Mrs. Beauvais:

"Listen dear Mommy, after my first 'presentation' I got scarlet fever. The gentleman was in a hurry. He was married before I had even recovered. After another presentation I had paratyphoid, and the gentleman got married. If you continue to make these 'presentations' to me...perhaps it will be best that for the third time the good Lord takes me home..." (Interview, Suzanne Favrot-Beauvais, pp. 39–41, May 29, 1956, no. 245). ✒

Yvonne's parents, Lucie Beauvais (née Brulé) and Alfred Beauvais

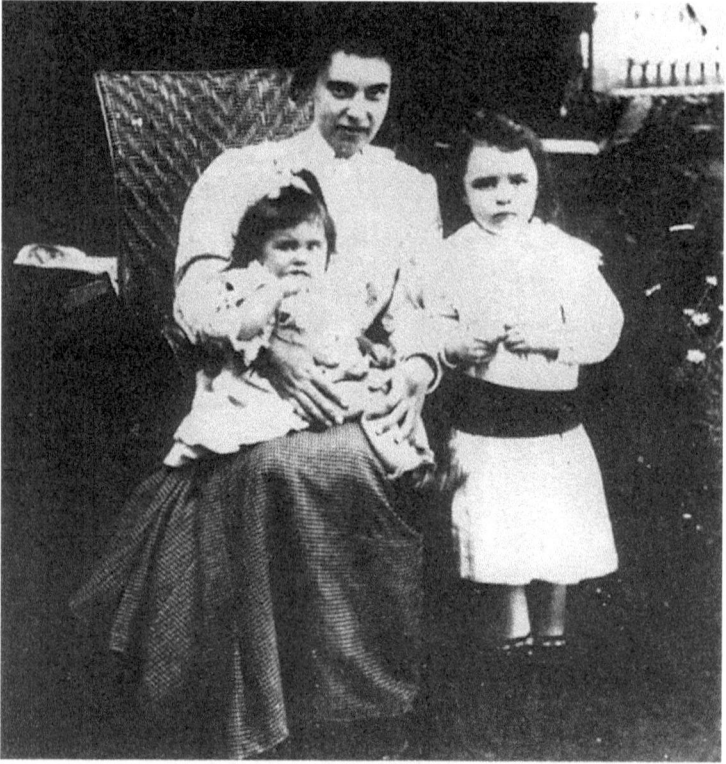

Lucie Beauvais and her two daughters, Yvonne and Suzanne (1902)

Yvonne at 18 months

Yvonne aged 3 years

1904

Yvonne knew every cat in the neighborhood—and they knew her!

With her grandmother Brulé

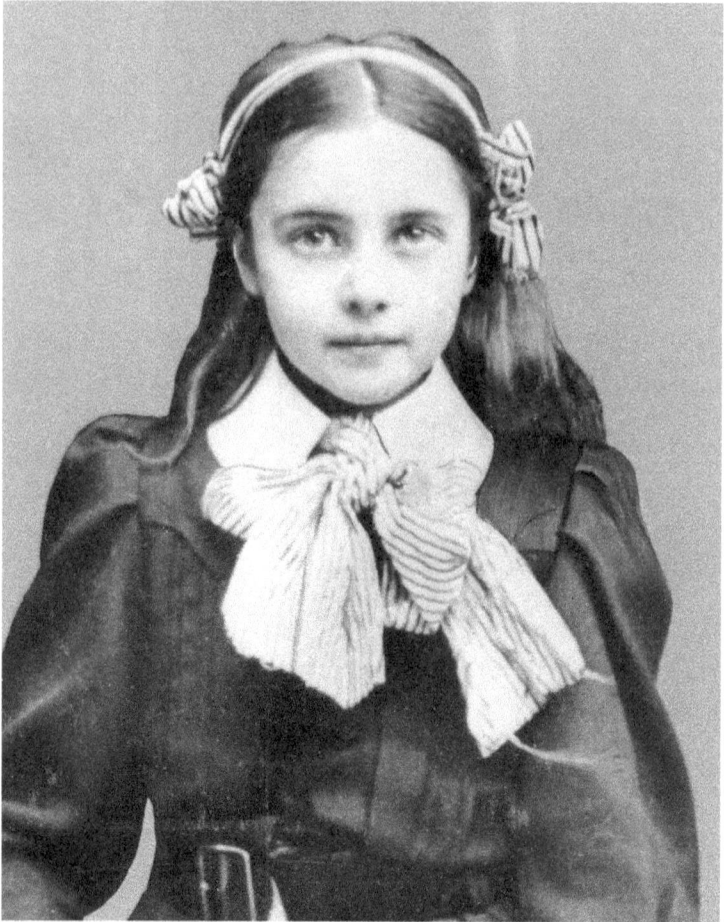

First Communion (December 30, 1910)

Solemn First Communion (May 11, 1913)

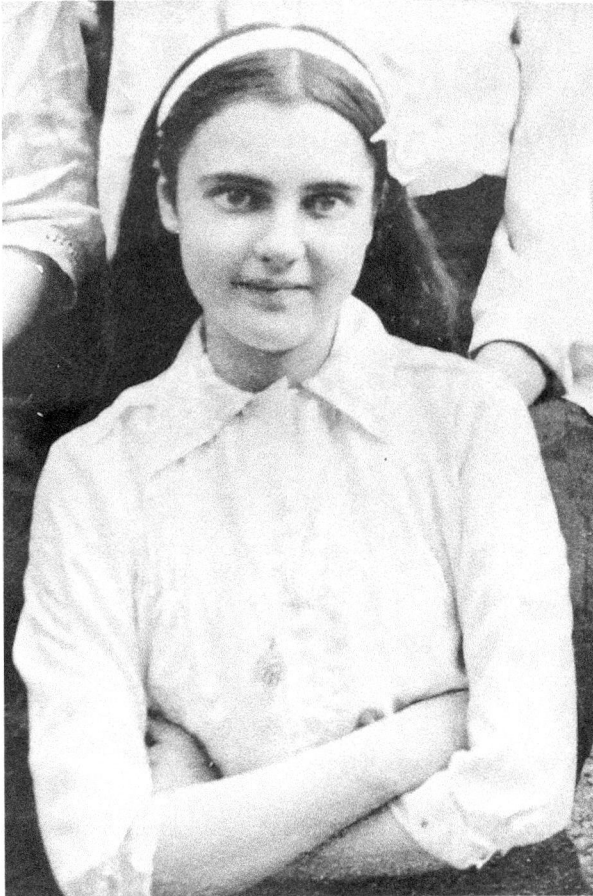

At school in England. She flourished in the
British boarding-school style of all-round education

Age 15 on her return to France and back to the first
boarding school of her childhood; the Lair-Lamotte Institute

Yvonne age 17

O Jésus, Roi d'Amour,
j'ai confiance en votre
Miséricordieuse Bonté.

Jesus King of Love. Drawing and prayer done by Yvonne.
(Later indulgenced by two popes.)

Yvonne (center) in evening wear with cousins and friends at a party thrown by a relative (1921)

*At Malestroit around the time
of her spiritual betrothal (1922)*

*In 1923, when she was forbidden to visit
her beloved convent at Malestroit*

In garden of the Home in Paris, looking somewhat
careworn while working as a maid-of-all-work and
tending her poor in the shanty towns of the Red Zone

In bridal attire before being clothed in the religious habit

Her father shortly before his death

II

Vocation

II

First Stay at Malestroit; Convalescence

MARCH 19 TO JUNE 12, 1922

THE PARATYPHOID DISEASE WHICH HAD put her suitor to flight had taken its toll on Yvonne's health. The doctor advised a period of convalescence in the countryside.

"Where should I go?" Yvonne asked Miss Bato.

"Go to Malestroit, to the nursing home of the Augustinian Sisters. My sister is there. You'll be made very welcome there."

But then the "young Miss" began to backtrack, in light of the cloudy and gloomy February weather.

"Er, no. It's not the right time of year. The weather won't be very nice and you won't see Brittany at its best. No, it's not the right time. Don't go to Malestroit."

"Yvonne looked at me fixedly," testified Miss Bato.

"Well, in fact, yes! I do want to go to Malestroit! I sure do want to meet the sister of my dear Miss" (Interview of Miss Bato, May 3, 1956, no. 220).

So Yvonne Bato wrote to her sister, Mother Madeleine of the Sacred Heart, recommending that she accept this charming young lady for "a complete rest."

On March 18, 1922, Yvonne took the express train to Rennes and then the coach to Bohinière, and then the old jalopy of a bus that went to Malestroit. There she found, on the edge of town, beside the Nantes-Brest canal, an old convent that was going to change her life forever.

She stayed in the little hospital attached to the convent. She was on the second floor, room number three, "A large and lovely south-facing room... Superb view over the countryside," she wrote to Andrea Labéraudrie. "The air is excellent. I'll return from here very strong and well" (March 19, 1922, no. 65).

The ancient Congregation of Augustinian Hospitallers of the Mercy of Jesus dated from the Middle Ages. It combined cloistered life with the care of the sick. The first Breton branch had been founded at Vannes by the convent of Dieppe in 1635, and took over the running of the town's general hospital. But problems with the municipal authorities led to them transferring to Malestroit in 1866.

They settled in the former Ursuline convent, which had been saved from ruin some thirty years earlier by Father Jean-Marie de Lammenais, founder of the Brothers of Christian Instruction.

The convent was antiquated but it had potential. Sister Marie-Anne of Jesus and the aforementioned Sister Madeleine of the Sacred Heart dreamed of modernization. A hospital with operating theaters had just been inaugurated in November 1920.

Yvonne, "the Parisienne," was found to be straightforward and charming. Friendships grew up with the young women patients and with the nuns. They appreciated her discretion. They didn't detect in her "any extraordinary piety" (Diary of Germaine Piacentini, May 1929, no. 195).

But her health was not great. From June 13, her fever often reached 104 degrees Fahrenheit. The doctors were bewildered. Was it a new flare-up of paratyphoid? wondered Doctor Maubin. It was not clear. On June 13 he consulted a renowned neurologist, Professor Charles Miraillé of Nantes, who dismissed the hypothesis of meningitis or of a nervous disease. "This young lady is extremely well balanced from the point of view of nerves, and in her case there is nothing that comes under my specialty," he concluded. (Mother Marie-Anne, Ordinary Process, Vannes, folio 462 v, October 7, 1957, no. 315)

At Pentecost (June 4) she met Father Théodore Crété, SJ, a sought-after confessor, rector of the Saint Francis Xavier college (a boys' school at Vannes), a preacher, but above all a spiritual director.

He was a spiritual guide who, under a gruff exterior, was both demanding and insightful.

Yvonne, who had been without spiritual direction since Father Trégard's death (November 11, 1921), opened up to him for the first time.

From their first encounter he discerned in her a deep vocation which those around her did not. (See his first letter, June 19, 1922, no. 95.)

Did he encourage her to pick up her plans of a vocation? It's unlikely. The vital spark came suddenly, from within. ⟐

12

Mystical Blossoming

JUNE 12–SEPTEMBER 2, 1922

AND SO WE ARRIVE AT A KEY MOMENT in Yvonne's life.

THE GRACE OF JUNE 12, 1922

On the morning of June 12, 1922, Trinity Sunday, she felt totally overwhelmed by Divine Love.

"I don't know how it happened. At Mass this morning, Jesus suddenly took hold of me. That was it. I could see only him, hear only him. I was no longer even aware of where I was. Fortunately, I stood up and knelt down at the right times but I was reeling; I wasn't really there. Returning to my place after Holy Communion, I had to sit down, so as not to betray the strength of my emotions; to contain my thumping heartbeats. Oh my God, how happy I am. How I know that it is truly you who is in me" (*Notebook*, June 1922, no. 90).

She responded to this secret grace with an uninhibited surge of fervor:

"My Jesus, I love you. What do you want of me?" (*Ibid.*, p. 2)

The experience of the young Samuel (1 Sam 3:4) was recurring afresh in the twentieth century, with no fanfare, without words.

Yvonne understood that she had to give herself anew, and totally. There was simply no other desire within her. It meant, however, a doubly-sad rupture—for the fiancé that she chose is the person she loved most in the world, and this rupture would be heartbreaking for him, however it were carried out.

> This evening, in my room, on my knees and holding my crucifix in my hand and covering it with kisses, I began the prayers of immolation.

"Lord Jesus, from this moment on, I renounce being loved."

It seemed to me that something in me broke, that the earth suddenly became empty, cold and as if covered in darkness.

"My God, what loneliness, what silence, what night!

"Oh my Jesus, your love sustains me in spite of everything. As long as you remain in me, I am content, and that's enough! It is the greatest sacrifice that I could make for you.

"You gave me a loving soul, and I feel the need to love and to be loved. Up to now, I don't think that a sentiment too human has entered my affections, nor any burst of self-love—but I am so weak that I could fall if I didn't take care, Lord Jesus, to give you all my heart." (*Notebook*, June 19, 1922, no. 97)

Father Crété, a man of much spiritual experience, followed this evolution clearly and calmly, strewn as it was with multiple health incidents which confounded the doctors. From his very first letter, he wrote with humor: "You have made your nurses suffer and thrown them into anguish. Don't start up again. I will be very happy to see you again, either sooner or later. But still, I think that the Lord Jesus wants you for himself" (Letter of June 19, 1922, no. 95).

THE CALL AND THE CROSS

On July 5 there was a call. A new dialogue began. On this day, she noted:

I had been in bed for about ten minutes when I clearly heard my name.

"Yvonne!"

I turned my head toward the fireplace as the voice seemed to come from there. There was no one there. I was mistaken. I settled down again and tried to sleep.

A second time, I heard: "Yvonne!"

I was afraid, very afraid and I put my head under the covers and began to recite the Our Father out loud. When I reached the words "Forgive us our trespasses as we forgive those who trespass against us," the voice again made itself heard:

"Yvonne!"

I went onto my knees...and from the direction of the fireplace I saw a glow. Nothing natural caused it.

Then a cross formed as a voice of extreme gentleness said,

"Do you wish to carry it?"

"Oh yes, Lord," I replied.

I felt at that very moment overcome by an immense happiness.

The voice spoke again:

"Be an abandoned soul. Accept the trials that I shall send you as the greatest grace and the greatest favor given to the souls that I love. Accept them without complaint, without examining their nature or their duration! Without claiming anything. Pay no attention to what will mortify you or humiliate you. Look at me: I love you. Isn't that enough for your heart?"

"Oh yes, Lord," I responded. "I love you. But is it really you who deigns to speak to me and to think of your little creature? Tell me, Lord Jesus; is it really you?"

Then I saw a hand advance toward the cross, pluck a lily and give it to me. At that moment I experienced such a rush of joy and love that I almost fainted. But that seemed to me to last just a moment; my soul, though, was filled with peace. (Notebook, July 10, 1922, no. 110)

Mother Madeleine then entered the room. She was astonished to find Yvonne kneeling on her bed. Did the flower that was there disturb her sleep? She reproached her gently:

"It's not good to have kept that flower, when I took the flower arrangement away from you (yesterday evening)."

"I didn't pick it, Mother," replied Yvonne. (Letter of Mother Madeleine of the Sacred Heart, to Father Crété, July 9, 1922, no. 109)

The lily, sitting on top of a piece of furniture, intrigued the nun.

It didn't fade, she noticed.

She carried out a test—she placed alongside it a similar lily from the garden with no vase or water. That flower soon withered. Yvonne's remained as fresh as on the first day. (Ibid.)

On July 13 Yvonne heard this word: "I'm taking my lily, so as to pour love into other souls" (Letter of Yvonne to Father Crété, July 14, 1922, no. 119).

The lily disappeared.

Witnesses of that summer of 1922 were numerous. They observed, sometimes without understanding, ecstasies accompanied by abundant signs. Flowers, rings, and perfumes created an atmosphere of betrothal. They stirred up the fervor and generosity of Yvonne, but not exaltation. Yvonne took these gifts as they came, without lingering over them. The Lord alone absorbed her in a total abandonment of herself. She desired to suffer with Christ crucified, out of love and to save sinners.

Profound suffering, physical, emotional and spiritual, came to meet her offering. And yet she radiated a sure and shining joy.

On July 11 Yvonne received the following message from the Lord:

"I love you my dear little Yvonne, and to all those I love I do not spare suffering. I, your God, I suffered joyfully for your sins. Won't you suffer joyfully for love? Won't you have my intimate love, an eternity of glory, as reward for a few years of combat and trials?" (*Notebook*, July 11, 1922, no. 111)

Yvonne responded unhesitatingly:

"Oh my Jesus, I love you with all my soul and I want to love you more than everyone else. Let them beat me in anything else, but not this."

It was literally the first expression of her vocation as a child, at the time of her First Holy Communion (see earlier, p. 21). This grace emerged from its chrysalis. But it was the same grace, in the same spirit. Yvonne in no way put herself above others but she recognized no limit and wanted to give not less than everything. And she did not forget her neighbor.

She added: "Oh Lord, I love you most tenderly but grant that I may make you better known, served, and loved" (Ibid.).

The next day, July 12, a week after the vision of the luminous cross, Yvonne went to see Father Crété in Vannes. She wrote in her notebook: "I'm so happy to have gone to Confession to him. Thank you Lord Jesus" (*Notebook*, July 12, 1922, no. 113).

The new relationship between Yvonne and Christ was not simply a loving heart-to-heart. Progressively she received a mission to give her life for mankind, especially sinners, and more especially priests, over whom she would exercise a considerable and varied influence. She was called upon to visit several of them, at difficult times of temptation or of danger.

This overwhelming growth of her whole being did not proceed without a hitch. On July 13 her fever rose to 104 degrees Fahrenheit. She was delirious all night long. Mother Madeleine kept watch over her from four o'clock in the morning.

This delirium was full of meaning, she understood. She went back up to Yvonne's room after morning Mass:

"I knelt down by her bed to finish my thanksgiving and to say my Office. Almost immediately, she began to speak.... I don't know what force kept me there.

"In short phrases, interspersed with long silences, she recounted ... passages of the Lord Jesus. Then what the Lord had to say to me" (Letter of Mother Madeleine to Father Crété, July 19, 1922, no. 138).

The words of Our Lord for Mother Madeleine are noted in Yvonne's notebook, dated July 11.

"I love her! Tell her. She is generous but I want her to be completely humble. I expect much of her because she has received much" (Notebook, July 11, 1922, no. 111).

On July 14 a new encounter, which she related to Father Crété only by allusion:

"Jesus is not waiting until I have entered into his eternity to fill me completely. You could say that he is eager to come and take his poor little creature to himself. It seems that he needs her love, as if he felt all alone, isolated" (Notes, July 14, 1922, no. 119).

SPIRITUAL BETROTHAL

The encounters of July 5 and the following days corresponded to what mystical theology terms "Spiritual Betrothal." These meetings were sometimes strewn with tangible signs, which humanly express love and strengthen it. These signs (somewhat disconcerting, even though found in the annals of mysticism) are accessories. They make concrete in everyday life the reality of a bond of love which renews and transforms the life of the person. It was the starting-point toward a more definitive and even deeper union which was going to come about, through many trials and episodes. She was led more than she led. She was worked upon more than she worked. She was filled with a gift which overwhelmed her.

These signs (which too quickly occupied the attention of the first biographers) remained unknown to the community of Augustinians. To them only the essential shone out—Yvonne's lively charity and her counsels. She carried this community in prayer. She felt urged to enter into contact, to wander into the corridor of the hospital, next door to the cloister. "Mary of the holy cloister," they dubbed her. She firmly denounced the petty gossiping and the diversions of human weakness which so often reduced communities dedicated to God to an all-encompassing mediocrity.

On July 16, 1922 Yvonne Beauvais turned twenty-one years old. Now she was officially an adult, according to the law. And off she sailed, launched by God into a love which absorbed her whole life, and left no place for her human betrothal.

That evening, again, Jesus appeared to her during Vespers of Our Lady of Mount Carmel:

"A light, a clarity so strong that at first I couldn't bear to look into it. Bit by bit this light took a human form. And then I recognized the outline of my Jesus. Without seeing the small details, I could see the changing expressions on his divine face. He...stretched out his hands in a sign of blessing. Then, going toward the Oratory, he put his hand on my head, brought it close to his heart, and disappeared" (*Notebook*, July 16, 1922, no. 127).

EVEN MORE!

July 18, a new encounter. Jesus appeared sad, because of a sinner.

"I love him and he makes me suffer," he confided. "Make reparation and give him to me."

"Lord," I said, "I offer to you the sacrifice of all my joys
on earth, of all my affections. I immolate all the desires of
my heart, all the delights of nature. I want to love you as
much as two people."

"Give me *even more*, my little Yvonne," he answered. (*Notebook*,
July 18, 1922, no. 137)

The next day, July 19, he appeared again, less sad, and asked:

"What are you giving me this evening?"

"But everything I have is for you, Lord. What do you want
from me?"

"Even more!" (no. 137)

Two days later, he repeated:.

"My little Beloved, *even more!*" (*Notebook*, July 22, 1922, no. 143)

This call to participate ever more in the Cross of Christ
remained enigmatic. Yvonne wrote to Father Crété:

"Jesus is asking me for something. What is it, Father? I
have offered up everything to him. I can only think of one
other thing, but I dare not offer it, as I was forbidden to
do so. It is my health, my strength, my life.... May I offer
it to my God? Isn't that what he is wanting? I await your
permission" (July 23, 1922, no. 145).

Father replied by return of post:

"If he repeats to you the 'even more,' reply to him, 'Lord
Jesus, everything that you wish!'

"Keep me up to date with everything. Be very humble...and
also...very grateful...and finally keep very calm" (July 25,
no. 150).

She was living a close relationship with Jesus at every
moment.

"I tell him a hundred times a day that I love him.... I work
on becoming small, forgetting myself. You are not mistaken
Father; I am not humble, but I'm working at becoming so for
the love of my God! He has told me so many times that he loves
the little ones" (Letter to Father Crété, July 23, 1922, no. 145).

Yvonne hungered for humility within herself, according to
the same reasons that Saint Teresa of Avila elucidated thus:

"Why does Our Lord love the virtue of humility so much?...

It is because God is the supreme Truth, and humility is to walk in the Truth. Yes, it is a very great truth that of ourselves we have nothing good, but only misery and nothingness.... The more one understands this, the more one is pleasing to the Sovereign Truth" (*Interior Castle*, Sixth Mansion, chap. 10, no. 7).

The Lord, who was enlightening her about her humility, invited her to see in it neither a decline nor a cause of sadness. On July 23 he encouraged her:

> Why are you so downcast? It pains me to see you like this. Your current imperfections and your past faults, because you hate them, cannot displease me. Make use of them to raise yourself up to me. You have known how to humble yourself and I have run to you. Humble yourself more, continually, always. I want you to be humble.
>
> Love being capable of nothing by yourself, because that incapacity puts you under the sweet obligation to keep yourself united to my heart through love, gratitude, and prayer.
>
> Love to be nothing of yourself because this nothingness places you in complete dependence on your Beloved.
>
> Yes, I took pity on your weakness, because you are of good will. Trust yourself to me, do not trust in yourself, and you will be a saint. (*Notebook* July 23, 1922, no. 144, where the words "be capable of nothing" and "be nothing" are underlined.)

Fr Crété observed:

"The Lord *renders* humble all those he draws near to" (Father Crété to Yvonne, July 25, 1922, no. 150).

Yvonne also received words of encouragement:

"If you only knew, my Beloved, how much my heart delights and rejoices when it meets a human heart that believes in my divine love.... I thirst for the love of mankind" (*Notebook*, July 26, 1922, no. 152).

The visits of the Lord Jesus were daily and could occur up to four times per day. Yvonne was overwhelmed with gratitude:

"Other souls, more generous and more fervent than I am would know better how to benefit from all your favors... and you chose me! You are not difficult, my good Jesus.... I love you madly. I beg you to have me make you loved passionately, my Beloved Jesus. My heart is racing. I beg you to accept each heartbeat as an act of love" (Notebook, July 25, 1922, no. 149).

"I am happy with the spiritual consolations that you deign to grant me but if one day it should please you to leave me in spiritual aridity, I shall still be trusting. It will be pure love... I will love you without any sensible satisfaction, with no other motive than your infinite goodness. I will love you solely because you deserve to be loved, without me bothering about my own contentment.... That is what will please your divine heart, isn't it, my sweet Jesus? Purify my soul of this sense of satisfaction which could degenerate into self-love" (Notebook, July 26, 1922, no. 152).

The apparitions of Jesus had only allowed her to make out a luminous silhouette, without seeing his features. She dared to ask to see him.

Her prayer was granted, on July 22, 1922:

> I saw my Jesus. I saw him. He deigned to respond to the desire I had expressed to him the other day.
> His features were illuminated. His deep eyes looked into my eyes and he smiled at me. He was dressed in white.... His eyes were quite dark; they appeared to be golden brown, and yet they had glints of green and blue. His brown hair, with golden glints, was wavy and fell onto his shoulders. I saw his facial expression change: I saw it become in turn a look of happiness, of joy—and then of infinite sadness. (Notebook, July 22, 1922, no. 143)

This sadness was no doubt because of the sins of the world, like that which Saint Bernadette saw on the face of Our Lady.

"He said it to me again! 'Even more, my Beloved.'

"And I replied as Father had advised me to reply: 'Everything that you wish, Lord.'

"Then his expression changed and he smiled at me. I felt

his love penetrate me completely and there was no longer Yvonne...nothing but Aimée de Jésus"[1] (*Notebook*, July 27, 1922, no. 154).

This perfect union of wills fulfilled the desire that God had aroused in Yvonne at her First Holy Communion: *I will always want what you want.*

She wrote, on July 29:

"My Jesus I love you and because I love you I want to have with you one single will. What you want, I want; what you do not want, I do not want..." (*Notebook*, July 29, 1922, no. 158).

Still this intention expressed since childhood (see earlier, p. 21) which was not voluntarism but pure love.

"Everything that pleases you, everything that you wish, Oh my God, I accept with full generosity, because it is your will. And this acceptance is not just an acceptance out of necessity, it is an acceptance out of love" (*Notebook*, August 1, 1922, no. 163).

It was not a simple heart-to-heart conversation, but a burning desire to communicate this love to the world:

"I love you tenderly, my Lord Jesus, and I would like to make you loved by the whole universe. I would like to embrace all hearts, draw all people to you. I would like that all men love you as a father" (Notes of Yvonne, July [13], 1922, no. 116).

Since July 13, Yvonne noted...

"I have not had feverish temperatures...but I've had barely any sleep, despite doing all I can to get to sleep. And for the past four days especially I've been suffering excruciating headaches. Last night it lasted for two hours and was really painful. I was somewhat afraid I wouldn't get through it. But I am so happy to suffer, Father" (Letter to Father Crété, July 23, 1922, no. 145).

The profound transformation was subjecting her whole being to a harsh trial. On July 28 she wrote:

"My nights are quite difficult, for there are times that I suffer a lot. And then, when the crisis has passed, I sometimes feel so worn out that sleep cannot come... But I am happy,

---

[1] "Beloved of Jesus."

very happy, Father, because I am at peace and because my
Good Jesus is with me, because he loves me and I love him"
(To Father Crété, July 28, 1922, no. 156).

She felt like "a little green fruit, unripened, that the Lord
Jesus lays on the straw, waiting for its perfect ripeness.... But
I shall wait patiently until the day it pleases Jesus to choose
me" (Letter to Father Crété, July 23, 1922, no. 145).

The giant step that she had taken on unknown paths, the
profound development that she was undergoing, frightened
her. It frightened her as the earlier prospect of marriage, or
of the monastic enclosure, had done, but on another level.

> Suffering, both physical and emotional, terrifies me.
> And yet, to suffering, as to everything, I say to you
> from the bottom of my heart, with the full and loving
> generosity of the Blessed Virgin, my good Mother:
>   Ecce ancilla D(omini), fiat mihi secundum verbum
> tuum. (Lk 1:38)
>   (Behold, I am the handmaid of the Lord; let it be
> to me according to your word.)
>   Your servant, oh my God, always, always. (Notebook,
> August 1, 1922, no. 163)

She did not look for any lessening or easing, but for
"patience in suffering," and also the grace "that no one may
notice that my poor body often suffers so much. I would
like that only you would see me suffer...and they've said
to me several times that I look sad! Oh, my Jesus, grant me
enough self-control so as to calm my expression, and that
my face won't reflect the suffering—but rather the joy that
I have in suffering so as to gain you souls" (Notebook, July
23, 1922, no. 144).

She received this reply:

"I will clothe you with my strength. But I shall also give
you suffering. I like to see those I love put up a fight. It will
be private suffering, hidden suffering, so that I shall be your
only consoler. Creatures will not always understand you, but
I'll be there! They will persecute you, they will contradict
you...they will not believe you, but I will console you" (Ibid.).

REVENGE AND COUNTER-ATTACK

Yvonne went to see her spiritual director on August 1. He forewarned her that she might expect assaults by the Evil One in revenge for all these graces. This presentiment surprised her.

"I saw Father for a long time and it did me good. But is it possible, Lord, that the Devil would come to torment me? Everything that pleases you, everything that you wish, oh my God, I accept" (*Notebook*, August 1, 1922, no. 163).

Two days later, those battles began.

"Father, you were prophetic," she wrote on August 3. "The Devil came to torment me last night" (Letter to Father Crété, August 3, 1922, no. 165).

The Prince of Darkness, who normally works in obscurity, manifested himself to her with a strange violence. She felt blows and injuries. And some witnesses saw the wounds form before their very eyes. Her friend Suzanne Guéry, a young intern from the Paris hospitals, who had the bedroom next to Yvonne's, came to her aid during the night several times in 1924, under conditions which exclude any self-harming.[2]

"And to think that there are learned people who deny the existence of the Devil," Yvonne would say to Father Labutte. (Labutte 2, p. 71)

How could the Lord, who fills with love those who love him unreservedly, allow the prince of this world these outbursts?

It is difficult to understand. But is it not the same scandal and the same mystery as that of the Cross? How could God the Father allow the horrendous suffering that was inflicted upon his Son? And we doubtless reassure ourselves rather

---

[2] This is not the place to detail these phenomena, of which we have begun another methodical study. So inexplicable were they that it seems impossible to be able to dismiss them with the usual clichés — automutilation, for example. Several witnesses saw blood gush and seep through Sister Yvonne-Aimée's wimple without any action on her part being able to explain it. And Doctor Queinnec, surgeon at the Malestroit hospital, who often examined, and even operated upon, Sister Yvonne-Aimée, observed the welts that had been left on her body. He left a precise description of them after a fresh verification during the exhumation. (Expert Certification, March 24, 1957, no. 79)

quickly with comfortable rationalism in reducing it to some
metaphor or literary symbol: the "thorn in the flesh" that
Saint Paul speaks of, and that "Angel of Satan that he asked
three times to be rid of. (2 Cor 12:7)

HUMAN BETROTHAL IN SUFFERING

These facts precipitated the breaking-off of the betrothal
to Robert. Yvonne was completely absorbed by another love,
a spiritual and immeasurable love. From the end of April
1922 she had tried to return his "troth," his promise, to Robert, to release him from his word. She used the fact of her
health and her relapses. This reason would have allowed a
separating with no drama, even though there would still
be pain on both their parts. But the previous year (in June
1921) when Robert, struck down with tuberculosis, had given
Yvonne's troth back to her, she had turned down this generous
offer. And in the face of that tragic situation of her fiancé,
love had begun to grow in her. At the moment of the final
detachment, before entering the convent, she confided to
Jesus in these private notes:

"You developed my friendship for Robert and, at the desired
moment, that friendship was transformed into love, so that
I could sacrifice it to you more completely. It pained me
horribly to cause him suffering, even more than my own
suffering" (Notebook, March 13, 1927, no. 138).

But the freedom which Yvonne now wanted to render
to Robert by reason of her health problems, he refused to
accept—just has she herself had refused when he offered
to return her freedom in June 1921. Now in July 1922, she
insisted on it. He tried to reason with her. He tried to seek
out elsewhere the real reason. Could she really be so afraid
of marriage? She replied honestly:

"Yes, the duties of marriage terrified me. That's true, but I
would not have withdrawn from all that if my vocation had
been there" (Letter 5, end of July 1922, no. 161).

"Religious life terrifies me just as much as married life
but...I am sure of its call. I'm telling you again, my dear

Robert, because I don't want to deceive you. Break off from me" (Letter of August 8, 1922, no. 179).

On August 14 he pleaded:

"You played with my heart and now you reject it because you think you've discovered a better life, less mundane? Do you even know what religious life is? You maintain that it terrifies you? To see you become a 'puppet mummy'!! You see, I know them, these good sisters...and I don't like them. You, who love freedom and beauty, adieu! You, my Vonnette, become a good sister, it's not possible!" (Letter of Robert to Yvonne, August 14, 1922, no. 198)

There was heartbreak on both their parts, for their affection was real. It had become, for her too, more than a friendship. She was telling the truth when she wrote:

"I am heartbroken at your suffering. To hurt you causes me incredible suffering. It pains me to be the cause of such a great sorrow when I've always wanted to give you happiness, joy, and peace. It was imprudent of me to come and offer myself to you, I should have waited. I ask your forgiveness" (Letter of August 1922, no. 179).

"Is there any other path to Heaven apart from that of the Cross?" Yvonne asked herself. (1922, no. 563)

Which caused her to reiterate:

> I don't take back any of the things I said to you and I assure you that I love you with all my heart, but neither did I ever hide from you my love for God. Now I feel this love grow more and more and filling me to such a point that everything that is human is effaced, wiped out. You can't be jealous of God...
>
> You are the person that I love most on earth, I'm completely aware of that. But God has the first place in my heart...I cannot resist this voice that is calling me. I break your heart and that pains me enormously. Forgive me but let me go. (Fifth Letter of Yvonne, end of July 1922, no. 161)

"Try not to think of me anymore" (Sixth Letter, August 1922, no. 179).

Later on, Yvonne would draw these conclusions:

"No, it would be impossible to give myself to anyone other than him (the Lord Jesus) and that is not because I don't know what it is to love...I have loved and I still love, but affection, however deep, is so pale alongside what I feel for him!...I want my joys to come from him. I desire to find my joy in his will, that is, in suffering, for I know nothing but to do his will; it is to suffer, it is to die to self constantly" (Retreat of June 3, 1926, no. 353).

The fiancé, full of tact, did not come to Malestroit, so as not to give any scandal.

VISIT OF MARY (AUGUST 15, 1922)

Miss Bato now arrived, on Sunday, August 6. At the railway station she found Yvonne "as thin as a rake." She was disappointed that the rest cure, taken on her advice, had not given a better result. She was "amazed to see Yvonne become more and more marvelously 'simple'" (Sister Madeleine of the Sacred Heart to Father Crété, August 8, 1922, no. 180).

And so she learned about Yvonne's new life. As Leader, or President, of the Association of Mary Immaculate she gave her permission to make her consecration during the High Mass on the feast of the Assumption. That very evening, Yvonne received the new grace of an encounter with Our Lady.

"I saw her clearly. She resembles Jesus, but her eyes are blue...'You are,' she said, 'my privileged child. Have recourse to me in all your needs. I will come to your aid.' Then she disappeared, leaving me an immense joy and a sweet peace" (Letter to Father Crété, August 16, 1922, no. 203).

Yvonne's humility remained total. And her down-to-earth love extended in a realistic manner to all those whom Christ loved and wished to save.

"Oh how good he is, the Lord Jesus, to spoil me so, for I don't deserve it.... But I am convinced that it is so that it will be useful to others" (Letter to Father Crété, August 18, 1922, no. 206).

PREMONITORY DREAMS

Yvonne was wakening to a new world. Her sleep was interspersed with dreams which seemed to her to have a meaning. She who never dreamed! (At least so she thought!) She whose teachers regretted her "lack of imagination" (Labutte 1, p. 233, Note 52). On July 15, 1922 she wrote to Father Crété, who had encouraged her to tell him everything, about a dream that she had "more than a month" before he knew her. Jesus was inviting her to work and entrusted to her a group of doves, some spotless, the others very wounded. The dream came back several times. The second time, she said, "as I was not in the habit of dreaming, I spoke about it to Mother Madeleine, who told me to pay no attention to it" (Letter to Father Crété, July 15, 1922, no. 124).

In August her spiritual director asked her to note down her dreams from now on. He guessed they had a meaning, however incomprehensible they seemed to Yvonne herself. And however humiliating it might be for her to write such absurdities.

What criteria did Father Crété apply (personal experience rather than the classic rules?) when he replied to Yvonne,

"When you can't forget them, these dreams are not ordinary and we have to realize that" (Letter of December 22, 1922, no. 533).

And so Yvonne began, without any embellishment, writing down her dreams, which were incomprehensible to her. The "white doves" which were entrusted to her, the "white cross" which Jesus put around her neck (which would happen when she became president of the future federation).

> Then I saw myself attending the consecration of a bishop in a church that I didn't know and Jesus was saying, "This bishop will be good for you and you will support him by your prayers and sacrifices—especially when he will be in the region of Saint Thérèse of the Child Jesus."
> I also saw myself in prison and an angel came to set me free. It was only in the white cross (dream) that I was dressed as a religious. (Letter to Father Crété, August 18, 1922, no. 206)

The bishop she saw consecrated would be Monsignor Picaud, on July 1, 1925, at the Basilica of Saint Anne at Aurey. At the time of the prediction he was vicar general of Vannes. He would become bishop of Bayeux and Lisieux—the home of Saint Thérèse of the Child Jesus—in 1931. Her angelic deliverance from prison would occur on February 16, 1943, during the German occupation.

Yvonne's new state reminds one of what Saint Teresa of Avila says in the fifth chamber of her *Interior Castle*.

"Do not imagine that this chamber is sleep like the preceding one . . . Here . . . one is absolutely dead to the world so as to live more and more for God. It is a delicious death: the soul is freed from all dealings that it might have, while still being united to its body" (*Interior Castle*, Fifth Mansion, chap. 1, nos. 3–4).

"When it comes back to itself, it can have no doubt that it was in God and God in it" (Ibid., no. 9, p. 603).

But this passivity toward God was an active receptivity in the very depths of the soul. It was released in an intense service characterized by a free outpouring of active virtues and unexpected charisms. It produced an astonishing efficacity, at once both natural and supernatural, despite the astonishing amount of sufferings that Yvonne bore (illnesses, difficulties, attacks from hell) and the upheavals in the very depths of her soul which aroused its radical mystical adaptation to God. Her intense activity was rooted in the Cross of Christ.

Yvonne recounted, as Father had asked her to do:

"The Devil came several times to torment me," she wrote to him on August 10, 1922, "but I am no longer afraid. As regards my pain, it is very sore at certain times but Jesus allows no one to notice anything [except the few persons who looked after her], and I am so happy to be able to suffer for souls, for priests!" (Yvonne to Father Crété, August 10, 1922, no. 186)

It would be one of the objectives of her life and of the missions she would receive from the Lord. She remained abandoned to him, unreservedly.

"I am suffering but if you wish that I should suffer doubly

in order to win you souls, Oh my Good Jesus, strike and use that instrument that is both cruel and humiliating—the Devil! I accept, Lord. I just ask that you never let me succumb" (Notebook, August 11, 1922, no. 190).

All of that immersed her in humility, but never enough, it seemed to her:

"If my heart is often troubled, wounded, it is because I am not humble, and I am sensitive... If I upset myself and am impatient in view of my numerous faults, it is because I am not humble, because I think too highly of myself" (Notebook, August 1922, no. 225).

MISSION TO THE COMMUNITY

In this cloistered community where she was a passing visitor from the outside world, her influence became decisive. It was as if a "mission" had been given to her, with new gifts. Sometimes she could read people's hearts. On July 28, 1922 she related to Father Crété, as he had advised her to do:

> Jesus came to me several times... without speaking. He made me understand and grasp many things which are currently happening and which have already happened [in the community and elsewhere]. He made me see souls, hearts, consciences. He made me see those who repent, those of good will. And Jesus added:
>
> "Know the world and do good to it. I will use you to sow love in souls, to bring relief to those who suffer, to console those who weep, so that you will bring them all to me.
>
> "For that, I'll make you experience all manner of states but my little Beloved, fear nothing, I will be with you." (Notebook, July 28, 1922, no. 155)

On August 28, 1922, the patronal feast of the community, Yvonne received this message for the community which she was in some way supporting:

"Make, and tell them to make, many acts of love. Morning and evening, say this prayer—Oh Jesus, King of love, I trust in your merciful goodness" (Notebook, August 28, 1922, no. 225).

This brief and simple prayer would profoundly inspire the community to re-center everything on love, which at that time was a remarkable novelty, the answer to a deficiency. This popular prayer, widely circulated even today, was encouraged by an indulgence of Pope Pius XI, which Pope John XXIII extended to the universal Church. Yvonne-Aimée saw in it the sowing of a worldwide benefit (Letter of August 22, 1927, no. 480). And thus it was that at the coming of the War in 1940 she would draw the picture and the medal of Jesus King of Love, with the face of a child. This inspiration took concrete form in messages that Yvonne felt urged to communicate to the sisters and to Mother Madeleine herself:

"Jesus told me to speak to several sisters. He told me what I was to say to each of them. This really cost me; so much did I fear that it was not of him... But he desired to give me proofs... In the afternoon, I asked to see the sisters that Jesus had indicated to me" (*Notebook*, August 30, 1922, no. 229).

Yvonne noted down some of the messages transmitted on a page entitled "Words of the Good Jesus spoken these last days, and replies to my questions." They invited very simply to charity, according to the particular problems of each sister:

"That she always simply express her opinion without trying to make it dominate."

"That in conversation she avoid a trenchant and domineering tone."

"That she speak hardly ever about herself, and avoid saying what would be to her advantage" (*Notebook*, August 1922, no. 225).

The community at that time was much on the mind of Monsignor Gouraud, the Bishop of Vannes. Tensions and rivalries were paralyzing the normal rule of charity. The chaplain was caught up in the different cliques. The unusual young Parisienne—wasn't she going to aggravate the disturbances?

Contrary to his fears, the action of Yvonne inspired a profound resurgence of charity, with concrete and demanding consequences. With astonishing perspicacity she rooted out gossip, bitterness, and causes of division. Those who benefited from her counsels were amazed, bowled over, while at the same time filled with a great peace.

"My heart feels the need to tell you what you already know. It's that you have been the messenger of an immense happiness. My life is as if divided in two [i.e., a "before" and an "after"]. There is now only joy," wrote for example Mother Saint John Le Bot to Yvonne (September 10, 1922, no. 268).

And then for the whole community Yvonne received the following message that invited them to root out gossip. It was Jesus speaking:

> The causes of discord are ambition and envy, based on deceit, often on lies. These discords cause the death of fraternal union and ... prevent the sanctity of a Community. A tongue that sows discord kills charity. It puts to flight God himself.
>
> Gossip, you see, destroys the peace of a house, disturbs minds, kills obedience. She who gossips harms not only at the moment that she is speaking, those she lives with. How many absent persons does she wound? So many wounds can never be healed. Rumors, suspicions ... perpetuate themselves. See the disaster! ... I would like that what I am saying here will benefit your dear Community that I love and where I am loved. (Message dictated three times: August 31, September 1 and 5, 1922, no. 230 and 244)

To seven religious sisters, witnesses of the exceptional graces and trials, Yvonne would send, four months later, this message:

"Redouble your goodness, charity, indulgence toward Mother Assistant and Mother Agnes.... Let Jesus radiate through you. All of you, the initiated, the little group chosen by Jesus, you are called by him to be the soul of the Community, the strength which he will use ... to spread ... his love in the hearts of all your sisters" (Letter to Mother Saint Paul, January 4, 1923, no. 13).

THE SIXTEEN STAYS OF YVONNE AT MALESTROIT

1922

1. March 19–September 3: rest

1923

2. April 20–August 20: rest
3. October 4, (19h15 7.15pm)–October 5, morning: overnight stay

1924

4. January 10–February 2
5. May 5–9
6. August 16–September 22: sent by her mother, faints at Doctor Daversin's

1925

7. January 3–April 8: sent by her mother

1926

8. January 16–February 22
9. April 22–May 10
10. August 3–24
11. September 1–22
12. October 19–26
13. November 11–15 At this point, Yvonne had spent six rest stays at Malestroit in 1926, with nothing notable
14. December 27–31: with Mrs. Beauvais, visit to Bishop Gouraud on December 27

1927

15. January 31–February 1: official admission
16. March 18: definitive entry

13
Surrounded by Doubt

SEPTEMBER 3, 1922–SEPTEMBER 1923

PROLONGED CONVALESCENCE AT ANGLET

On September 3, 1922 Yvonne left Malestroit to rejoin her family at Varades and at Le Mans. On October 9 she resumed her life in Paris. She rejoined her poor.

But her health had not recovered. On October 20 she was sent to rest in Anglet, near Bayonne, where her stay would be prolonged in the Stella Maris religious boarding house until March 1923. A "Mrs. B." and her daughter became friends with her and learned her secret. They were stunned by it:

"You will always be my little girl," the mother would say to Yvonne.

"You will abandon me one day," she heard Yvonne reply gently.

The Lord had warned her that she would be let down in friendship. She knew it and resigned herself to the fact, for him alone (according to her own words quoted in the notebook of Mother Madeleine, August 18, 1922, no. 210).

At rest, Yvonne played the piano, and took walks among the pine trees and along the seashore. Her life, devoid of work, was absorbed by the Lord. There she began a new notebook. Her interior life was intense and filled with more activities than it would appear. Her mission of messenger found itself transferred from the community of Malestroit to unknown persons that she would go to meet, before knowing where they were. A first mission sent her from Anglet to Bordeaux,[1] on January 4, 1923. She set off, not understanding anything, on the 2:00 P.M. train and arrived in the big city at 6:00 P.M. The next morning she went to the 6:00 A.M. Mass in

---

[1] About 120 miles.

the cathedral and found there the person she was to meet, and who seemed to be secretly waiting for something. She was carrying within her a fault which she hadn't dared to admit in Confession. It had become the hell of her life. She attended church in remorse and devoid of hope. That very evening she went to Confession.

Yvonne faithfully reported this mission to Father Crété: "It cost me. But I must go, and come, paying no heed to my own reluctance. I am the unworthy little instrument that Jesus wishes to use. Oh my Beloved! I remain embarrassed and grateful for your mercy, which wished to choose me...me the most poor and incapable of everyone, to be the executor of your divine wishes" (*Notebook*, January 5, 1923, no. 7; cf. Letter to Father Crété, January 4, 1923, no. 12).

Jesus showed her his satisfaction.

In mid-March she returned to Paris, to her mother who since October 1922 had been living with Yvonne's sister Suzanne at the Temporary Home, run by the Daughters of Saint Francis de Sales at Auteuil. It was a refuge for distressed gentlefolk. Mrs. Beauvais had been engaged there as Deputy Director, under the leadership of forty-eight-year-old Miss Villemont who knew about Yvonne's situation.

MISSIONS

In Paris, as at Anglet, Yvonne felt driven into "missions" which led her, without her really knowing where she was going, to persons who profaned consecrated hosts. She was horrified at this level of sacrilege. The perpetrators were dumbfounded when, after a polite introduction, she would ask them for what they secretly possessed. They resisted and sometimes sneered at her, then they would sob and own up. Out of obedience, she recounted to Father Crété:

"It was an evening, at 6:45 P.M.... I was not well received, but the poor woman ended up by giving me the Host...The next afternoon Jesus showed me another dwelling so that there too I should go and get him back. This poor woman was certainly possessed. I was shaking as I looked at her, so terrifying was her face and so full of hatred. I ended up, nevertheless, by having my Jesus. That happened not far from rue Monsieur. And I went there in order to get a corporal in which to wrap the Host, and then I went to take it to Father Grizard" (Letter of April 10, 1923, no. 220).

As might be expected, confessors were astonished and had their doubts. Father Grizard, a Holy Ghost father, who was Miss Villemont's spiritual director and Yvonne's confessor, would long remain perplexed and would ask the Lord to enlighten him. And the following year, without him having said anything to either of them, it so happened that Miss Bato accompanied Yvonne on one such mission and came back with her to bring the Host to him. He was reassured by this verification. So it was not a case of imagination. (*Notebook* and account of Y. Bato, November 13, 1924, nos. 822 and 823)

SECOND STAY AT MALESTROIT (APRIL 20–AUGUST 20, 1923)

But Yvonne's health was just not recovering. The pains in her kidneys that she had suffered since her scarlet fever had now become unbearable. Mrs. Beauvais sent her to rest at Malestroit. She returned there willingly, for her heart had remained there.

She found herself once again being a convalescent, idle, and apparently cheery in the walks with her friends where she spoke neither of illness nor religion.

But the kidney pains had got worse. And another heart-break came back to her. Robert's love was ineradicable. He apologized for his strong letter of August 18 (you! A good sister!?) but he was unable to resign himself to the separation and the distance between them. Yvonne's break-off had plunged him into a glacial winter. Her wrote to her again to say:

"My soul is as cold as the weather. It resembles the season. It is somber and full of clouds" (Letter of Robert, November 1922, no. 399).

"I can't sleep; nights seem to be interminable. I rest better by working, for in those times I don't think" (Letter of December 1922, no. 471).

Regarding her stay at Anglet, he had received news that alarmed him. On April 21, 1923, he wrote:

"Ah! Now I understand why you ditched me! It seems that the young man that you meet at Biarritz is a very fine man. He has a title. He has the latest model Voisin car and appears, so I'm told, very deferential toward you. Why didn't you tell me all that right away? Perhaps I wouldn't have understood but after all, however brutal the facts are, it would have been less painful than to hear the whole story from other people. You are free to love whomever you wish.... But why did you deceive me...?" (Letter of Robert to Yvonne, April 21, 1923, no. 240)

Yvonne replied on April 25:

> You have been very badly misinformed. Here is the truth:
>
> The young man with whom I go out is the brother of Madeleine. It's my cousin Xavier de Beauvais. He has fallen for me, it's true, and he proposed to me exactly two weeks ago. But I told him that I already have a fiancé—the Lord Jesus—and that despite how I like him, he can have no hope of marrying me.
>
> I did not tell him about our love, between you and me, because we agreed not to speak about it.... Xavier was amazed at my resolve but accepted it. I saw him again two days ago. He was pleasant; we spoke about religion, nothing else. (Letter of Yvonne to Robert, April 25, 1923, no. 247)

Robert begged her forgiveness:

"At heart, I didn't really suspect you, but...I wanted to get back at you, cause you pain. Yes, alas! I had wanted you to get angry on reading my letter and then write me a letter full of silly and foolish remarks. Instead, I received a letter that was completely calm, completely clear, wherein the truth breathed from every line. Conclusion: my love, that I wanted to diminish by this incident, is freshly stirred up. Did it need any stirring up?" (Letter from Robert to Yvonne, April 29, 1923, no. 257)

How to take Yvonne's conclusion?

"Let's love each other like the old days, when we were children. Let's love each other simply in sight of the good Lord and give to him all the excess of our love.... You only have the good Lord as a rival.

"You have a bright future ahead of you, believe me, and you can still know happiness" (Letter of Yvonne, April 25, 1923, no. 247).

THE BISHOP'S FEARS

In May, now none other than Monsignor Gouraud, the bishop of Vannes, was worried about the unusual importance being given to Yvonne. Father Crété and a nun from Vannes had spoken too much about her, even though it was in confidence. The murmurings had reached as far as the bishop.

"Please don't speak about me too much," Yvonne would write to Father Crété. "Later on they will give me so many problems about my activities. (She already had an idea about the future.) Bless your child, who desires to remain hidden" (Letter of September 3, 1923, no. 544).

Yvonne was summoned to the bishop's office. Monsignor Gouraud (sixty-seven years old) was one of the fourteen bishops consecrated in Rome by Pope Pius X in 1906 to be the vanguard of the resistance[2] after the French government's unilateral breaking of the 1801 Concordat [between the Church and the French State]. He had a reputation of being impressive and stern.

"This visit certainly didn't put a smile on my face," wrote Yvonne to Miss Lefèvre, Director of the motherhouse of the Daughters of Saint Francis de Sales, on June 1, 1923.

> Monsignor is reputed to be excessively cold and somewhat frightening...and it's true. My father [Father

---

[2] Not the same as the French Resistance of WWII.

Crété] told me that he had spent two hours with him
and that His Excellency was frightened by so much
of the extraordinary and was dumbstruck before it
all. I don't find that difficult to believe, for in fact
it's the impression it would make on anyone learning
about all of these things in one go. Despite everything, I remained calm, being completely sure that
my good Jesus would support me in this difficult
moment . . . and, in fact, Mother, this interview went
very well. It lasted an hour and a quarter and it was
only in the last quarter of an hour that Monsignor
came over as less dry and a bit kindly. Until then, he
questioned me without helping me, having me recount
so many details to him. And yet, I have to say, the
fact of being a little Daughter of Saint Francis de
Sales helped oil the wheels a bit . . . as he himself is
a Salesian priest.

After an hour of conversation with him, I dared
to ask him if in fact he believed it really was Jesus
who acted in me and through me. He answered me:

"I have no reason to doubt it, my child. But your
path is so extraordinary! And then again, we have to
say that the Devil sometimes dupes us; in wishing
to do evil, he produces a good."

"But only a temporary good," I replied. "Jesus would
not allow a lasting good."

"That's clear," Monsignor replied.

Then, as I was getting up to leave, His Excellency
said to me that he would receive me any time I
wanted to speak with him. I was touched by this
kindness. . . .

The visit was obviously a bit difficult, but I felt
my good Jesus with me. He had promised to help
me. And so why would I fear Monsignor? He rep-
resents the Church . . . and I have no fear whatsoever
of being supervised by Her. As long as I had always
acted with loyalty, heeding only my conscience, even
if they should accuse me of acting falsely, I would be
ready to accept this humiliation, which would only
increase the beauty of my life in him. I desire only
the truth. (no. 334)

On June 5 the bishop visited Malestroit, where the tension between the two camps (that of the chaplain, and the other side) was still not solved.

YVONNE'S NIGHT AND FEARS

Meanwhile, Yvonne was going through a dark period. The devil showed himself no longer by violent attacks but by doubts, accompanied by a sudden inability to pray. She wrote to Father Crété.

"Father, I'm afraid of all the extraordinary stuff in my life. I don't want to deceive you and I believe I'm a fraud. I see in me only misery and sin. I'm afraid of leading you into error by telling you about all that I see and hear, all that I understand. To be fraudulent would be my agony... The Devil tried to persuade me that I'm not right, that it is him deluding me" (July 6, 1923, no. 401).

Seized by moments of terrible anguish, she spoke to Mother Madeleine, and in somewhat excessive terms. To the words of consolation, she could only reply with aggressive words or a false laugh which was not like her at all. She was seized by a desire to flee Malestroit. Mother Madeleine was worried. Father Crété came from Vannes to conduct an exorcism which brought a momentary calm. But she remained plunged in a great darkness.

On August 1, 1923 she went to Kermaria for the religious clothing of her friend Sister Yvonne Bamélis, and met Father Questel, SJ, who had prepared her for her First Holy Communion (above, p. 19).

"He reminded me of the facts of my three days of retreat. Jesus had already taken possession of my heart and my soul" (Letter to Father Crété, August 1, 1923, no. 471).

But she felt no nostalgia for those days. On December 30 she wrote to Jeanne Boiszenou, mentioning the thirteenth anniversary of that Communion. "I already really loved him at that time, my good Jesus. But since then we love each other even more. We also know each other better" (Letter of December 30, 1923, no. 815).

VACATION AT LE MANS

On August 20, 1923 Yvonne joined her mother and her sister at Le Mans. On September 13 her aunt held a dance for all the young people, from 8:00 P. M. to 10:30 P. M. She joined in with gusto but wrote:

"If I must do the same as everyone else so as not to make myself stand out, and in fact there is no harm in dancing like that, my thoughts are well occupied with other things. I think that in acting this way I'm doing the will of God. That is everything to me" (Letter to a friend, September 14, 1923, no. 568).

During her vacation she made herself the cook at her grandmother's, which was no trifling matter as there were often eleven at table.

A premonitory dream (which she reported faithfully to Father Crété as he had advised) took hold of her when she was on the train from her Aunt Lemoine's place, the castle of Chahaignes, to Le Mans:

"I saw myself in religious habit and travelling. I was in the Augustinian habit (and at that time the Augustinians did not travel) and I saw airplanes throwing large cylinders onto trains, onto railway stations and destroying and burning down everything. I saw men dressed in green getting on and off the train. They looked like military suits...I was afraid and I heard a serious and gentle voice which was saying, 'It will be a trial, a great trial. Pray. Pray much, especially for the priests and for the prisoners.' I woke up with a jolt. It was just the train stopping" (Letter to Father Crété, September 29, no. 607).

The war of 1940 was still far off, and the German army was not yet dressed in green.

14

No Man's Land

PARIS, LATE SEPTEMBER 1923–EARLY JANUARY 1924

On her return to rue Montoise at Le Mans on September 29, Yvonne found a letter from Mother Madeleine (which has not been preserved). Bishop Gouraud temporarily forbade her to have any contact with the hospital and the convent at Malestroit. This caused her suffering such as she never thought possible, but she submitted unhesitatingly.

"Monsignor's decision is that of the divine Master, and he will be obeyed faithfully, loyally and joyfully. If at the moment my tears flow, my Beloved knows that they are not bitter tears. I will love you to my dying breath and even more so when I'm in heaven... If the doors of your cloister are closed to me here on earth, in his heaven Jesus will place me among the Augustinians of Malestroit" (Letter to Mother Madeleine, September 29, 1923, no. 68).

Yvonne had overcome her health problems. She went back among her poor in a new state, where she sometimes felt pulled between her demanding activities and the contemplative prayer which so absorbed her in her time of enforced leisure.

Her help to the poor brought back money worries. How to acquire funds? She enlisted with an employment agency for temporary domestic staff. She would be a bit embarrassed one day. She was standing in for the house cook and one of the lunch guests came and slipped a tip into her hand. Instinctively, she pulled her hand away.

"Yes, yes, take it my child," insisted the generous guest.

She suddenly realized that she was no longer Miss Yvonne but Vonnie the cook. And so, as if to explain her gesture of pulling away, she quickly dried her hands on her large cook's apron and accepted—for her poor—her first tip. (According to Father de la Chevasnerie, *Monette et ses pauvres*,[1] p. 59)

To raise the necessary funds, she came up with 101 different jobs. She painted a number of holy pictures for a shop in the Saint-Sulpice neighborhood. She would soon publish novels (under the pen name of Dyvonne) beginning with *Joujou se marie*[2] (Paris: Plon, 1924). A story about betrothal informed by her own experience.

Gifted at music and expert at piano (with her English diploma) she took up violin lessons, which she felt had more immediate possibilities of being useful. While she was still learning, she dared to give concerts at the homes of her friends.

It's hard to grasp how she managed to take on so many things. For the service of the poor was no walk in the park: one must identify the most urgent requirements; buy, parcel up, and deliver goods; sort out so many urgent needs and problems.

It was this ubiquity that inspired Father de la Chevasnerie to write his successful book *Monette et ses pauvres* (Paris: Mignard, 1931), which sold more than 100,000 copies.

It was at this time that, along with the poor that she herself had sought out and discovered, there were added those to whom she found herself being sent.

> Ever since Jesus has been speaking to me, I learn from him about impoverished households. I go to visit them and in each home I do what Jesus orders me to do. In one there is a sick person to tend; in another a sorrow to console, a morale to be built up. In a third it's a material help to be given.
>
> These poor people are so often to be found in the most miserable neighborhoods of the city. I couldn't go there alone without a divine order; it would be dangerous for my soul as well as my body.

She knew this from bitter experience, and yet she added: "But once Jesus has spoken, I go through these streets without being noticed. Nobody looks at me, so much so

---

[1] "Monette and her poor."
[2] "Dolly gets married."

that I really think that I am invisible to everyone. And so I reach the indicated place unhindered. But my poor are often astonished that I've been able to find their poor hovel without asking anyone for directions" (*Autobiographical Notebook*, pp. 94–95, 1924, no. 859).

All this was done without any fuss, in a clear-sighted fear. Her letter of August 25, 1923 to Miss Bato expresses it well:

"I live by memories...and when the memories disappear, I live by faith. This faith reassures me that he still loves me. I hang on to that despite the best efforts of the Devil to make me let go" (no. 523).

CONFLICT OF OBEDIENCE

Yvonne had made the sacrifice of her beloved Malestroit (just until heaven) without giving up hope that the bishop would one day decide otherwise. And then, didn't her own mother, Mrs. Beauvais, push her, imperiously and prematurely, toward her dear convent? On September 30, recounted Yvonne,

> Mommy came into my bedroom...
> "Yvonne, I'm sure that you're troubled. You've been very pale these past two days. One doesn't just change like that for no reason..."
> "Well, yes, I'm upset because His Excellency doesn't want me to have anything to do with my convent...and how I love my convent!"
> And Mommy...
> "Oh, my poor Vonnette...it won't last.... It will only be for a while. I'll pray that the good Lord consoles you."
> A few minutes later, she comes back into my room and says to me:
> "In any case, my dear Vonnette, you'll see your mothers (the nuns) in January. A nursing home can still receive patients, after all! And then, you also have to attend the clothing (reception of religious habit) of your friend. I insist." (Letter of Yvonne to Rosalie Morand, October 1, 1923, no. 611)

The friend was Elisabeth de Kervenoael. And her clothing wasn't until January 10.

THIRD STAY (OCTOBER 4–5)

So what happened? Did Mrs. Beauvais order an immediate stay (at Malestroit) as she would do later on? Whatever the case, Yvonne was pushed by circumstances that the archives do not shed any light on, to find herself three days later outside the door of the chapel at Malestroit. She did not ring the bell. And yet, Rosalie Morand heard the doorbell ring. (Account of Rosalie Morand, probably November 4, no. 616)

Mother Madeleine was informed, and was perplexed.

"Knowing nothing about this trip...I could not bring her into the hospital because of the bishop's prohibition.... To send the child to a hotel could set tongues wagging. I made a bed for her on the floor of the linen room" (Account given October 5, 1923, no. 620).

The numerous witnesses to this scene seemed to be taken by surprise and at the same time were somewhat awed at this result of a convergence of circumstances that they knew nothing of. Obedience prevailed, despite the surprise. The next day, at six o'clock in the morning, Yvonne was on the train which would deliver her to Angers at three o'clock in the afternoon. Thus ended her third trip to Malestroit, the shortest one, and the most disturbing—for the others as well as for her.

Informed of events, Father Crété was perplexed:

"This scenario is odd. In fact, Yvonne did not disobey. She did not want this trip. She tried to get out of it.... All that remains mysterious...improbable. As for doubting the child, how could I do that?" (Letter of Father Crété to Mother Madeleine, October 7, 1923, no. 622)

He struggles to reconcile two pieces of evidence: Yvonne did not want to disobey. And yet she found herself outside obedience. Could she have been a victim of the devil, he asks himself.[3] He is as perplexed as she is.

---

[3] On January 3, 1924 (no. 6) Father Crété writes: "The Devil could have transported Yvonne." On January 7, 1924 the hypothesis torments him "that the Demon has deceived or duped our little daughter since the end of June" (no. 12). January 14, 1924, his diagnosis and his advice

Yvonne was being led into the unknown. It caused her suffering. She wrote on December 29, 1923: "I think I can say, like little Thérèse of the Child Jesus: I am a little ball riddled with pinholes" (Letter of Yvonne to Father Crété, December 29, 1923, no. 813).

FOURTH STAY (JANUARY 10–FEBRUARY 2, 1924)

And so we come to the journey of January 10 insisted upon by her mother: "You must go to the clothing of your friend Elisabeth Kervenoael."

Father Crété did not want Mrs. Beauvais to know about the mysterious paths of her daughter. And this created unavoidable tensions for Yvonne. How to obey at the same time both the bishop and her mother? She tried. She took the train, "not for Malestroit as Mommy thinks, but to Vannes where Father Crété is waiting for me," she wrote to Miss Lefèvre. "Once at Vannes I'll be enlightened as to what I must do next" (January 5, 1924, no. 8).

She got there on January 10, at 6:30 P.M. The next day she went to the bishop's house.

"I saw His Excellency this morning at 9 o'clock. I stayed a half hour with him. First of all he didn't want to let me go, and I told him I would obey him, whatever he decided. And only a few minutes before I left he told me that I could go there on one condition: to speak about absolutely nothing spiritual with the nuns. It will be hard, but I will obey.... I leave this evening for Malestroit on the 7:15 Express. You can imagine my joy!" (Letter to Yvonne Bato, January 11, 1924, no. 17)

Bishop Gouraud was an intransigent man; he didn't easily change his mind. So how to explain this about-turn? The vicar general, François-Marie Picaud, could not hide his astonishment from Father Crété who then reported their conversation to Mother Madeleine:

---

remain strangely embarrassed: "Did you disobey on October 4? Perhaps, But not clearly disobeyed. You would not, as much as I know you, have clearly disobeyed. But you didn't obey as you should have" (no. 32). His spiritual insight doesn't quite clear up a certain fogginess.

"He confided to me that it is something completely illogical and unexpected that His Excellency did. He very easily permitted Yvonne to return to you and (according to Monsignor Picaud) he should not have done so, so decided was he. I wanted to tell you quickly so as to cheer you, you and our daughter" (Letter of Father Crété to Mother Madeleine of the Sacred Heart, January 14, 1924, no. 32, confirmed by the notation of Father Crété on the letter of Yvonne dated January 12, no. 21).

Bishop Gouraud therefore acquiesced to Mrs. Beauvais' plan, with this single restriction: "Go, then, because your mother is sending you but do not speak about any spiritual matter" (Letter of Sister Saint Paul to Miss Villemont, January 15, 1924, no. 40).

THE TRIAL OF SILENCE

The stay at Malestroit would be prolonged by more than three weeks—up to February 2, 1924. But the warnings or cautions of the bishop and the distance that he established between Yvonne and the community stirred up the critical spirit of Sister Madeleine. She began to doubt. Yvonne didn't complain, nor was she surprised. "How could I defend myself, I being the first to doubt," she would later write to Father Crété, on December 7, 1924 (no. 870).

She herself had been the first to feel these same objections now felt by Sister Madeleine. She liked what was reasonable and the actions that dragged her into these other ways upset her and cost her. If she didn't abandon herself to the doubt it was because the fruits were convincing and because her spiritual director confirmed her insights. In the middle of this arid stay, when "Mary of the holy corridor" found herself excluded, she wrote to Father Crété:

"If in my life there are—both in the present and in the future—shadows, question marks, it is so as to increase my faith, my trust, and that of others. There will be for the humble, which will always include you, irrefutable proofs of the merciful Goodness toward me.

"The Devil will often be quite malicious and seek to discredit me, but he will not always be the stronger one. I am not saying that I shan't suffer before the truth is discovered, but all truth will out one day" (Letter to Father Crété, January 20, 1924, no. 53).

Graces of light and understanding occasionally came to comfort her:

"These happy moments bring me a great peace in my soul, a lasting peace. I am deeply happy.

"More than ever, however, I am having to fight at this time. I am constantly tempted in so many different ways, but my involuntary faults ... do not trouble me. They humble me, and that is good" (Letter to Father Crété, January 25, 1924, no. 70).

PARIS

On February 2, 1924, she resumed her hectic and busy life in Paris. On February 22 Misses Villemont and Boiszenou were witnesses to attacks that she mysteriously suffered:

"Her arm and especially her hands were as cold and stiff as a corpse," wrote Miss Boiszenou on February 22, 1924 (no. 175).

Yvonne felt as if she were pierced. She could no longer see where she was going, she couldn't make sense of anything. However, she concluded in her account to Father Crété (February 24, 1924):

"Jesus came to tell me that he was happy, and that I had worked well. He told me to leave and go see my poor.

"When he had disappeared I got up to leave. Once again I couldn't see. I made an act of faith. I dressed.... At that moment the light returned" (no. 17).

TRANSFER OF SUFFERINGS

On February 29 she entered into participation in the Passion of Christ, especially the crowning with thorns. Witnesses (Miss Villemont and Miss Boiszenou) saw droplets of blood flowing on her forehead. She was sharing in the suffering of Christ for the sins of the world, to a degree that sometimes caused the stigmata, as has happened beginning with Saint Francis of Assisi.

On March 4, 1924 she wrote to Father Crété:

> When I hear of a soul who offends him or who suffers
> without loving him, or even a soul that the Devil is
> torturing, allow me to win that soul for him by my
> sufferings, to pay for it or to suffer in its place the
> pains that it is undergoing.
>
> Up to now I had no right to ask for sufferings: I
> just accepted those that it pleased him to send me.
> Nor would I have dared to ask for them ... that would
> have been presumption on my part.
>
> But now it is different. Because it is Jesus who
> acts, he will give me the necessary strength.... I suffer
> greatly, but I trust my Beloved ... and I am so happy
> to suffer. I believe strongly in the redemption of souls
> by suffering.... It is my way, the apostolate that I
> love. (Letter to Father Crété, March 4, 1924, no. 209)

On March 9 she received the requested authorization, without fuss or fanfare.

To a correspondent who was inclined to dolorism, out of the same concern for reparation, she wrote:

"You tell me that you are inclined to offer yourself for certain souls. Yes, there is a call there.... That does not mean that you will suffer in an extraordinary way. To redeem souls, the principal thing is to unite oneself: unite our nothings to his All, unite our actions, our sorrows, our joys and even our smiles to ... Our Lord" (Letter to Mrs. Quéroy, April 9, 1924, no. 309).

To another friend, attracted to the same ways, she wrote:

"Love suffering, but don't lean on it, don't measure it, for Jesus doesn't like that. In looking at oneself one is tempted to exaggerate everything. One calls 'suffering' what is in fact nothing but our fallen nature and wounded self-love. That is not good suffering" (Letter to Louise Lépron, April 7, 1924, no. 301).

Only love matters. That is what she lived. That is what she counseled, with nothing extraneous. It is what made everything worthwhile and it was the source of her strength.

AT THE TABLE OF SINNERS

On Saturday March 8, 1924, vigil of the first Sunday in Lent—when we read the Gospel of the temptation of Christ—at about 9:30 P.M. she was assaulted by the violence of the one who transported Jesus to the summit of the Temple. Her bedroom was on the third floor. It was a tough fight. She was thrown from the balcony. Her spinal column would retain painful consequences that would last her whole life. At that time of night the doors of the Chalet were locked shut. Yvonne had to knock on the door of Miss Villemont the Director, who put her up in her own bedroom.

The next day, Sunday, she had a fever of 39.5 degrees Celsius (103.1 Fahrenheit) and had several bruises. She got up, with difficulty, for Mass. A sprained ankle made her walking painful. The next day a fever of 39.8°C (103.6°F) and the enemy continued his attacks. She described to Father Crété: "The Lord sent me the humiliating suffering of being possessed by the Devil" (Letter of March 9, 1924, no. 227).

It was her way of sitting at "the table of sinners." To the external attacks, the devil added interior temptations. And yet the spiritual fruits continued to be evident.

"Jesus wanted to make use of me to do good to souls, may he be blessed!" she concludes in her letter to Father Crété. (Ibid.)

STIGMATA

> The temptations of the repugnant enemy alternated with a spiritual and physical entering into the Passion of Christ. On Friday March 14 she wrote: "On Friday, at 2 o'clock, I began to suffer a lot on my left side just near my heart (the lance)—then in my feet, but especially my hands from which blood flowed; also my side, the blood flowed quite copiously from there.
>
> "At 3:30 the sufferings stopped and Jesus came—two or three minutes at most—to encourage me and smiled at me" (Letter to Angèle Mabin, March 15, 1924, no. 243).

"A small wound, about four centimeters long and
quite narrow" was visible at the site of her heart,
specifies her letter to Father Crété (March 17, 1924,
no. 246).

For Yvonne, everything was grace, including suffering. She
wrote on April 7: "He chose me as his instrument because I
was all weakness, all ignorance and because his mercy was
waiting, it seems, for the poorest of all creatures to pour
himself out on. In this way he would have more glory! Little
by little, he absorbed me. Now I no longer live, I live Jesus"
(Letter to Miss Louise Lépron, March 7, 1924, no. 301).

FIFTH STAY AT MALESTROIT (MAY 5–9, 1924)
From May 5 to 9 Yvonne felt impelled to go to Malestroit,
to help a young friend, Angèle, who was close to the convent. Her father was against her vocation. Before going there,
during a day filled with other missions and duties, she wrote
about it to Father Crété.

The authorization given by the bishop, under condition of
not speaking to the community, remained in place.

"I wish to obey it, faithfully and generously," Yvonne wrote
to Father Crété on May 4, 1924 (no. 366).

This brief stay was a source of graces for many. She left
for Alençon, with the conviction that "she'll come back soon"
(Account of Mother Madeleine, May 5, 1924, no. 383).

HUMILIATING SYMPTOMS
In that springtime of 1924 she bore with humor a distress-
ing physical condition:

"My health is . . . not great and—a funny thing—I've grown
to an enormous size. Otherwise, everybody compliments me
on my complexion, and my rosy cheeks and how chubby they
are! Who could doubt it?" (Letter to Angèle Mabin, April 28,
1924, no. 353)

It was an albumin imbalance that was swelling her up so
much. It affected her natural beauty. She was aware of that,
but her life was now beyond self-regard.

JESUS'S SLEEP

The summer of 1924 was marked by trials of abandonment. She wrote to Father Crété on July 11, 1924:

"I try, in the midst of my busy life, to keep myself very united to Jesus. But it is dark and I feel even darker than the night that I'm in. He stays quiet and he sleeps. Let him rest. I will do nothing to wake him, even though his absence weighs on me" (no. 520).

She wrote in her notebook of July 20–26:

> I couldn't write all this week as I've been suffering so much—physically a lot and emotionally even more. Is it the trial foretold by the Lord Jesus? No one will understand you so no one will be able to console you. You will suffer from a strange pain such that no one will be able to understand it, no more than you will be able to express it. This so that not one heart will empathize with your sorrow, and not one word will lift your courage and that abandonment by God himself will be your supreme desolation.
>
> I think that this moment has come. Since Sunday my suffering is to the maximum and when I try to make it known to those whom I should, I cannot.
>
> I think that I'll be able to share what's weighing on me and tormenting me and when I try to do so, I remember nothing, I'm struck dumb. It's just today that I've remembered the words Jesus spoke to me on July 12 last year, and that gives me back a little strength: the abandonment by God himself will be your supreme desolation.
>
> I have not communicated [received Communion] all week. Every morning, when I try to get up I fall to the floor. I start again, and I fall a second time. A third time brings no success either. I'm in agony that I'm not dying. I go into every church, while doing my shopping. I remain right at the back, like the publican. Am I not, in fact, a poor publican? God, who sees right into my heart, knows that I'm sincere and I'm waiting—in vain—for a word from his mercy.
>
> I don't say anything to him. I don't know what to say to him.

I remain there at his feet. Like a little sick dog at
its master's feet. I wait, not a crumb of bread, I'm not
worthy of it, but some crumbs and a remedy. I am
harassed, tormented by the spirit of evil....

I hear these words: "The possessed person speaks
and acts as if it were nature acting on its own when
in fact it is another influence and the patient's will
can't do anything."

Who is saying this to me? Is it a good angel? A
bad one? Am I or am I not guilty? I am torn and
broken by the interior battle. So, is my conscience
so corrupted that I can no longer see if I have or
have not acted wrongly?

In any case, Lord Jesus, sorry for all the pain I
cause you, sorry from the bottom of my heart. How
I wish I were a soul that consoles you, and I cause
you to weep. And I cry too, for I've abused your
kindnesses.

These words that I've just written are nothing,
absolutely nothing, compared to my actual suffering.
It seems to me that if I write what I'm suffering
then I might be at least partially relieved—and Jesus
doesn't want any easing. (Notebook, July 20–26, 1924,
no. 553)

NEW CONFLICT OF OBEDIENCE

On August 15, 1924 Mrs. Beauvais, who Yvonne was to
accompany to Lourdes, suddenly decided to send her directly
to Malestroit. It would be less tiring for her and could only
do her good, she wrote to Mother Madeleine (August 15, 1924,
no. 589). She still knew nothing about her daughter's exceptional graces and the fierce opposition of Bishop Gouraud
who had banned her from Malestroit. The sisters and Father
Crété kept everything private.

On August 16, just as she was leaving, the mailman delivered a letter from Father Crété. Yvonne took it with her and
only opened it once she was on the train. The bishop had
forbidden her to go to Malestroit! She was confused.

SIXTH STAY (AUGUST 16–SEPTEMBER 22, 1924)

The sisters of the hospital had decided to pick her up at Ploërmel and take her to the bishop. (Account of Mother Madeleine, August 16, 1924, no. 594) But by a combination of circumstances she was unwell when she arrived at Ploërmel and Doctor Daversin found her unconscious in his waiting room. She had a fever of 40 degrees Celsius (104°F). It was 7:30 P. M. He brought her to Malestroit. In the circumstances, they took care of her there. And so, on August 17 she was once again at the bishop's house.

"I uphold my decision, he began. You will not set foot again in Malestroit.

Certainly, Your Excellency, but please give me the means to obey you while also obeying Mommy.

Tell your mother.

My spiritual director forbids me to. Mommy should have seen a hundred times by now everything that happens. Jesus lets her see nothing" (Letter to Miss Villemont, August 18, 1924, no. 598).

Yvonne reminded him what he had said to her during a previous conversation:

"My child, in obeying your mother you won't go wrong, and you will do the will of the good Lord" (Ibid.).

The bishop spoke some harsh words:

"I think the Devil has done everything in you," et cetera. (Letter of Yvonne to Father Crété, August 19, 1924, no. 603)

And yet, against all expectations, he concluded:

"Obey your mother. I have no right to prevent you obeying her...."

"His Excellency is very tired. I'm going to pray a lot for him and Jesus will enlighten him," concludes Yvonne. (to Miss Villemont, no. 598)

And yet, Bishop Gouraud's doubts and reasons had struck her:

"I am holding on to everything you tell me, so as not to doubt," she wrote to Father Crété. (Letter of August 19, 1924, no. 603)

The push and pull between obedience to Jesus and obedience to the contrary views of authority was a real blow to her innermost being. How to emerge from such a confusion?

At Malestroit, Mother Madeleine was cold and distant with her, even more than the previous time. The bishop's doubts and critical observations, which she had assumed in interior obedience, had made her reticent.

MISSIONS AND PREMONITIONS

During this sixth stay (August 16–September 22) asked to be discreet toward the community, she felt sent—as in Paris and at Anglet—to unknown persons, profaners—in Vannes, Rochefort-en-Terre, Nantes, Josselin, Saint-Anne d'Auroy, and Carnac. She was sometimes accompanied by Suzanne Guéry, who confirms for us the dates and the itineraries.

Certain premonitions struck her. The Lord made her understand "that the persons I love most in the world will make me suffer much" (Letter to Father Crété, September 9, 1924, no. 579).

In mid-October another prediction was given to her: her little mother, Sister Madeleine of the Sacred Heart, "will die aged 52 and a half, in 1929." She believed she had to tell her and Sister Madeleine "announced it in the middle of recreation" to the astonishment of Mother Marie of the Sacred Heart, who noted it in her diary that day, October 18, 1924 (no. 765).

In Paris, these premonitions continued. On October 25, Yvonne saw herself presiding over an assembly of Augustinian nuns, in front of a book marked "31." This mysterious number makes sense today. It was in 1931 that Rome gave approval to the Constitutions of the Congregation of Augustinian Sisters, which she herself had played a determining role in revising.

She was embarrassed to have to tell Father Crété this strange "proud thought" that had come to her, though how she did not know.

"I wish all these imaginings would go away. And to think that it happens to me always, or almost always, when I'm praying! As I don't take any notice of them, my prayers are still good, aren't they?...

"Yesterday again I wept at not being like everyone else" (Letter to Father Crété, October 26, 1924, no. 778).

At Houilles on October 25 Father Crété informed her in person that he was likely to be banned from dealing with her. (Letter of Yvonne to Angèle Mabin, October 26, 1924, no. 780)

It was the will of Bishop Gouraud, but he didn't want to be the one to command him. He preferred that the decision would come from Father Crété's religious superiors.

Yvonne wrote to Mother Madeleine a few days later:

"The Father Provincial is not giving this order himself but has written to Rome to the Father General, who will order the separation. While we are waiting we are not allowed to write each other as we did before, and in a short time not at all" (Letter to Mother Madeleine, November 3, 1924, no. 791).

On November 15, 1924 she submitted to Father Crété the self-criticism to which she was prone, as invited by the bishop, and she ended up by saying:

"Could it be possible, Father, that the Devil deceives me while I do everything I possibly can to avoid his trickery? Aren't prayer and mortification powerful agents upon the heart of Jesus which force him to give his light?... Could he leave me living in error while all I seek and desire is the truth? No, he loves me and I believe in his love which cannot deceive" (Letter to Father Crété, November 15, 1924, no. 827).

She remained in the appreciation which she expressed thus on September 9, 1924: "It is good, delightfully good, but also terrible to be so loved by the Lord Jesus" (Letter to Father Crété, September 9, 1924, no. 579).

And it was then that the action from hell became something interior. From aggression it became temptation, and dangerously so. There were temptations to suicide, the means of which were given to her. Miss Doublet, of the Home, has left two accounts of the temptation of October 28 in her letter to Miss Boiszenou (October 30) and to Mother Madeleine of the Sacred Heart (November 4, 1924, no. 796).

Her friends from Anglet (see above, p. 75), who had been so moved by their contact with her, turned away from her. On December 4 she told Father Crété:

"They are the first to leave me, others will follow...To you, Father, I can say quietly that I've had rejections in my convent and, perhaps because of my convent, among those who most loved me, most supported me, most helped me to achieve in their early stages the plans of the Lord Jesus" (Letter to Father Crété of December 4, 1924, no. 861).

And yet she remained at peace.

"If these rejections are for me a cause of more sanctity and glory, then I suppose I could put up for an eternity with the lessening of their love" (Ibid.).

UNDER THE CRITICISM OF THE EXORCIST

On November 3 she had a premonitory dream. She saw herself in front of a bearded religious priest with blue eyes. He was questioning her harshly and he increased the number of summonses to appear before him. It is what came about on December 19, 1924.

By order of Bishop Gouraud, who wanted an investigation, she found herself before Father Joseph de Tonquédec, SJ, a noted philosopher and the exorcist of the diocese of Paris. His task was in fact to be like an examining magistrate.

"Have you never thought that all that was the result of your imagination?"

The question did not surprise her. She had never stopped asking herself this question, nor awaiting with perplexity the signs of an answer. This interview restarted her troubles. But, from the very next day, signs sustained her. In the chapel of the Home she saw drops of blood flow from the side of the statue of the Sacred Heart. Other women present in the chapel soaked up the blood onto a piece of linen, which they preserved. (Notebook, December 20, 1924, no. 886. Letter to Angèle Mabin, December 24, 1924, no. 896. Account given by Miss Doublet and Miss Lépron, December 20, 1924, no. 889.)

TO THE AID OF A PRIEST IN PERIL

She continued to be inspired interiorly to visit Christians in danger, sometimes by being transported rapidly which astonished her. This cost her:

"Father, I suffer a lot when he has me do what you know about for priests [stop them when they are about to commit a sin]. I was impelled to do what I did. I did what I believed was for the best. I could still be mistaken" (Letter to Father Crété, December 7, 1924, no. 870).

She spoke about it again in her letter of December 17:

"This poor priest that Mitou spoke to you about on my behalf, wrote to me.... I'm sending you that letter, take care of it Father. He is still sick.... Soon the soul of this priest will enter into its eternity" (no. 879).

His letter (December 10, 1924), preserved in the archives at Malestroit, reveals his conversion.

"You saved my soul, a priest's soul," he wrote to Yvonne. "I went to Confession. It is thanks to you, dear Miss, that I didn't fall and I will always be conscious of that.

"It is difficult for me to entrust to paper what I would like to say to you. I need to see you. I know that you are the Lord's messenger and that you will bring me strength, courage and patience to repair the harm that I caused, and have done to myself. Please accept my apology and my deep respect, A. B., priest" (no. 874).

This priest died a month later, at the very beginning of January 1925. To Father Crété, who was always keen on precise details, Yvonne wrote on January 16, 1925:

Dear Father, you want me to tell you about this priest who died about two weeks ago. I came to know him about five months ago. I had gone into a church to make a visit to the Blessed Sacrament when quite suddenly I knew that I had to go toward this priest who was just a few steps away from me, and to tell him not to go where he was intending to that same evening, that he would fall. Then another communication of a more private nature. He was very surprised and moved. His plan (for that evening) was known only to himself. He asked me how I knew what I had just told him.

I replied that I had just now had the revelation while praying and that I had immediately come over to him. He thanked me very much. I did not introduce myself to him.

The second time I was again in a church. The Lord said to me:

"Go out, and tell this priest to be careful this evening."

I obeyed this voice. I recognized the priest from the previous time and I repeated to him what Jesus had told me to say to him.

A third time I gave him a somewhat similar message. That time I was walking along the street and in front of a certain house I became sort of immobilized, incapable of going any further. At that moment a voice told me to go up to a certain floor where I would find this priest preparing to receive a visit and that I was to ask him to let me tell him such and such a thing. This I did. (Letter to Father Crété, two weeks after the death of the said priest, January 16, 1925, no. 31)

As she realized it was time for the mail collection, she finished her letter mentioning a fourth meeting which she had already several times "recounted in detail" (in her letters of December 7 and 15, 1924, nos. 870 and 879).

GOD ALONE

On January 1, 1925 she renewed her abandonment to God alone:

What will be my great resolution at the dawn of this new year? I have none other than to abandon myself completely to God, to lose myself in him so as to do everything that he wants.

If God orders me to do the impossible, I will undertake the impossible and he will accept my effort. If God commands, what can I do other than obey? If he tells me to go and move a mountain, I'll get up in the morning, I'll go and lay siege to the foot of the giant and if I lack pick and shovel, then armed only with my two hands, I'll still go.... I want to see your will everywhere. I want to love you and make you loved with all my efforts, oh my God. (*Notebook*, January 1, 1925, no. 2)

SEVENTH STAY AT MALESTROIT (JANUARY 3–APRIL 8, 1925)

On January 3 Yvonne returned to Malestroit. It was her mother who sent her there—and she obeyed, as Bishop Gouraud had decided was the right thing to do. But Father Crété, who did not receive her letter, was against her coming to the convent, where the bishop had asked him no longer to be a confessor.

On January 5 Yvonne submitted the problem to Father Picaud, superior of the Malestroit community, who had come to visit her.

He was a short man (1.53 meters, barely five feet). He had an inferiority complex about it. But his presence was imposing: a penetrating gaze, a deep and expressive voice, and a "frightening intellect," according to the dean of the chapter.

He could combine a sharp logic with a lively sensitivity, and a keen critical sense with an open realism. The wide range of controversies that he addressed and mastered led him to judgments that were respected. An expert theologian (former teacher of dogma, then of sacred scripture, at the major seminary in Vannes), he had gained the trust of his bishop and of the clergy. He had been vicar general since 1917.

"He was very good for me, despite his haughty air of an examining magistrate," Yvonne wrote to Miss Lefèvre after her first meeting, January 6, 1925 (no. 13).

And to Father Crété:

"I don't know what impression I made on Father Picaud. I shan't worry about it too much. I prayed Jesus to make me answer exactly and very precisely all the questions he asked me" (Letter of January 7, 1925, no. 15).

He allowed her to remain at Malestroit. She was astonished. (Ibid.) He saw her again on January 11:

"I told her again my objections and my fears. She suffered a lot, shedding copious tears. Obviously I terrify her. She left downhearted," he noted. (April 10, 1925, no. 289)

For her part, Yvonne noted:

"Everything that he tells me as spokesman of His Excellency is very painful to hear" (Letter to Miss Bato, January 15, 1925, no. 29).

"Father Vicar General doesn't believe what I tell him. I trust in Jesus. If it is he who wants me to speak, he will see to it that what he wants is accomplished" (Notebook, January 12, 1925, no. 22).

Monsignor Picaud was amazed when she asked him for the modernization of the hospital and not her entry to Malestroit. She dared to do so the next day, January 12, in the evening. Monsignor Picaud replied:

"The extraordinary phenomena which you are subject to are incompatible with the life of the Community" (Signed notes of F. Picaud, April 10, 1925, no. 289).

But that very day Monsignor Picaud perceived signs which began to convince him. (Ibid.)

On January 13 Yvonne noted this dialogue with Christ:

"Lord, I'm hungry."

And he answered me:

"Just a little more time and you will be satisfied" (Notebook, January 13, 1925, no. 23).

In this beginning of January 1925, Father de Tonquédec visited the Home to inquire among the young women who saw Yvonne in daily life:

"He was thorough, strict and good, and judged Yvonne to be simple, obedient, balanced, good and incapable of being devious. But he is disconcerted in the face of the extraordinary facts and, obviously, he doesn't believe" (Testimony of Miss Villemont, transcribed in Yvonne's letter to Father Crété, January 16, 1925, no. 31).

On February 1 Yvonne told her spiritual director about new premonitions, as he had instructed her to.

"Jesus told me some secrets: I don't want to tell you

everything because it concerns certain souls. But I can tell you about what has to do with me.

"I will have troubles—a lot—through Mother Madeleine, and through the convent chaplain. Through a priest who will be for me at first a friend and benefactor for the works of God and who...will later on do me much harm.... I didn't understand. I entrust myself to Jesus," she concluded. (Letter to Father Crété, February 1, 1925, no. 77)

She didn't forget her poor, from whom she was separated by distance.

> Poor Alice!... I've only got 20 francs. What to do? I saw her, my poor Alice, holding her two children close to her and walking along the banks right beside—oh so close to!—the Seine. She even went down via the little staircase beside the bridge. Her feet got soaked in the water. Mimie screamed and little Jean cried. She realized her carelessness. She went back up the steps. So as not to pay for a hotel room, she stayed outside all night. She prefers to eat and not to rest. Oh my God, have pity on her, you who have the heart of a mother.... Mother Superior kindly loaned me the money. I sent it to her right away. May it arrive in time. I trust in you, Jesus! (*Notebook*, February 11, 1925, no. 115)

How to earn the money necessary to meet these needs? Her health no longer allowed her to work as a maid or a cook. And Father Crété had just forbidden her a more advantageous solution that she had found—to publish novels and short stories: "It will cost me, to no longer write for my poor. That's no doubt why Jesus is asking this sacrifice from me," she noted in her *Notebook*, February 13, 1925 (no. 121).

She also painted pictures and sold them to a shop in the Saint-Sulpice neighborhood. But at the beginning of March, "the shop which took my pictures has changed hands and the new owner isn't going to sell pictures! Jesus is taking away from me all the means of earning the money for my poor! And yet I need to! What am I to do?" (*Notebook*, March 7, 1925, no. 180)

She was invited to give a concert, on the approaching March 19, in the salon of a nearby house. Father Crété encouraged her to do this: "So, I'll go, unprepared! I don't know what I should play. I have neither music nor violin to rehearse some pieces. Ah! If it were not for the poor!" (*Notebook*, March 5, 1925, no. 172)

The day after the concert, March 20, she noted:

> I was extremely praised and complimented; but these tributes passed over me as if they were meant for someone else....
>
> I was thinking of Jesus.... I was playing and singing for him....
>
> When I play, all my love goes into my bow, I make every chord resonate with love. I make my violin translate my soul, my faith, my hope, my love...he understands and that's enough for me.
>
> The audience, not used to this particular game, I assume, applauds. They don't know that it's my soul that plays and that all these tunes are canticles of love. That's why I have success. It's because of him. (*Notebook*, March 25, 1925, no. 213)

This cost her more and more but it was the only solution left to her to succor those whom she helped from afar.

TRAPPISTINE, POOR CLARE, CARMELITE...OR AUGUSTINIAN?

The uncertainty of her future weighed upon her. She wrote to Miss Bato:

"The bishop's resistance is perhaps willed by God to prevent me entering Malestroit because I'm meant to go somewhere else...

"My heart, obviously, tends toward Malestroit. It's my convent.... I have suffered so much and even still suffer so much for it. But a more austere life would suit me better. I thirst for silence and solitude" (Letter to Miss Bato, March 5, 1925, no. 173).

She asked Jesus: "Where do you want me? As a Trappistine, with the Poor Clares, or in Carmel, or with my dear

Augustinians? Where do you want me, Lord?...I am so Augustinian in my heart, even while having no taste for what they're doing in my dear convent!" (*Notebook*, March 11, 1925, no. 186)

But she thought she saw that Malestroit might become possible.

CONVERGENCE OF SIGNS

On March 17 Father Picaud asked her prayers for a serious decision that he had to make, and which he kept absolutely secret. (Bishop Gouraud had asked him to be auxiliary bishop of Vannes.) Yvonne replied to him the next day:

"I heard Saint Joseph saying, while placing his two hands upon the head of a priest, who seemed to be you...

'With a new title, he will be my son.'

"I assure you that I didn't understand much in all that" (Letter to Father Picaud, March 20, 1925, no. 215).

That which Yvonne hadn't understood was, though, full of meaning for its recipient. The convergence of signs struck him.

BEFORE THE EXORCIST

On Holy Thursday, April 9, Father de Tonquédec was in Le Mans. He was preaching in the town's church of Notre-Dame-du-Pré. He had Yvonne come to see him.

"He was good; dry and cold. He wonders if I'm telling the truth or am I not quite simply an actress.... He wants to see something. If he doesn't see anything, he won't believe" (Letter to Father Picaud, April 9, 1925, no. 282).

On Easter Sunday he mellowed a bit.

"He was very good."

Yvonne always said of those who made her suffer that "they are good." Note here her nuance—"very good." She continued: "He told me that he didn't mean to call me an actress but that it was his duty not to take at face value what I told him, that is, not to believe without proof. He told me that it was necessary for me to see a doctor, who will examine me to see if the wounds that I have were not caused by any sort of instrument and inflicted by myself. It's also necessary for him to pronounce on my case that he see some phenomena taking place" (Letter to Mother Madeleine, April 12, 1925, no. 295).

This request was alien to Yvonne. None of this was done to order, or on demand. It was alien to her grace, to her dynamism and to the risks of her difficult life. But, here again, she tried to obey, tirelessly: "I well understand that he cannot just believe me on my word. His duty is to judge me rather than to approve me. Approve what first of all?! The graces that I receive! See if all that comes from Jesus?" (Letter to Father Crété, April 14, 1925, no. 301)

The medical examinations, insisted upon by Father de Tonquédec, cost her. They were "humiliating," she wrote to Father Crété. (He made her undergo a bladder probe.)

She added:

"I like the father. He told me he was not ill-intentioned. And I have no trouble believing that. He has a very onerous duty to carry out for, obviously without wanting to, he must cause grief to people and that is always disagreeable.

"I'm going to pray a lot for him and then, if you allow me, I'll offer an hour of my sufferings every day for his intentions. I won't specify why to Jesus. He will use my suffering for whatever cause he wants."

These benevolent expressions represented her victory over an extreme repugnance. Sister Marie of the Trinity still remembers the shudder of fear that came over her when one day she happened to run into Father de Tonquédec—she who was afraid of nothing.

The questionnaires which were conscientiously multiplied by the investigator, the introspection that he required, were contrary to an essential demand of her spiritual life—not to look at oneself. All these demands for explanations, for proofs to be furnished, led her toward introspection, to the past which one should forget in order to go forward as the Lord interiorly invited her to do. Such that she would write a year later to Miss Villemont:

"I didn't want to fall into the trap of analyzing myself too much.... It pains me to think about myself. That prevents the soul from rising, for, as long as one is turned in on oneself, one doesn't look at him; the more one speaks about me, the less one speaks about him" (Letter to Miss Villemont, March 21, 1926, no. 208).

The service of the poor, the mystical graces, and the spiritual battles continued, nevertheless. On Holy Thursday, April 9, after an interview with Father de Tonquédec which had somewhat disconcerted her, she shared both interiorly and physically in the Passion of Christ.

"At the moment I was beginning my holy hour, I felt a really strong anguish overtake me.... I suffered an agony. I felt alone, exhausted, suffering all over, especially of thirst.... My heart felt as if squeezed in a vise, and my eyes flowed with tears of blood" (*Notebook*, April 11, 1925, no. 290).

REMOVAL OF FATHER CRÉTÉ (APRIL 1925)

After Easter, Vicar General Picaud communicated to her an order from Bishop Gouraud: cease all contact with her spiritual director Father Crété, assumed to be the instigator of this profusion of signs and wonders. Yvonne courageously took the initiative in this rupture demanded by obedience. But with such delicacy:

"My father, and that you will always be, whatever happens.

"You taught me, my father, to be generous, to know how to obey. I wish to bow with no objection or bitterness before the will of a hierarchical authority.

"I also want to prove to Jesus that I love him, by offering him generously the greatest sacrifice that he's asking of me" (April 25, 1925, no. 327).

PERPLEXITIES OF THE EXORCIST

Father de Tonquédec remained skeptical. These extraordinary signs that others witnessed, why did they never happen in front of him? He asked for them. Then, at the beginning of May, one day when Yvonne received the grace of participating in the crowning with thorns, he saw blood flowing from her forehead. But, in fact, this sign was not needed for him to give his approval.

"He told me that he believed.... that I was a good child, and that I really loved Jesus" (Letter to Mother Madeleine, May 9, 1925, no. 360).

MEETING POPE PIUS XI (MAY 1925)

On May 11 Yvonne and her mother set off for Rome. They were going to attend the canonization of Thérèse of the Child Jesus, who Yvonne had felt close to since her childhood. She summarized thus the fruits of this journey:

"I suffered there and received great graces. The atmosphere in Saint Peter's transports you from earth. I was flooded with joy, with light, with hope upon approaching the 'confession'...where rests Peter, the Prince of the Apostles" (Letter to Father Picaud, May 28, 1925, no. 401).

"If I could tell you...everything that I felt, heard, everything that this temple of God revealed to me!...but I don't know how. I would need to speak another language.... I already loved the Church a lot but now, this love has grown so much that for Her I would suffer the greatest martyrdom.... With Jesus nothing is impossible" (Letter to Mother Madeleine, May 31, 1925, no. 406).

The pilgrimage leader, an Assumptionist priest, invited each one to ask for a specific grace. On this day of her glorification, Saint Thérèse will be graced with a special power and will be able to refuse no one! Yvonne asked for "the grace to do something for France." She even dared to ask for a sign that her request had been heard: that the *sedia gestatoria* would stop in front of them and that the Pope would bless them specially. To Mrs. Beauvais this seemed an enormous request. And yet that is what happened. Pius XI emerging through the crowds upon the heavy portable throne, traced the sign of the cross over her and her companions.

Two days later, during the papal audience, he fixed an attentive gaze on her. She had the impression that he recognized her.

"In this gaze," Yvonne would say later, "we said many things to one another" (*Articles*, p. 41).

VISITING THÉRÈSE AT LISIEUX

On their return, June 15, she went to Lisieux. "I asked the little Thérèse, who like me knew the pain of waiting, to help me to bear it well" (Letter to Mother Madeleine, June 15, 1925, no. 434).

NEW MEDICAL EXAMINATIONS

Father de Tonquédec increased his requests. After the examination by Doctor Pasteau came one by Doctor Vinchon, a neurologist. He found her "very normal" (Letter to Mrs. Quéroy, July 16, 1925, no. 485).

Yvonne reminded Mother Madeleine that Professor Miraillé had already reached the same conclusion: "They have never told me that I was neurotic," she concludes. (Letter to Mother Madeleine, July 19, 1925, no. 490)

PROVIDENTIAL AMNESIA

Father de Tonquédec didn't leave her alone. Yvonne had predicted the death of her twenty-two-year-old cousin Marie-Madeleine de Beauvais, which came about on July 16.[4]

Father de Tonquédec asked for the address of the deceased. But before her death, on July 12 Yvonne had promised Madeleine complete discretion, with an oath sworn on a crucifix. Father Grizard, the confessor, invited Yvonne to keep the promised secret. She was relieved, she who wrote on March 4, 1925, about an indiscretion that she was the subject of:

"While everyone is a master of his own secrets, he is not master of others' secrets" (Notebook, no. 169).

Father de Tonquédec was convinced of his rights. He insisted:

---

[4] On this well-documented episode:
   —Diary of Miss Boiszenou, July 10, 15, 17 and 18 (nos. 479, 483, 487, 489)
   —Letter to Mrs. Quéroy, July 16 (no. 485)
   —Letter to Marie-Reine de Beauvais, not preserved but known via the Boiszenou diary, July 18 (no. 489)
   —Letter to Mother Madeleine of the Sacred Heart, July 19, 1925 (no. 490)
   —Telegram to Fr Crété, July 16 (no. 484)

"It seems that under the seal of Confession I can speak without breaking my oath," writes Yvonne. "I tried to do it but at that moment something very strange happened in me: a void in my head, so total that I could only just manage with difficulty to pronounce these words:

'I can't. I can't'" (Letter to Mother Madeleine of the Sacred Heart July 19, 1925, no. 490).

This type of amnesia casts light on the mysterious case of Catherine Labouré who suffered the same inability when her director commanded her to respond to the investigation instigated by the archbishop of Paris. Yvonne tried to obey, unaware of the casuistry of these types of secret. An interior dam prevented her. But this blockage made a poor impression on the investigator. Evasion, acting, he believed.

He insisted, and he threatened:

"In all this I do not see the divine spirit. I will tell Bishop Gouraud that you have disobeyed" (Yvonne to Bishop Picaud, September 14, 1925, no. 602).

It was a harsh shock to her.

On July 1, 1925 Monsignor Picaud was consecrated auxiliary bishop of Vannes, at Sainte-Anne d'Auray. Yvonne was there. The event clarified premonitions which she had received without understanding them (see earlier, p. 105). But she remained in the dark night.

On August 3 she wrote to the new bishop: "I am assailed by doubts, by anguish. The Devil uses everything to discourage me; good as well as bad actions, and I have to struggle hard to keep my soul in peace" (Letter of August 3, 1925, no. 521).

Then she received from the Lord a grace of peace. (Notebook, August 5, 1925 and Letter to Miss Villemont, August 7, 1925, no. 530)

A VERY SURPRISED MOMMY

Mrs. Beauvais still knew nothing of Yvonne's extraordinary life. That made no sense, insisted Father de Tonquédec; it was a source of misunderstandings. You have to tell her. Yvonne had held off, for fear of multiplying the indiscretions and complications, which were already too many. She entrusted this delicate mission to Father Grizard. He carried it out. It was a shock to Mrs. Beauvais. She screamed. Father Grizard provided her with proofs. Suzanne had already heard, due to an indiscreet remark, at the end of September.

"At first Mommy was appalled," Yvonne wrote to Mother Madeleine, "now she is happy.... My sister appears to believe.... May Jesus turn everything to his glory" (Letter of October 8, 1925, no. 664).

When they saw each other again, on her return from Le Mans, Yvonne explained to her:

"You know, dear Mommy, God works wonders in all souls and it is unseen. With me, it is seen and that is the only difference" (Testimony recorded by Father Viry-Dacheux, OP, in 1959, which expands on the somewhat less specific testimony of Mrs. Beauvais in her notes of April 1957, no. 125, p. 32).

Her smile and her joyful appearance drew a veil over the trial that she was bearing. She wrote, on March 16, 1926:

"Someone said to me today:

'Oh, how you're spoiled, indulged, pampered. You don't know what it is to suffer.'

"I smiled interiorly. I looked at the crucifix that was in front of me, and I kept quiet. What could I have said?" (Notebook, March 16, 1926, no. 197)

BISHOP PICAUD'S INVESTIGATION

On October 17, 1925, Bishop Picaud was passing through Paris en route to Rome. He took the opportunity to make enquiries at the Home, at Miss Villemont's, and at rue Monsieur at the Daughters of Saint Francis de Sales: Misses Bato, Lefèvre, et cetera.

"I wanted to understand if I were dealing with cranks, with neurotics and if there wasn't a certain naïveté, a certain gullibility in their case. And instead I found myself confronted with declarations of a perfect clarity and completely consistent. I found myself, taking them one by one, dealing with persons who are perfectly balanced" (Bishop Picaud to Father Louis Barral, October 5, 1954, no. 176).

He couldn't reach Father de Tonquédec but he met Father Grizard. His conviction was strengthened.

On October 29, the day of his audience with the Pope, Yvonne thought she saw him at the feet of the Holy Father. (Letter to Bishop Picaud, October 29, no. 694)

EIGHTH STAY (JANUARY 16–FEBRUARY 22, 1926)

On January 16, 1926 Yvonne returned to Malestroit to have a rest there, with the authorization of Bishop Picaud. It was the eighth stay.

From February 4 to 22, 1926, she suffered from harsh assaults from hell, attested to by several witnesses. She fortified her courage by even harsher penitential acts, which Miss Villemont discovered by accident on February 6. (Villemont Diary of that date, no. 98)

PILGRIMAGE AND SMALL TALK IN SERVICE OF THE POOR (APRIL 9, 1926)

April 9, Yvonne spent the day at Lisieux and returned to play the violin in the evening at the house of "Madame de R," as always for her poor. She was feeling more and more alien to these social events.

"And to think that . . . this evening I'm going to have to play the piano and the violin, to give pleasure! I'm going to have to dress up and make small talk. . . . It's for you, my God! But I much prefer the evening that I spent yesterday, the dinner at the home of my poor—my miserable soaked clothes, my worn-out shoes—to all the luxury of this evening (and yet I do like this luxury). I prefer the thatched cottages or the old shacks, because you would have preferred them! I prefer them because there everything is true . . . and there my heart feels at ease" (Notebook, April 10, 1926, no. 269).

INTENSIVE PRAYER

Yvonne continued to pray in all serenity for those who, without meaning to, increased her sufferings. On May 23, the feast of Pentecost, she wrote: "I prayed a lot to the Holy Spirit this morning, for those I love, for my big sister [Miss Villemont] and for Their Excellencies Gouraud and Picaud, Father Crété, Father de Tonquédec, those who are involved in guiding me in the way of Truth" (Notebook, May 23, 1926, no. 322).

From May 31 to June 4 on retreat at Versailles, she did not forget the future of Malestroit. She wrote to Mother Madeleine of the Sacred Heart, who had become superior of the House: "For your plans, first of all obey what Bishop Picaud has to say on the matter" (Letter of June 1, 1926, no. 340).

And to Bishop Picaud: "I am convinced that Our Lord wishes to make Malestroit a rather important work. Why? I don't know, but it is incredible how much he loves this convent" (Letter of June 6, 1926, no. 358).

Miss Bato enrolled her for a retreat for young girls at Lisieux. Yvonne met up with her at Trouville, where she was "sent to someone": a new spiritual mission which was not elaborated upon. (Letter of Miss Bato to Mother Madeleine, June 21, 1926, nos. 385 and Notebook, June 29, 1926, no. 410)

She was being led more and more to forget herself for the sake of others: "Nothing gives me greater joy than the joy we give to those we love, and the way to give me happiness is to really make my friends smile.... It is quite sure, nevertheless, that I do not live for myself, nor for what happens to me, but rather for everything that affects and happens to others. My life is not my own; it belongs to God and to the others" (Notebook, June 26, 1926, no. 399).

At the end of June she was burdened with cares—urgent orders for paintings, but especially her sick in the red zone: "In the past two weeks, four deaths among my poor. It's a lot.... It's misery.... Always misery!... Thanks be to God, I was able to pay for the four burials, but I had a hard time. I hurt my foot and had to slow down my visits" (Letter to Mother Madeleine, June 28, 1926, no. 407).

On July 5, 1926, the fourth anniversary of her first mystical graces, she saw the same cross but with red rays. (Notebook, July 5, 1926, no. 429, and account given by Miss Augris, no. 430)

On July 22 a somber premonition was given to her: her little mother, Madeleine of the Sacred Heart, the Superior of

Malestroit, was going to turn against her. "Why is my heart so sorrowful when I think of my 'little mother' Madeleine? I have the impression that I'll suffer a lot through her. I already told her this but I keep quiet now because the idea is hurtful to her. She assures me that she'll never doubt me. As for me, I'm afraid for the coming years of 1927, 1928 and 1929" (Notebook, July 22, 1926, no. 470).

Her premonitions came to her in a darkness, which contrasted with the clarity they took on after they had been fulfilled.

On September 18 she began to speak about her entry to Malestroit in the following March. Yet, everything was against it, in the Chancery of Vannes as well as in Paris. Nevertheless she prepared her bridal trousseau. On September 20 she confirmed: "I am sure that I'll enter next March. I don't know how it's going to come about, but I feel that Jesus wants it" (Diary 1926, September 20, no. 570).

On October 4 she received from a wealthy friend a substantial material and moral assistance for one of the priests she looked after.

On November 13, during her stay at Malestroit, she was again invited to play the violin at the home of a neighboring "marchioness," no doubt Madame de Boynes, at Campénéac, for the benefit of her poor. This cost her more and more:

> Ah Lord, if were not for you, I would send them all packing. It's tiring to be sociable and chatty all the time. And to be true! This evening I can't take it.... Yet I promised to go to the house of the Marchioness of X to play the violin. Three times I was about to telephone to say I was too tired, that they shouldn't expect me. Thank you Lord for not letting me give in to the temptation. I'll go. I'll make myself up and be sociable. I'll wear my white silk dress and my pearl necklace. I will put a smile on my face, and I'll be able to keep it there by thinking of you, my Jesus. I'll be gentle, patient, joyful and I will introduce souls to you while sipping... a cup of tea. (Notebook, November 13, 1926, no. 643)

A DEFINITIVE REFUSAL

On January 5, 1927 a letter signed by Bishop Picaud brought Yvonne a refusal with no hope of appeal:

> In agreement with Bishop Gouraud, I write to inform you that you must no longer think of being admitted to the convent of Augustinians at Malestroit. I know how painful this news will be to you, but I am sure that your supernatural spirit will lead you to accept this decision.
>
> You may, however, enter any other community of Augustinians that you wish, and write at once to the superior to request admission. Pointless to speak of extraordinary facts. I myself will inform whoever needs to know. (Letter partially burnt, preserved in the archives, January 4, 1927, no. 6 and reconstruction sent by Yvonne to Bishop Picaud on March 3, 1927, no. 113)

On receipt of this letter, explained Mrs. Beauvais,

"We looked again, more carefully, at the letter and the envelope...Yvonne put these documents carefully into her bag, with a medal, so as to send them back to you...

"This morning, at the start of breakfast: 'The Devil must be about to play a trick on me,' said Yvonne. 'He is not pleased.'

"At the same moment, we saw the letter in the fire. A fragment had fallen beside the fireplace. I kept it carefully..." (Letter of Mrs. Beauvais to Bishop Picaud, January 6, 1927, no. 12).

That study of the letter, snatched from the fire, revealed anomalies that can still be observed today. It was indeed the handwriting of Bishop Picaud (perfectly imitated). But the cross that he always put at the top of his letters was missing. "Fearing fresh incidents, we immediately prepared it to send to Bishop Picaud. The letter was rolled around a little statue of Our Lady so that thus protected it would reach its destination" (Account by Mrs. Beauvais, March 1956, no. 145).

On receipt of the damaged letter, Bishop Picaud quickly replied: "The Devil has been caught red-handed. Once I received Mrs. Beauvais' letter and yours I thought that this rage of the Devil against you, and more precisely your entry into Malestroit, could be considered an argument in favor of your entry. So I recounted to the Bishop what had happened and let him read both letters. His Excellency was really impressed and gave me authorization to approach the question of your admission favorably" (Letter of January 7, 1927, no. 16).

So Yvonne said her goodbyes at Le Mans and then in Paris. Her mother accompanied her to Malestroit. She presented herself at the convent on March 18, 1927 at four o'clock in the afternoon. (*Notebook* of Mother Ange Gardien, March 18, 1927, no. 151)

Bishop Gouraud made no mystery of his hesitations and about-turns, which were not at all his usual manner of acting.

On August 29 he wrote to Mrs. Beauvais: "I have taken too much of an interest in the soul of your child to forget it at such a serious moment of her life. May she, in her turn, remember in her prayers a priest who only wanted her good, even if his methods of procuring this for her did not always seem obvious. But God is master of his lights" (no. 508).

And he wrote to Mother Madeleine a year later: "I may have appeared harsh at certain times, but my harshness had its excuse in my good will and in the difficulty that I had to always see clearly in such a delicate matter. Her prayers will help to obtain my forgiveness" (September 6, 1928, no. 664).

CONSISTENCY OF THE INCONSISTENT

What a strange No Man's Land those five years were between the first graces received at Malestroit (June–July 1922) and the long-delayed entry into this convent!

The succession of events seems random, disparate, inconsistent, oddly opposing:

—A harmonious human engagement but irreversibly broken off.

—Wondrous gifts of love from Christ, adorned with unusual outward signs, alternating with long spiritual nights and an extreme solitude.

—Effective and fruitful missions regarding priests at risk, and confusion at the physical and psychological attacks by the devil.

—Coexistence of severe illnesses and long convalescences with an energetic activity in service of the poor.

—Jobs, either glamorous or mundane, undertaken to earn money to bring relief to those poor: concerts and paintings, articles and novels, cooking and cleaning, et cetera.

—The union of this all-consuming service with an intense contemplative life, and the stigmata of the Passion.

—Overflowing creativity, despite oppressive ecclesiastical and medical investigations.

—Easily-changing periods of admiration and opposition.

—Dazzling, even binding, signs revealed to many (the young women at the Home, Father Crété, several sisters, even Bishop Picaud and Bishop Gouraud).

—The lack of knowledge of Mrs. Beauvais, despite her being an attentive and perceptive mother.

—The absurdity of unimaginable premonitions that Yvonne wrote down out of obedience, with the humiliation of understanding nothing about them, and the clarity that they then reveal when fulfilled.

Normally, these opposing forces should have produced breakdown, dissociation, disintegration, the destruction of this young woman, carried away beyond all common sense. And yet, these contradictions weave a coherent fabric. They lead irresistibly to a goal. The contradictory orders of her mother and the bishop create an inextricable conflict of obedience but these opposing arrows resolve into a straight line. Everything ends up in the achievement of an impossible vocation. How did that vocation that was so opposed, challenged, and attacked in every way, come to be achieved with a sort of inevitability?

It is an even more pertinent question in that this broken line is Yvonne's day-to-day life. Every day she had to deal with, in patience and obedience, these changes of view, this being pulled in opposite directions, these extraordinary graces which could have engendered a luciferian pride, and hellish temptations even to suicide and apostasy. She could have ended up either in exaltation or in despair.

Her strength was, beyond total self-giving, an abandonment to God alone, in a love prepared for anything. She experienced deeply what Saint Paul said, "We know that in everything God works for good with those who love him" (Rom 8:28).

In this dizzying adventure, with no plan or program on her part, Yvonne was led more than she did lead. Through the baffling shocks and contrasts that she took on in an active abandonment, Providence, which toys with human plans, resolved the crooked lines into a straight line, according to another dimension.

The last paradox: step by step, everything did come through Yvonne's free will. She reacted well to harsh testing but everything was given to her. That coinciding, which is the most basic experience of Christianity, is the secret of that life. God "stirs us so that we'll stir ourselves, not so that we will cease to stir" (*Aguntur enim ut agant, non ut ipsi nihil agant,* as said Saint Augustine. *De correptione et gratia,* chap. 2, no. 4).

An intelligent reader warned me about the inconsistent nature of this chapter and the need to put order into it. In rereading this impressionist fresco that I allowed to take shape as the source documents dictated, in reviewing as a whole this interlinking of battered, bruised, and disparate facts, I remain sure that to impose an order and a human coherency would be to betray what is essential. Here, as when we read the Passion, we are taking part in coherence of the incoherent, the wisdom of this folly that is the unquenchable love of God.

Let him understand who will.

Yvonne's life illustrates the solution of the problem raised by Ecclesiastes long before Jean-Paul Sartre—the absurdity of human life, riven with contradictions:

> A time to be born, and a time to die;
> a time to plant, and a time to pluck up what is planted;
> a time to kill, and a time to heal;
> a time to break down, and a time to build up;
> a time to weep, and a time to laugh. (Eccles 3:2–4)

Yvonne was subjected to particularly violent and paroxystic contradictions but was able to accept them in love—the great and the small, grand projects and tiny ones, joy and suffering, gifts from God (which could have gone to her head, as in Lucifer's case) and attacks from the devil. However submerged, however exalted or depressed that she could have been by all that, her fundamental love was never quenched. It took on everything without the slightest hesitation, without the slightest regret. She was also as far away as possible from the lamentations of Job, torn by the contradictions of this life and the apparent withdrawal of God.

It was love that gave a meaning to the disparate points of her life and turned them into a straight line. Her life as well as her works manifested the consistency with which God can "write straight with crooked lines" as the Portuguese proverb dear to Claudel says. The curved space of freedoms, of events, of suffering, and even of sin can be a straight path toward God. ᴥ

III

Religious Life
in Malestroit

15
Novitiate

THE "GOOD SISTER"

March 18, 1927, four o'clock in the afternoon. Yvonne left behind the gentle sunlight reflecting off the Nantes to Brest Canal, and the Breton countryside. In the convent chapel they had just finished praying the Stations of the Cross. The bell was tolling the thirty chimes traditional for the entry of a new postulant. Yvonne, accompanied by her mother and Miss Bato, made her way to the entrance to the enclosure. The door opened to reveal the forty-nine sisters of the community, black cape over a white robe and veils over their eyes.

Yvonne knelt at the threshold. Mother Madeleine of the Sacred Heart asked the customary question:

"What do you ask?"

"Reverend Mother, I very humbly beseech you to allow me admission to this holy house."

In reply, the superior held out a crucifix. Yvonne kissed it and stepped over the threshold. The door closed.

The community silently began to process in two lines toward the chapel. Yvonne followed. She knelt in the choir while the community chanted the hymn to the Holy Spirit, *Veni Creator Spiritus*. Then the forty-nine sisters came one by one to embrace Yvonne, smiles of welcome on their faces.

The new postulant was entrusted to the novice mistress, Mother Ange Gardien (Guardian Angel), a former superior. She was led to her cell. She changed her secular clothes for the long black dress reaching her ankles, the short cape, the apron and the little piped bonnet, which she secured under her chin by its ribbons.

The grave of vanity, they called it.

She was happy. Here is where Christ wanted her to be. She had had the proof. But what a shock!

"When I think that of the two of us it's I who will be the Good Sister!," she used to say laughingly to her friend the doctor, Suzanne Guéry, just a short while previously.

This name, the "Good Sister," implied everything jaded and artificial in institutions where they buried treasures of generosity. Yvonne was thoroughly modern in her tastes, her culture, her Parisian and English education. In 1923, during her second stay at Malestroit, she had had the vision of a new modern hospital. (Letter to Father Crété, August 1, 1923, no. 471)

The environment was foreign to her. Everything in her was rejecting it. The gentle efforts of everyone to soften this harsh change didn't help, even though she was also forcing herself to love everything there.

In the refectory, faced with the earthenware dish and the wooden spoon, to the sound of the *recto tono* reading of a text, she swallowed the monastic soup of soaked bread, pieces of carrot, leek, potatoes, and braised cabbage with buttermilk. At recreation, she struggled to remain upright next to a window. Back in her cell, with no heater, by the light of a little oil lamp, the cabbage and buttermilk made their reappearance. An attack of asthma was choking her.

Nothing was more contrary to her free and roaming nature than the enclosure. She began to think: "So, when is the next train for Paris?" (Testimony of Father Labutte)

Nothing was more contrary to her modernity than this dilapidated house, where everything was from a bygone age. Mother Madeleine soon recognized that Yvonne "is at her limit and is having a hard time."

The endlessly repeated rings of the bell that chopped up the time and imperiously interrupted all activity, stirred up in her the anguish of those bad days. "It wears you down, that bell!"

On March 25 she wrote to Yvonne Bato, who had accompanied her right to the threshold:

My dear little Miss.

Phew!...I'm not going to hear the bell for another hour, so I'm making use of this time to write to you.

This "Phew" doesn't mean that I've had enough of all this! No, I'm very happy but I have terrible battles that my little mother Madeleine is unaware of.... The Devil is mean, hateful! Well, the good Lord Jesus is surely content, because I am not rejoicing at all! Oh! Not at all!...Still, I feel that I'm learning the ropes, even if it is just by the color of my knees. They're all black and blue! I greet the choir grille correctly enough, it seems, and I'm beginning to come to grips with the prayers. Oh, there goes another bell. I'll go find out what it's for. Another time, I'll write to you more seriously.... (no. 167)

On May 19, she confirmed: "I don't regret anything, despite from time to time when...I'm finding it all a bit too much, I say: 'I would love Jesus better in the world, I should go back there.' But, in fact, it isn't true. I gave him more, perhaps, but I loved him less" (no. 289).

It is in this spirit that she took on the customs and traditions, the timetable, the permissions, the seclusion, that she had never known before: "At first, I didn't really like the enclosure. I had chosen it because I was convinced, sure that he wanted me here.... I understood later that the enclosure—at least 'the spirit of the enclosure'—is the guardian of the interior life of recollection, of prayer" (Her last talk, given on March 23, 1933, no. 204).

It seemed that her life should be anywhere but here. But she stayed. One thing surprised her: "I've never prayed less well than since I've been here." She knew why. "First, I'm always hurting somewhere: on my knees I'm sometimes ready to scream; standing up I've got so many pains all over the place that I struggle to stand up straight—and even to sit upright, for heaven's sake! It's getting a little better but, still, I can't get any rest. So I offer everything to the Good Lord. It's the only prayer that I can make. I give him loads of smiles, even though I always feel like crying" (Letter to Yvonne Bato, March 25, 1927, no. 167).

Her health broke down. She had blackouts. It was impossible for her to practice the whole Rule. She rued the exceptions which were applied to her:

"At table…a special diet…. In choir…to sit down when everyone else is on their knees, and so many other things! I understand and have accepted this path on which Jesus wishes to lead me. It is crucifying, but I love it because it is he who chose it. Therefore I want to practice abandonment to a high degree. Since making this resolution, I feel better" (Letter to Gilberte de Sartiges, May 4, 1927, no. 262).

Clear-sighted about her difficulties, she wrote to Jeanne Boiszenou, another friend from the Home:

"What can I tell you from my end? Not much. I'm getting used to the Rule and the customs. Everything is very new for me. Ah!…it truly is only for the Good Lord that one enters a convent! If it weren't, one wouldn't have the strength to remain" (Letter of May 16, 1927, no. 281).

Her life was marked by ecstasies, by missions. The fights with the powers of darkness, well known to Saint Paul, for her took on violent and bloody forms.

Mother Madeleine of the Sacred Heart was able to distinguish these various extraordinary events from the essential: "The life of Sister Yvonne is still a tapestry of wonders, miracles and graces," she wrote. But she quickly added, "She is a saint not because of extraordinary manifestations, but above all because of her great virtue. What a grace to be part of her life" (Letter to Germaine Piacentini, July 27, 1927, no. 431).

Sister Yvonne-Aimée would soon ask the Lord to deliver her from all that was extraordinary. "I would like to keep my treasure a secret," she wrote in her notebook. (Notebook, August 1, 1927, no. 442)

And that despite the crippling monotony which caused her to say, "How bored I am! Oh, how bored…!"

> I've been switched off from the outside…I feel cramped, hemmed in. I'm like a bird in a cage! A poor bird, very unhappy humanly speaking, and I didn't think that just six months of convent life

would change me to this extent. I no longer laugh, I no longer sing, I no longer speak. And when I do risk saying something, I'm afraid; I look at Mother Mistress to see whether I've done something good or bad. No more spontaneity, no one to open up to freely without constraint. I'm always afraid of doing something wrong.... What gives me strength and gives me the courage to remain here despite everything, is the thought that I'm presenting to my Jesus the maximum amount of sufferings, and that I'm happy to be unhappy. (Letter to Odette de Montlo, August 18, 1927, no. 477)

Another trial soon arose: Mother Madeleine was worried about these extraordinary graces, which confounded reason, and she suspected they were traps of the devil. Sister Yvonne-Aimée still felt compelled to pass on messages, but was no longer listened to: "Mother Madeleine thinks it is my own opinion that I'm giving. And that's why she contradicts it. For if she thought it really does come from the Lord, she would immediately accept it," she wrote. "Whenever I risk delivering something to her, or giving her my opinion, I always do it under a formal command of the Lord Jesus. I told her that. She didn't believe me.... She is completely at liberty not to believe me; after all it is only a matter of prudence" (Ibid.).

The scope of her generosity had hardly begun: "I feel more and more inclined to offer myself to receive all sorrows, and when I pray my being gets caught up in the single idea of God" (Letter to Bishop Picaud, August 22, 1927, no. 488).

The very depth of the love that she was living preserved her from all introspection. This love was even a sort of trial to her, as a type of weakness or powerlessness. In Confession she wants to accuse herself "like everybody," but she observed: "When I'm trying to call to mind my faults, I can't fix on anything, can't specify anything. My mind gets all mixed up, and I say to Jesus 'I love you' as if it weren't actually the time to be asking him for forgiveness.... My mind gets lost in the love. My sins too, no doubt.... When I come back to myself, I begin afresh to examine my conscience. In fact, the last time, I spent the whole night from Monday to Tuesday doing that" (Letter to Odette de Montlo, August 25, 1927, no. 498).

The duration of this "I love you" absorbed her life. She confided to the same friend that she was "continually think-ing of God despite the many activities.... Neither work, nor reading, nor mealtimes interrupt my prayer. Everything speaks to me of love.... Jesus draws me and I give myself: and the more I give myself the more he draws me" (Ibid.).

CLOTHING IN THE HABIT

It was in this happy and unhappy state that her transfor-mation deepened. On September 10, 1927 she was clothed in the religious habit. Bishop Picaud presided, standing in for Bishop Gouraud who was unwell. Father de Tonquédec and Father Grizard were unable to attend but sent their best wishes. Father Crété, who Bishop Gouraud had removed as spiritual director, was the preacher at this clothing. He dared to compare Sister Yvonne-Aimée's vocation to that of the little Thérèse. He exhorts her mother to sing the Magnificat like Mr Martin, Thérèse's father, "when his last daughter announced her vocation." Without recalling that he had offered himself as a victim and had undergone the unimaginable humiliation of the insane asylum, Father Crété urged Mrs. Beauvais to imitate his thanksgiving:

"So sing your Magnificat ... oh happy mother of Jesus's Beloved (in French *Bienaimée*) who not only accepted the choice of the Lord Jesus but who actually so helped it ... *Ben-edicta tu inter mulieres et benedictus fructus ventris tui* (You are blessed among women and blessed is the fruit of your womb. Lk 1:42)."

To Sister Yvonne-Aimée he recalled the luminous and inde-cipherable night of the journey that had finally led her to the goal after such a long wait:

> Was it from your earliest years that you heard the
> call of the Spouse of souls? I wouldn't dare to assert

it ... It was right here in this hospital ... where so many bodies had been healed ... where so many souls had been comforted by nurses who were at the same time real spouses of the Lord Jesus. It was right here that the Lord Jesus whispered in your ear while showing you his cross (July 5, 1922):

"Do you want to carry it?"

And you replied generously,

"Yes, Lord."

Since then, five years have passed. So today it's already been five long years that you've been hoping to put on this white robe that the tenderness of your divine Fiancé had reserved for you. Certainly, this delay felt long to your heart and to ours. But let us not regret anything. In fact, pleased with your consent, the Lord Jesus, as well as doing what he normally does, put all creatures at the service of your love. And to remind you of his tenderness and to adorn your soul, at the moment foreseen by him everything came; sorrows and joys, sufferings and temptations, angels, men, demons bringing blows or bringing caresses meant to render the little fiancée less unworthy of the Lord Jesus. May he be forever praised! One day, in Heaven, my dear brethren, we will be able to understand this marvelous work for which the divine Craftsman simply asks our coop- eration.... Let's allow ourselves to be carved at will, because ... it is love alone that guides the hand of the heavenly artist. For you, my dear daughter, the less you hinder it, the less you resist him, so also the less time and effort that created and uncreated love that is here and that loves you so much will take to perfect his work. Oh! Allow him to accomplish the whole marvelous design of love that he has conceived in calling you both into existence and into religious life in his dear community of Malestroit.... May you teach us all that science that he himself taught you ... God is love. And there is nothing better than consenting to carry his cross and to become here below first and then in Heaven, an "Aimée de Jésus" ["Beloved of Jesus"]. Amen (no. 540)

The inspired insight of this sermon, which so well distilled the essential, coincided with other allusions that were clear to Sister Yvonne-Aimée. The song composed for the occasion by Father René Piacentini alluded to the exceptional grace which had irreversibly prompted her vocation: "I saw in the night your luminous cross" (Song for the reception of the habit, September 10, 1927, no. 541).

The novitiate resumed. Mother Ange Gardien, the novice mistress, was a benevolent nun but aged, steady, austere—the complete opposite of the young, exuberant, and spontaneous novice. Everything was coming together to plunge her into a dark interior night.

BUSINESS TRIP

Her influence and advice had become so appreciated that the superior, Mother Madeleine, and Mother Anne of Jesus brought her with them on a long trip to visit the hospitals of the twelve Augustinian houses in Brittany and Normandy. It was rather surprising that a novice, in the white veil, was taken out of the monastic enclosure so soon in order to deal with planning of a practical nature. And it would last for two weeks, October 26 to November 15, 1927. It was already back in 1923, before she had even entered the novitiate, that Sister Yvonne-Aimée had recognized the need and stressed the necessity of modernizing the somewhat dated clinic. It was thanks to her insights that the project took shape, both the grand scheme and the details. She had become indispensable. Bishop Gouraud himself, having so long opposed her project as being too ambitious, had given the order to the superiors to bring her with them.

It was Sister Yvonne-Aimée's word that had finally convinced the bishop, who was worried about the cost. "The funds will come because the Lord Jesus wants this work," she said. (Note-book, September 13, 1926, no. 551)

This explains the surprising dispensations from canon law.

Soon after their return the donations rolled in: 200,000 francs at Christmas 1927. Then on December 29, 700,000 francs from Mr Bolloré, an industrialist from Finistère.

"ON THE VERGE OF DEATH"

On November 28, 1927, Sister Yvonne-Aimée fell sick. She was delirious. Her temperature reached 40.9°C (105.6°F), then 42°C (107.6°F). She was still smiling, but she was suffering. Her friend Suzanne Guéry, intern from the Paris Hospitals, was looking after her. They thought she was going to die. She was happy about that. Father Bruneau, the convent chaplain, prepared her to make her religious Profession "on the verge of death."

On December 1 in the infirmary decorated with hangings and greenery, Bishop Picaud received her commitment before the assembled community.

The next day, December 2, her condition worsened. Yvonne received Extreme Unction (the Anointing of the Sick) in the presence of the community gathered around her once again. Bishop Picaud was there.

At 2:20 P.M. Doctor Suzanne Guéry diagnosed the symptoms of imminent death. At 2:40 P.M. an auscultation, a sounding of her chest, revealed something strange: "two distinctly different types of cardiac noise, one weak, the other vigorous, separated in time the one from the other."

Doctor Guéry would never have an explanation for this extraordinary physical phenomenon. She never encountered another case of it in her long life and medical career. A mystical explanation, with reference to the heart of Christ, seemed best to her in this case. (Report of Doctor S. Guéry, p. 9, December 3, 1927, no. 777. She retained a vivid memory of that inexplicable auscultation when she personally recounted the experience to the author preparing this book in the 1980s.)

BACK TO LIFE

"Jesus, come quickly!" murmured Yvonne.

Then, after a silence:

"As you wish...I don't want to choose anything....I want what you want....I want your greater glory....Your love will be my heaven on earth" (Letters nos. 760 and 762).

The Superior questioned her: "I'm not going to die," replied Sister Yvonne-Aimée. "Jesus is leaving me with you" (Letter of

Mother Madeleine of the Sacred Heart to Mother Bernard at Rennes, no. 760).

At 3:00 P.M. her "cyanosed" face returned to its normal coloration. She asked for something to eat and drink. It was time for Vespers. While the community was assembling, she got dressed. She was there in the chapel for Benediction.

In her ecstasy she had understood that, "In remaining here below, I could make him more loved. I chose the sacrifice after seeing how good it is up there" (Letter of Sister Yvonne-Aimée to Father Crété, two days later, December 4, 1927, no. 762).

Her return to health annulled her Profession *in articulo mortis*, on the verge of death. Yvonne returned to being a quiet novice. She rarely spoke "without having been asked something," testified one of her companions, Sister Mary of the Cross. (Testimony gathered by Father Louis Barral, 1956, no. 181)

She was lively, smiling, attentive to others: "Jesus will help you in the measure that you help your sisters. Mutual assistance is the most beautiful almsgiving of a religious sister," she wrote. (Sheet of a notebook, end of August 1929, no. 392)

She remained totally available to others.

FOR A RETURN TO NORMAL LIFE

The concern of her superiors was still the extraordinary aspect of her life: ecstasies, stigmata, and so on. Yvonne prayed for a return to "a normal life." She received this reply: "I grant what you have asked me... For a while. I suspend your mission and change your path" (*Notebook*, May 30, 1928, no. 475).

The Lord invited her to back up this grace with mortifications, no doubt to neutralize the irrational influences of the spiritual realm. The list, in accord with the customs of the time, is quite scary:

"With permission, you will spend your nights stretched out on the floor.

"You will give yourself 100 lashes of the cord discipline every day, except Sunday.

"You will, in addition, give yourself 300 lashes with the metal one on Fridays and 200 on Saturdays.

"You will wear the cilice eight days in a row, etc."

And this is not taking into account "bracelets, belts," "hearts of iron" (which were all part of the arsenal of that time), and severe fasts. (Ibid.)

Despite her health problems, she managed to follow the Rule pretty strictly. And with joy: "I go to all the Offices, except Matins. I have a real happiness in following my sisters.... So far, nothing costs me. In fact, it's not difficult. I'm not hurting anywhere" (*Notebook*, June 1, 1928, no. 484).

Alas! Ten days later the pains and difficulties returned. Mother Madeleine had to put her back on the regime of dispensation—from the morning rising of 5:30 A. M., the Office, and sometimes the Mass. These exceptions pained Sister Yvonne-Aimée, even to the point of tears.

ARCHITECT

These vicissitudes did not change her influence, and her interventions were decisive for the building of a new hospital. The architects were progressing slowly, as the marshy terrain was problematic for the foundations. Sister Yvonne-Aimée prayed to the Lord: "If you wish that this be done, show us how."

The next day: "she drew up the plans for the future buildings and submitted them to the architect," recounted Father Bruneau.

"I remember that on the way back to Rennes with him, he told me: 'They are amazing, your nuns! It is they who did the work that I am carrying. I only had to establish the proportions, put everything to scale and my plan was done'" (Testimony of Father Bruneau, Autumn 1951, no. 145).

It was indeed that part of the land that could support a building on it.

From May 1928 she assisted the new treasurer, Sister Marie Anne of Jesus.

On June 21, Bishop Picaud blessed the foundation stone.

ACTRESS

Yvonne led the recreation on a feast day. She performed a comic sketch, *The Loriot*. "She really made us laugh," noted Sister Marie-Anne. (Letter to the community at Guingamp, June 29, 1928, no. 554)

WHEN EVERYTHING WORKS

They had been worrying about furniture. But before the building was even finished, it was filling up as if by magic. "We were seeing beds arriving, cupboards, armchairs, linen, and crockery" (Sister Marie-Anne to the community of Guingamp, September 9, 1928, no. 672).

The hospital opened in mid-June 1929. Two months later (August 18) it already housed fifty-three patients. The utopian plan "received" by Yvonne in 1923 had become a reality. Everything was going well for the community, materially and spiritually. Everything was renewed.

THE PRICE THAT HAD TO BE PAID

And yet Sister Yvonne-Aimée's own trials and burdens increased.

During the summer of 1928, the bone disease that afflicted Mother Madeleine worsened. She asked Yvonne for her healing as "the" proof of the divine authenticity of her mission. The signs which had previously convinced her no longer counted.

Yvonne prayed, but with no result. She exhausted herself to ask the impossible: "Oh, what a night," she wrote. "Oh my God, you've gone and perhaps I'll never see you again!... I had no right to your favors.... I come to ask you for peace" (*Notebook*, August 20, 1928, no. 643).

PROFESSION, SEPTEMBER 29, 1928

It was in this desolation that she professed her first vows. Just before her Profession retreat, she was gripped by doubts about her vocation. She missed her direct apostolate. (*Notebook*, September 17, 1928, no. 685)

"I'm going into retreat tomorrow," she wrote on September

17. "Two months ago I wanted this retreat so much! Now it frightens me.... The silence and the solitude terrify me. Once I'm alone, I get frightened. Jesus is no longer there and I'm left with my thoughts and temptations that are so strong and obsessive that I don't know what to do to take my mind off them" (*Notebook*, September 19, 1928, no. 689).

She abandoned herself to the Lord: "Break, cut, slice, annihilate me by your divine torments of love. My nature will often complain, but my heart never" (*Notebook*, September 23, 1928, no. 693).

In the harsh distance at which Mother Madeleine now kept her, she wrote:

"Shouldn't I be happy to have so many opportunities given by her, things to offer up for her?" (*Notebook*, September 11, 1928, no. 679).

"I entrust myself to him, to my God, totally. One must. I want it; abandonment, trust, peace" (*Notebook*, September 23, 1928, no. 693).

On September 29, in contrast with the brilliant light of her clothing ceremony, she professed her temporary vows of three years in complete aridity. Her calm face reflected the fact.

DEATH OF ODETTE

The death of a close friend, Odette, who had supported her, made the night even worse for her. (Letter from Sister Yvonne-Aimée to Miss Villemont, October 19, 1928, no. 570)

Odette had annotated for Yvonne the first biography of Sister Marie of Jesus Crucified, an Arab convert to the Faith who became a Carmelite nun. The marvels of her life had long been hidden under a bushel. (John Paul II beatified her on November 13, 1983.) In this book by Father Denis Buzy (Paris, 1921) preserved in the archives at Malestroit, Odette underlined, piece by piece, the similarity between the astonishing graces of the little Carmelite and those of Sister Yvonne-Aimée. Odette had shared in and supported Yvonne on her path. (Letter of Father J. Bruneau, June 6, 1928, no. 490)

REJECTED BY MOTHER MADELEINE

Mother Madeleine's state of health deteriorated. But she no longer wanted to be cared for by the one she used to call her "little daughter." "Not even good enough to perform a little service, such as to lend an arm to my dear little mother, or to apply to her a compress of Lourdes water," she wrote. (Notebook, September 11, 1928, no. 679)

Mother Madeleine's coldness increased. Sister Yvonne-Aimée remembered the warning she had received: "Your best friends, even those who were meant to support you, will let you down, leave you. Doubt will assail them and you will be suspected and misunderstood. Oh, my God, if it is you who told me that...then I must expect to suffer.... When that time comes, give me the strength!" (Notebook, October 11, 1928, no. 734)

She added: "How I should wish for what you say. Because suffering is a sign of predilection, more than ecstasies and all the rest" (Ibid.).

> To love and to suffer. That's the law for those who want to become saints.... Oh! Hard and crucifying love of my Jesus, cause to die in me all my desires, my wants. May I only want to love you to folly, even not knowing the degree of my love. May I desire to be but one with you, in a total union of mind, heart and will....
>
> You want, O my Beloved, to act in my soul as it pleases you, and that my happiness be only to grant you this full and entire liberty.
>
> The humiliation that I must have in order to please you and become holy; on bended knee I ask you for it, I beg you for it. Impose it on me. (Notebook, October 12, 1928, no. 738)

OPPOSITION OF THE CHAPLAIN

The warm friendship with the chaplain also faded away. Since her entry he had been her only confessor and spiritual director and had helped her a lot. Now he challenged her and rebuffed her friendship. Yvonne had already felt this change coming on during the last months of 1928. In some confusion, she wrote in her notebook:

"How I am tempted, how my mind is filled with ugly thoughts. God, help me to chase all that away!... I can't believe that my father would end up doubting me! Even if he hears nasty things said about me!... He told me that he would always support me. That's surely the Devil who's planting these nasty ideas (in my head) so as to discourage me. To think that about him, who God willed to be the chaplain here for me...is mean!" (*Notebook*, October 15, 1928, no. 744)

Yet, for all that, from April 19, 1929 the drama erupted. The chaplain, overwhelmed with worries in the face of these unusual phenomena which he was unable to verify, accused Sister Yvonne-Aimée of deception. Bishop Picaud was there. He recounted: "The three of us were there: he like a judge, stern and sure of his task, mastering it with the weight of his own convictions.... He spread out before me a number of letters" (Interview of August 1, 1954, no. 145).

They were the letters from Odette, Yvonne's friend, which used to arrive mysteriously at critical moments. The chaplain, Father Bruneau, challenged their authenticity. The bishop urged the nun to defend herself. She confirmed her honesty without refuting the charges against her: "Remember when I was about to die [during her Profession *in extremis*] I swore that I have always told the truth. That was the case, and it still is!" she confirmed in her letter to Bishop Picaud the following Monday, April 22, 1929 (no. 123).

"I suffered horribly after you left. I also suffered interiorly for your suffering," she added.

"My child, I trust you completely," concluded Bishop Picaud. (Account of July 22, 1954, no. 131)

The shock left her inhibited and distraught. "My soul is squeezed as if in a vise. I no longer know who to confide in; Father Crété and Bishop Picaud, they believe in me. Mother Marie-Anne too but I am no longer able to confide, and then I'm always afraid of being mistaken" (*Notebook*, June 3, 1929, no. 199).

Father Bruneau said to her: "You are proud, impressionable, your imagination makes you see and hear things that aren't really there. So admit that you're wrong. You sulk; you want to be noticed, you don't know how to obey. So, be brave and have the courage to admit for once and for all; the good Lord will forget all about it and you will have peace" (*Notebook*, March 25, 1929, no. 98).

She remained confused: "To accuse myself of something that I don't see, of what I don't believe I'm doing, would be a sin! And yet, the saints did not sin... and they accused themselves of lots of things.... If this goes on, I'm going to go out of my mind, or leave. It would be better to die," she concluded. (*Notebook*, June 3, 1929, no. 199)

PREMONITION

On June 4 she glimpsed with the end of Sister Madeleine's coldness, the more difficult trial of her death.

"In a month you will suffer a lot," Jesus told me, "but it will also be the end of a trial which is also about to become more intense in these times" (*Notebook*, June 4, 1929, no. 200).

REST AND GRACE

On June 12 Mother Marie-Anne brought her to Lannion, where she would stay for ten days. This time of rest was also a time of graces and spiritual refreshment, which marked the Hospitaller community.

She sent daily notes to Mother Madeleine, whose condition was deteriorating. Nothing in return. This wall of silence was crushing her....

RECONCILIATIONS

And then, in the mail of June 16–17, at the bottom of a letter from Mother Marie-Anne, these shaky words from Mother Madeleine: "I love you dearly my darling Vovonne" (Letter of June 15, 1929, received on June 16 or 17, no. 239).

Sister Yvonne-Aimée returned to Malestroit on June 22, for the blessing of the hospital. After two long months, Mother Madeleine had revived their friendship but didn't have the strength to express it. On July 4 she entered into a terrible agony, which resolved itself in serenity. They finally heard her

murmur: "I'm going toward the light, toward home; I'm happy."
(These were her last words, printed on the *In Memoriam* card.)

The next day, July 5, 1929, was the seventh anniversary
of the foundational grace received by Sister Yvonne-Aimée
(July 5, 1922).

On July 15 Father Bruneau similarly reconciled with Yvonne:
"I give you back my trust and leave the past to one side."

But, by an "incredible illogicality," said Bishop Picaud from
whom he had withdrawn (Labutte 3, p. 89), he remained
distant, suspicious.

Confessions with Father Bruneau remained a real trial and
sometimes Sister Yvonne-Aimée even left them in tears. There
was no longer any relationship with him who had helped her
so much. It was only in 1932 that Bishop Tréhiou (the succes-
sor of Bishop Gouraud, who died in October 1928) removed
him from Malestroit to become Parish Pastor of Carentoir.

"Father Chaplain, with whom I spoke for quite a while,
this time was very kind to me," wrote Sister Yvonne-Aimée.
"He seemed moved to be leaving me and asked my forgive-
ness for having made me suffer.... I felt his pain. And now
I remember only the good things he did for me" (Letter to
Bishop Picaud, December 10, 1932, no. 776).

Shortly before his death (November 28, 1954) Father
Bruneau said to one of his former directees, Sister Marie-
Dominique: "Ah, if only I had always trusted Mother Yvonne-
Aimée! If only I had always had faith in her!" (Testimony of
Sister Marie-Dominique, January 6, 1955, no. 3)

DISTANCE AND MISTRUST

But, meanwhile, the confessional was a hard trial for her.
During the summer of 1929 Father Joseph Henry, SJ, preacher
of the retreat, invited no doubt to test Sister Yvonne-Aimée,
gave her a penance. Every evening for a year she was to pray
the Litany of the Sacred Heart. (Testimony of Bishop Picaud
and of two nuns.) He ordered her to write to Bishop Picaud
to play down her extraordinary graces and to ask him not
to speak of them anymore. This order was quite superfluous

for Sister Yvonne-Aimée never stopped writing to those who were indiscreet, calling them to silence on the matter.[1]

"A BIT OF EVERYTHING"

Sister Yvonne-Aimée entered a period of activity that was intense and unrewarding. "Our little sister Yvonne-Aimée is doing a bit of everything at the moment, with the same simplicity and the same gentleness," wrote Mother Marie-Anne to the sisters at Guingamp, on November 10, 1929 (no. 484).

During the summer of 1929, following the departure of a cantankerous cook, Yvonne took on the role. She was quite the expert. But the complications were way beyond what she might have experienced before: "Eight different services at the same time; it's a real headache. And had I not made the good Jesus himself the director of my Pass,[2] I would be lost with all these menus and different dishes" (Letter to Sister Marie-Aimée of Jesus, an Augustinian at Guingamp, who had taken the name of Aimée because of Yvonne and whom Yvonne called "my goddaughter," November 10, 1929, no. 480).

Her assistants appreciated her: "To see her like this makes me believe in her holiness more than all the wonders," said one of them. (1929, no. 484)

Guests and patients praised her baveuse omelet, her stews and her home baking: cream pastries, "frozen matchsticks," and rice pudding. "Your hospital cook was obviously trained in Paris; you can tell," said a patient one day in front of Sister Yvonne-Aimée and her assistant Sister Bernadette, who reported it. (Testimony 1956, p. 3, no. 182)

Despite her status as "chef," she took part in the monotonous task of peeling vegetables and would intervene with

---

[1] Letters from Sister Yvonne-Aimée to Mother Saint Augustin at Lannion (February 12, 1929, no. 57); to Bishop Picaud (April 15, 1929, no. 116): "Your Excellency,... that Fr Chaplain doesn't speak about anything. Could you ask him.... I'm so upset with him at the moment... Would you also ask Canon Guillo not to speak about me"); to Miss Villemont (April 22, 1929, no. 124); to Fr de la Chevasnerie (March 1929, no. 78); texts quoted in Labutte 3, pp. 100–102.

[2] The "Pass" was the name of the place from where she directed her kitchen and expedited the prepared dishes.

the doctors to ensure they didn't visit the patients during their mealtimes. Her humor and her resourcefulness came to the fore during setbacks. On August 18, 1929 a power supply failure stopped the dumbwaiter from working at lunchtime. The finely regulated routines were put out of synch. Sister Yvonne-Aimée set to work, and did the job herself. Everything arrived perfectly—right to the bed of each patient.

On January 8 an earthquake seriously damaged the convent. The dilapidated building was falling to bits, observed Sister Yvonne-Aimée. "We love our poor house but she's taking her leave of us…. We had to evacuate twenty-two cells, the refectory, and other rooms…. We're going to have to think about rebuilding, for we're too numerous" (Letter of Sister Yvonne-Aimée to Miss Villemont, April 3, 1930, no. 98).

She was not content just to carry out repairs. She drew up plans for a new refectory which would close the square of buildings in the shape of a cloister. She was going to restore the chapter house in the style of a manor with its old wooden beams.

She designed an English garden for the relaxation of the convalescents—birch trees, cedars, and weeping willows would be reflected in the pond, which would have a little island in the middle.

She drew winding paths through groves and flowerbeds. The neighboring field would become the vegetable garden, with a bower for the community's walks. The walls were adorned with espaliers. Lawns and flowerbeds appeared in front of the new hospital. The money arrived according to each new need.

However, one evening in January the coffers were empty. And an invoice of 10,000 francs had to be paid urgently. A check arrived. It was for precisely the sum required. A friend had sent it to Sister Yvonne, "as a help, perhaps." (Letter of Sister Saint Paul to Father de la Chevasnerie, January 17, 1931, no. 46)

"The Lord Jesus guides everything. The measure of his liberality will be based on the measure of my trust and my abandonment," wrote Sister Yvonne-Aimée. (*Notebook*, February 10, 1931, no. 91)

Vocations continued to flow in. In November 1929 there were eight novices and four postulants. Two entries were foreseen for the following month. This was something new. The new bishop of Vannes, Monsignor Tréhiou, was amazed.

"MONETTE" A BESTSELLER

Enter Father René de la Chevasnerie, SJ, a friend of the House since 1927. He was dynamic, full of conviction. He had been put in charge of the religious programs on *Radio-Paris*. Tracing the footsteps of Father Lhande who had aroused public opinion for the "red zone" around Paris, and his first missionaries, he learned of the precursor apostolate of Yvonne.

We must write a book about it, he declared! And: her anonymity will be respected, he promised. Vonnette will be called Monette.

Sister Yvonne-Aimée had to make herself available to the priest to tell him everything he needed to know. It was no walk in the park. She had to recount everything to him, tell him all that would be useful to him. She had to deal with the various enthusiasms and hesitations of the writer-apostle, and reply to his sometimes indiscreet questions. She had to read over his texts, which he had the annoying obligation to disguise in order to protect her identity. At each moment, at every step, Sister Yvonne-Aimée was required for this urgent matter. "It's for the kingdom of God," he told her.

Sister Yvonne-Aimée recognized his sincerity. She was ready to do anything for the Lord, even to "hand herself over" as she had written a few months before. She cooperated as best she could and would retain a basically favorable opinion of that book whose bright and artificial style is no longer in vogue. On July 13, 1931 she wrote to her Jesus: "The first volume of *Monette* is finished. May this book, written for your glory, accomplish much good. You know, Lord that if this book comes out, it is for that reason. Bless this priest. He has worked hard" (*Notebook*, July 13, 1931, no. 238).

Her tranquility and the joy that she radiated was clear to everyone. But her own outlook remained somber. "It is night, total night. But I am trying to love the dark, and I'm beginning to get there. It's not easy" (Letter to Miss des Georges, May 10, 1930, no. 135).

Heart ailments disturbed her sleep but every morning she recovered her strength. During the summer of 1930 a pulmonary edema stopped her in her tracks. "If it were any other of my daughters, I wouldn't hesitate to get her the last sacraments," confided her superior. (Details gathered from the letter of Sister Saint-Paul to Mother Marie Bernard at Rennes, August 17, 1930, no. 215)

"AUGUSTINIAN YOUTH"

In 1931 she launched a newspaper for the community: *Augustinian Youth.* The title is in the style of the time. It was the era that saw the rise of all the Catholic "youth" societies—Young Catholic Farmers, Young Catholic Students, et cetera. The duplicated sheet, which was illustrated and full of humor, soon passed through the enclosure and became the link between Malestroit and the young religious sisters of the different convents. In a way, this link prepared the path for the future federation. The unsigned editorials were by Sister Yvonne-Aimée.

CANON LAWYER

And now she was indispensable for a new task. The Constitutions of the Augustinian sisters had to be revised. They dated from 1631 and were now obsolete. The project was foreseen from 1919 and firmly decided upon in 1924. Father Georges Sauvage, a Holy Cross priest and canon lawyer, was dealing with it in Rome along with others. It involved obtaining the approval of the Holy See amid all the difficulties and its legendary lethargy. Here again Sister Yvonne-Aimée felt led. Before the general chapter which would study the changes, she wrote to Bishop Picaud: "Push for the meeting to be held here please Your Excellency.... I believe it is the wish of the Lord Jesus because of the good that will be done here, or more precisely that Malestroit will do, for all those who will come here and who will then spread the spirit of joy and charity that they will have experienced here" (Letter to Bishop Picaud, November 11, 1930, no. 316).

The chapter was held there, at the end of April 1931, presided over by Bishop Picaud. Sister Yvonne-Aimée was unanimously elected secretary. She was the linchpin of the whole thing.

It involved conforming the Constitutions to the new Code of Canon Law created in 1917, and reforming usages and customs that had become impracticable. The vow of strict enclosure was abolished. The nurses were allowed to care for male patients (which had been forbidden until then). The habit was simplified and the obligation of wearing it was relaxed, according to functionality.

THE ANGEL OF MALESTROIT

During the chapter a play was put on. The "Protecting Angel" of each of the forty convents spoke. It was Sister Yvonne-Aimée who played the leading role.

"I am the Angel of Malestroit."

Witnesses admired her maturity, her availability, her ubiquity. This chapter left a deep impression. In July Sister Yvonne-Aimée worked with her superior and Bishop Picaud, auxiliary bishop of Vannes, on finalizing the definitive text of the Constitutions. She did all that while fighting an exhaustion we can barely imagine.

On July 16, for her thirtieth birthday, on the feast of Our Lady of Mount Carmel, she wrote: "Thirty! Oh, how old I am. Or, more precisely, how old I feel! Since I missed the train to Paradise in 1927, it seems you no longer want me up there. Are you, my God, going to leave me on earth for a long time? Whatever you like. If I have some longing to die as soon as possible for many good reasons, I have an even greater longing to want only your greater glory. And if that has to be for me old age, white hair, infirmities, alright; *Fiat*, joyful *Fiat!*" (*Notebook*, July 16, 1931, no. 241)

Yes, it was indeed joy that she radiated.

THE COMMITMENT

On September 29, 1931, she made her perpetual vows in the restored and enlarged chapel. Bishop Picaud presided over the ceremony. The preacher, Father Crété, referred to the sacrifice of the newly-professed who, for God alone, was going to bury behind this enclosure all her zeal for travel and wishing to serve on a worldwide scale. For God alone: "Oh, brides of the Lord Jesus...happy victims of love, it is you, yes it is you who are the Beloved (in French *Aimée*) of Jesus" (September 29, 1931, no. 313).

Sister Yvonne-Aimée was the first to receive (from Bishop Picaud) the gold wedding band that from then on the professed nuns would wear. (*Constitutions*, no. 26, p. 16)

ROME (OCTOBER 19–NOVEMBER 9, 1931)

On October 19, 1931 she left for Rome with her superior. Four days later, October 23, they were welcomed by Father Sauvage the canon lawyer. They hoped to have the approval, "very quickly, very quickly." The advisers smiled at their illusion. However, the unusual speed of the process was going to surprise them.

On October 27 the two religious were received in a private audience. In 1925, Yvonne had twice exchanged a look, a long look, with Pius XI. This time she could speak. She gave him an illuminated text that she had painted herself, copied from a twelfth-century manuscript, "that he might keep in his breviary."

"Oh! Welcome such a beautiful picture," he said warmly as he put it into the inside pocket of his white soutane; "over his heart." (Annual of Mother Marie-Anne, January 15, 1932, no. 42, p. 8)

That same October 28 Cardinal Lépicier went way beyond their wildest dreams. The cardinal urged:

> "Tell Father Sauvage to do it quickly, and as soon as
> he presents it I'll take care of it. I'll tell the Council
> that I want you to be dealt with as a priority..."
> Here everyone is shouting "miracle," except two people

(Yvonne and her superior) who don't understand any
of what's going on. (Letter of Mother Marie-Anne to
the community, October 30, 1931, no. 390)

And Sister Yvonne-Aimée: "Never, in the last three years,
has the Lord shown himself more tender and more merciful"
(Letter to Bishop Picaud, November 6, 1931, no. 420).

For her it was a new time of graces and trials, some of
them exceptional, with "tears of blood" (Account of Mother
Stanislas, Ursuline, October 29, 1931, no. 387).

On November 9, two weeks and three days after arriving
in Rome, a telegram was received at Malestroit: "The Constitutions are approved" (*Notebook* of Sister Mary of the Cross,
November 9, 1931, no. 439).

Before leaving Rome, Sister Yvonne-Aimée had been asking
for a forgotten title to be restored to the Augustinian sisters,
that of Canonesses Regular. She based her request on a bull
granted to the convent of Rouen, attached to the order since
1631. This was still proving problematic on the eve of her
departure. But she went to the Vatican Archives and received
from Monsignor Fideccichi a reply which dispelled any last
doubts. "It was quite unexpected," wrote Sister Yvonne-Aimée.
"But it is well worthy of him, of the Lord Jesus who watches
over us with his all-powerful and merciful Goodness!" (Letter
to the community, November 19, 1931, no. 488)

In record time the Canonesses Regular had obtained, with
their new title, new Constitutions, three centuries after those
of 1631.

On November 22 Sister Yvonne-Aimée, along with her
superior, began a visit to all the convents in France, for
the application of the new Constitutions. She returned to
her normal activities in January 1932. She wrote to Bishop
Picaud on January 28:

"I'm fine... My soul is not in the light but it is in peace"
(no. 75).

In her life buffeted and pulled in every direction the previous year, it was the very grace that she had earnestly asked
for. (*Notebook*, February 16, 1931, no. 113)

16

The Unstoppable Rise of Sister Yvonne-Aimée

1932–1936

FIRST RESPONSIBILITIES

Even before entering Malestroit, Yvonne had been the inspirer of renewals, first of all profound conversions, and then transformation of disagreement into harmonious unity. The changes were already clear to see. At the convent, observed Father Crété, until her entry, "everything was small; small was the chapel, small the nuns' choir, small the hospital, small the flock of little lambs in the novitiate; yes, really, everything was small, except the hearts and souls. Today, that is to say in three years, everything has become large, worthy of religious life and modern progress, worthy of a convent of the Immaculate Conception... the second-oldest of the convents of the Order" (Sermon at the Profession of Sister Yvonne-Aimée, September 29, 1931, no. 313).

Her secret was tirelessly to inspire love of Christ, with all its personal and practical consequences.

TRAINER AND TEACHER OF THE YOUNG SISTERS (1932–1935)

There were thirty-five sisters in the novitiate. It was an unprecedented success but also a burden. As a result, the group of sisters who had made their first, or temporary, vows (and curiously were called juniors) was separated from the young new arrivals (i.e., postulants and novices) and entrusted to the care of Sister Yvonne-Aimée, as of May 18, 1932.

Right from the start she exercised a strong presence there, at once stimulating and pacifying, without any polarization toward herself. She had asked the Lord for the grace "never

to keep for herself even a single fiber of the heart of her
daughters" (May 12, 1934, no. 241).

She aroused above all love for the Lord himself. In this she
integrated the rules of ascesis necessary to implant such a spir-
ituality. She was able to cloak her counsels with humor, even
poetry. At Christmas 1932 she gave each of the juniors a card
with a little flower that she had painted on it, each one bearing
a little advisory comment adapted to the individual person.

—To the waterlily: I shall water your heart with the delicious water of my heart.

—To the cornflower: Accept the clouds. I'm hiding behind
them. (No doubt for a novice suffering or being tested as
Sister Yvonne-Aimée herself had been.)

—To the jasmine: Perfume all those who approach you by
charity.

—To the bindweed: Bind yourself strongly to me. Forget
yourself ever more. Empty yourself of yourself.

The *Augustinian Youth* testifies to a healthy atmosphere:
"You need very little to brighten up the recreation of nuns.
When souls are in peace and when charity creates a union
of hearts, joy radiates easily on the faces; sometimes it even
erupts in great gales of laughter" (*Augustinian Youth*, January
1933, p. 5, no. 149).

It didn't mean the sort of hysterical laughter that denotes
an excess of nervous tension, observed another article. And
there was certainly no manic laughter when the power supply failed during the Office of Matins and two young sisters
prevented the interruption of the psalmody by gaily lighting
little tapers and candles all about the place. (Ibid., January
1934, p. 6, no. 74)

The notes left by Sister Yvonne-Aimée show her to be attentive to details that assure personal and community equilibrium:

—"enter and leave the choir sedately, without swinging
arms..."

—"when you're thirsty, put off taking the first sip of your
drink for a few seconds" (List of mortifications for Lent,
February 1933, no. 151).

—She considered recreation times as "The ideal moment to forget oneself by giving joy to those around you" (*Articles*, p. 161).

—"Take part in the conversation, especially on days when it means nothing to you," she recommended. (Mortifications of Lent, February 1933, no. 151)

—Her discretion allowed for "live and let live." She knew the importance and the cost of the long haul, the span of time: "I don't like a holiness that grows too quickly. It is cheap wood. It can lead to pride. Our failures give us experience and humility. Jesus loves souls who do not get discouraged but start again" (*Articles*, p. 125).

—She didn't like to reprimand and was able to wait: "I did something wrong," recounted a novice. "When I went to her to apologize, I also said to her, "But you knew, Mother. Why didn't you say anything?" "I was waiting and praying" (Ibid., p. 142).

—It cost her to be severe: "I am so sensitive and impressionable that to reprimand one of my daughters yesterday evening made me ill" (Letter to Father Crété, November 7, 1933, no. 670).

—She knew that the sabbath is made for man and not man for the sabbath.: "I said to my daughters in the Juvenate: When you feel tired, I order you, in the name of obedience, to come and ask me for a dispensation. I will always grant you it. I trust you" (Letter to a chaplain, quoted in *Articles*, p. 143).

—Her spiritual talks combined solid doctrinal bases with practical lessons, inspired by a "profound and nuanced knowledge of the human heart" (Ibid., p. 67). The style of her teaching (oral or written) progressed without repetition, in a direct and sober manner: "One had the impression that she was speaking the words that the Lord was giving to her," said one of her novices. (Ibid., p. 141)

—Yvonne confided: "I sense that the Good Jesus is there, that he is helping and leading me. I say 'I sense' but it is not a feeling, rather it is an observation. I do what, without grace, I could not do. I say, whether in a talk or at recreation, things that do them good, enlarges their soul and makes them love the Good Lord more. And all that, it's not from me, for often I use ideas that are new for me, expressions which are not usual for me. It's in that way I feel it" (Letter to Bishop Picaud, June 5, 1932, no. 333).

—She was astonished to be able to see into souls: "The Good Lord permits it ... It's useful to me." And she took it not too seriously but with humor: "Oh Mother, you're like the Curé of Ars," said a novice who felt "read" or seen into. "What intuitive daughters I have!" she replied. (Testimony of Sister Saint Jean Berchmans, April 1956, no. 187)

And that was the end of the matter.

Her multifaceted activity, astonishingly free, went from one of her charges to the other, and was just right for each one. Her gifts, which had played such a great role in the community, proved their worth in the formation or training of the juniors, at the service of the Lord alone. With her dynamism, no one would guess the trials that she was still suffering: "Oh Monsignor, if you knew the terrible hours I spend! And yet, if the surface of my soul is agitated, I believe that deep down a profound and even serene peace dwells in me. I want absolutely only what he wants and his will surpasses all my wants, all my desires" (Letter to Bishop Picaud, June 5, 1932, no. 333).

It cost her to remain available for so many different and useful tasks, which pulled her in so many different directions at once: "I am harassed, my time is chopped to bits. Oh, if only I could be like other people. But I desire nothing and I need to learn to say: It is what he wants that I love" (Notebook, September 3, 1932, no. 562).

There was no question of her continuing the spiritual journals that she had written out of obedience in the preceding years; she wouldn't have the time and she was no longer obliged to do so.

On August 10 she accompanied her Superior to England to present the new Constitutions there (Diary, August 10, 1932, no. 500). The novice mistress of another convent which accepted sisters from Malestroit on nursing internships admired their free and dynamic style: "I would be happy to spend some time at Malestroit to see how they train the sisters, and adopt their spirit. Here they mostly teach us to tremble and quake" (Conversation related by Mother Marie-Anne to Bishop Picaud, June 22, 1932, no. 375).

NOVICE MISTRESS (1933–1935)

After a year, her success with the young sisters saw her entrusted with the novitiate, on May 9, 1933. "A week ago I had no idea that the Lord Jesus would land this on me. Here I am appointed novice mistress; without any joy, I can assure you, Father," she wrote to Bishop Picaud on May 10, 1933. "On the contrary, I have a heavy heart. I'm scared of doing it badly and not having what it takes. It's true that the Lord Jesus is here and he must help me, and having only my weakness and inability he really has to clothe me with his strength and his wisdom. In fact, I abandon myself; may I make him loved and glorified" (no. 300).

The following month temptation came "to leave everything here, to leave."

"My responsibility has become so unbearable—thinking that I'm doing everything badly, that I'm wrongly directing the souls entrusted to me, not doing them any good, so much so that I really can't get any rest or sleep. I prayed hard to Our Lady to come to my aid as I couldn't go on. These temptations, I might say obsessions, so bad that I don't get any respite, have really tired me out" (Letter to Bishop Picaud, June 8, 1933, no. 365).

This temptation was completely interior. The novices were happy and her superiors amazed. "For me, it is a great relief to see the novitiate in good hands," wrote Mother Marie-Anne of Jesus. "If these children make the most of the grace that is given to them, we will have a generation of real religious sisters. But I feel sorry to see (Sister Yvonne-Aimée) so tired" (Letter of Mother Marie-Anne to Bishop Picaud, June 8, 1933, no. 369).

"She taught souls in depth ... sacrifice ... charity (she would summarize later). The training that she gave was both collective and individual, adapting itself to each person, to each one according to her gifts, her qualities, her possibilities, and making sure that she developed and brought out the best qualities in each different personality. She gave the novices a very lofty idea of the Order and our Constitutions" (*Obituary Notice* by Mother Marie-Anne, p. 25, 1951, no. 154).

"Despite her young age, Mother Yvonne-Aimée made her mark right away by the impact of her lovable and radiant virtue, and her goodness ... which won her the hearts of her daughters.... Around her there was no formality, but a free and open atmosphere" (Ibid., p. 24).

She remained an available instrument in the hands of the Lord, and was very faithful to the norms of her community— the rules, the spirit, and also the authority. "The more one has authority," she told another novice mistress, "the more one must submit to those who have authority over you.... To like control—that is such a misuse of responsibility! For me, I can assure you that this is what has drawn the favor of the Good Lord on my little flock" (*Articles*, p. 72).

She set about restoring the liturgy, according to the authentic tradition of her order. "We are learning to make the bows ... a bit deeper than before, but it's very beautiful. The chants were revised by the fathers of Solesmes. So everything is perfect and liturgical," she wrote to Miss Bato. (May 18, 1933, no. 319)

"To abandon oneself to the liturgy, isn't it to be led, lifted up, moved by love? Isn't it by the liturgy that you attract our attention, oh my Jesus, above all the initiatives of your love for us?" she would write later. (*Notebook*, April 18, 1942, no. 179)

She really lived and brought to life Christmas and Eastertide, which for her were times of graces and profound trials. She led others to discover that prayer is the source of union with God. What she could experience of the extraordinary could help nourish the ordinary in others: "When you don't pray, that is one degree less of love and glory for eternity. But no complicated methods—just do it!" (Testimony of Sister Mary of the Eucharist, 1956, no. 181)

"Yes, it is so good to pray. You see, we are not made to live alone. We need God. When we pray we receive so many graces and it is in fact our natural state to pray" (*Articles*, p. 118).

"Love him without self-regard and without measure" (Letter to Sister Marie-Paul Duflos, August 27, 1934, no. 418).

God lives only in a house of silence, she also said.

For her all doors were "made of velvet," testified one of her novices (Sister Marie-Paul Duflos, 1956, no. 191)—and that, even when she was busy or in a hurry.

She avoided analysis and complication: "Do we know if we are giving enough of ourself?" a nun at Malestroit asked her. "It's not difficult. You just have to give yourself to the present moment. You know when you are not doing it," she replied. (Testimony of Sister Rose of Lima, April 1956, no. 181)

In a letter written from Puy during a retreat led by Father de la Chevasnerie in September 1933, she confirmed: "Our sanctification is the work of each day. It is not to go over our past, which is left to the divine mercy. It is not to think of the future, which we abandon to the wisdom of the Good Lord. It is to content ourselves with the present manifestation of the divine love under whichever form it comes. It is now!" (Letter to the novitiate, September 9, 1933, no. 562)

She lightened the monotony of the cloistered life by celebrating the feast days. For the feast of "the kings," January 6, 1934, she gave to each of the thirty-three sisters the virtue most apt for her, in a pithy style:

> Zeal: My child, life is a small sum of money which you must spend only on the service of God.
>
> Humility: You will grow in holiness in the measure that you forget yourself. Jesus expects that from you.
>
> Detachment: Of the world, everything will crumble. There will remain only God and his elect.

Forgetfulness of self: The more you forget yourself, the more Jesus will take care of you.

Kindness: Above all, be kind. Kindness is what is most Godlike and most disarms people. (January 22, 1934, no. 50)

For Saint Anne's day (July 26) she again used her artistic skills as well as her humor. Each sister received a little picture of an animal, with a motto related to her personality or character:

I am a crayfish, but to be good I must be cooked well-seasoned. Tests and trials make me see clearly.

I am a jay, a bit chatty and rowdy, but devoted to my superiors and my sisters and I have such a good character.

I am a little pug. I bark a lot and I'm not always well-behaved, but I do my duty and work at correcting my faults.

I am a faithful dog. I want to sleep at the feet of my master, and poor little beast that I am, I wish to delight him with my loyalty.

I was an oyster, firmly attached to the rock of my own will. But the divine angler was able to take me...I shall be the pearl that he hopes to see come out of it.

I am a donkey. I know myself. I know my baseness but I enjoy the strokes of the cane. It's all I deserve. They will be worth it to one day look upon my little Jesus. (July 26, 1934, no. 326)

Her personalized counsels stimulated and penetrated hearts. Her interior trials radiated only joy. She confided them only to her spiritual director Bishop Picaud, with the complete openness that he asked of her:

Pitiful state...but I avoid speaking about it. Sometimes it's worth it to be ill, to often feel so tired. It's so wonderful in heaven, so wonderful. Isn't it the case, Father, that this thought sustains one? It is what

> picks us up better than the remedies, sachets, pills
> and all the works! For my part, my morale is fine,
> my soul is at peace. It's not without struggles. There
> are some days when it's really hard, because one asks
> oneself if the Lord Jesus is content, if there isn't too
> much of the human that slips into the actions, the
> words, the thoughts. Well, I want to believe that I
> love him, that I love him above all. (Letter to Bishop
> Picaud, January 27, 1934, no. 67)

Her superiors finally realized her alarming state of health:
"A high temperature of 39 degrees Celsius [102.2°F] and higher
in the evening. Complete rest is prescribed," wrote Mother
Marie-Anne to Mother Saint-Augustin. (August 26, 1934, no. 413)

During a journey in the south of France her superior,
Mother Marie-Anne of Jesus, took her to Castres to have a
rest with the Sisters of the Immaculate Conception. Their
superior general, Mother Sylvie, was there. Yvonne had met
her during the trip to Rome in 1931.

On August 24 Mother Sylvie had to leave, to go visit her
order's houses in Bisbal and at Lloret de Mar on the other
side of the Pyrenees. Sister Yvonne-Aimée was invited to
accompany her and thus she got to discover a part of Spain.
Her letters only share the happy aspects of her trip, while
her health continued to try her:

> This morning I went to draw from the well of truth.
> I was alone in the chapel. I stepped onto the sanc-
> tuary and sat on the step of the altar. There I drew
> on him, him the good Lord who has no other wish
> but to have us participate in his joy.
>
> So, my little sisters, let us be as one in the inti-
> mate joy of the Holy Trinity who lives in us; in the
> Father who in an eternal present now begets in us
> his Word; in the Word who, in us, never stops prais-
> ing the Father, in the Holy Spirit who, in us, is the
> substantial joy of the Father and of the Son. (Letter
> to the novitiate, September 4, 1934, no. 448)

Sister Yvonne-Aimée returned to Malestroit on September
11, via Paris and Dinan.

She had to deal with the new qualifications needed by the Hospitallers. The anti-clericalism of the time was creating inextricable problems in some nursing internships. Sister Yvonne-Aimée was searching for a solution.

She left hastily for Paris on Tuesday September 25 at 10:00 P. M. in order to see the Minister, Monsieur Marin. By chance, Wednesday was the only day he received visitors—but only by appointment. There, she happened upon Mother Sylvie, her guide in Spain, who just happened to have an appointment that very day. So, she saw the Minister of Health with the result that the sisters would henceforth be sent to exam centers that were less overtly hostile. (Letters of Sister Yvonne-Aimée to her mother and to Mother Sylvie, September 26, 1934, and a letter to Sister Marie-Aimée at Lannion, September 29, 1934, no. 493.)

On November 26 she left again, in order to visit Monsieur Bolloré, a significant benefactor of the convent, who was terminally ill. (Letter of Mother Marie-Anne to the community, November 27, 1934, no. 597)

January 16, 1935 she rushed back to his bedside and was there for his last breath. "He died like a saint," she said.

Her weekly lessons given to the novitiate were simple and profound. They promoted love of the religious spirit, poverty, joy, prayer, perseverance and humility: "To be humble is to be the same with God, with oneself, and with others" (Lesson of March 1, 1935, no. 106).

SUPERIOR OF MALESTROIT

On May 2, 1935 the sisters of Malestroit assembled to elect a superior, in accordance with the periodical renewal prescribed in canon law. Yvonne was elected unanimously. She was thirty-three years old. She was not of canonical age, nor had she been professed for the required number of years. A dispensation was immediately requested from Rome. Yvonne was known there. The favorable response arrived by telegram on May 6 (no. 226).

Mother Marie-Anne became her assistant and Mother Marie-Emmanuel the novice mistress.

Mother Yvonne-Aimée wrote to Bishop Picaud:

"I ask the Lord to keep his House in this atmosphere of charity and openness. May he use me to the maximum for his glory. That is my only desire" (May 11, 1935, no. 238).

Frightened by this burden, she turned to the Lord: "If I were to look at my faults and failings then there would be something to be scared of. But I found it simpler to entrust myself completely to him who wanted me here. If I had looked at myself too much I know that I would have lost my peace and my joy. But in looking at him I found strength and abandonment. And looking at my mothers and my sisters, who all appeared so happy, I felt my heart open wide.... My fears melted away in love" (Letter to the superior of Douarnenez, May 15, 1935, no. 246).

She was assailed on all sides by duties and distractions: "It's no bed of roses being superior.... Not that I have any problems with my dear community! All my sisters are so considerate and so good that on that front, it is complete peace. But I'm drowning in mail, visits, calls to the parlor, business, the building works and the former practical tasks that have not exactly left me" (Letter to Mother Marie Bernard at Rennes, June 16, 1935, no. 304).

She confided to Father Crété:

> My soul is at peace, but my heart is often heavy and burdened.... It feels like I'm not in my rightful place being superior. It costs me more and more to hold this position and I have to fight constantly to keep myself calm in the middle of so many different tasks, for which I am unsuited. Visits especially are my nightmare. I don't know what to say to people. I can't take an interest in what they're saying to me. I've only got Jesus on my mind and, once again, I can't speak. Well, if that is what Jesus wants, then I also want it but I need to sanctify myself to better carry out the duties of my state. (Letter to Father Crété, July 1, 1935, no. 331)

On August 5, 1935 the community celebrated the third centenary of the arrival of the Hospitallers in Brittany. Having settled in Vannes on August 3, 1635, they relocated to Malestroit in 1866. The House, which now numbered ninety-two nuns, that day celebrated two clothings in the religious habit, and three Professions of vows all in the presence of five bishops, three abbots and 100 priests, as well as representatives from several communities. The preacher was Father René de la Chevasnerie.

That celebration was a step toward the Federation of Augustinian Hospitallers of the Mercy of Jesus that Mother Yvonne-Aimée was beginning to instigate. Her visits, her correspondence, the *Augustinian Youth* had strengthened bonds.

The contagious atmosphere of the Malestroit convent, its numerous vocations and the services it provided, were making a mark. The future was there. But Mother Yvonne-Aimée's tasks multiplied. The increasing demands on her were taking their toll.

She took it all on despite her still-precarious health. Since October 31, 1935 she had had a fever (with rare moments of respite) of 39 and 40 degrees Celsius (102.2 and 104 Fahrenheit). It was still there at the start of 1936. (Letter to Bishop Picaud, January 25, 1936, no. 42)

Later on, Mother Marie-Anne wrote to Bishop Picaud: "Mother Yvonne-Aimée...knows that a faint can happen at any time and that she can't stand for long periods. But she remains calm and smiling and has a deep joy that she didn't have (before)" (June 1, 1936, no. 262).

On September 15, 1935 a blood sample revealed an abnormal level of albumin. (*Notebook* of Sister Marie of the Cross, September 15, 1935, no. 494)

Doctor Queinnec notes: "Mother Yvonne-Aimée cannot live long with this; at least without a special permission from Heaven" (Letter of Mother Marie-Anne to Mother Saint-Augustine at Lannion, September 15, 1935, no. 493).

Yvonne herself declared: "In the service of God, I prefer to feel weak rather than strong, for he carries the weak but allows the strong to walk" (handwritten on the back of a card).

And again: "The more Mary knew herself to be rich in graces, the more she humbled herself, remembering that she had received everything from God" (another handwritten note on a card).

In 1936 she, along with the superiors of the order, completed the revision of the liturgical books and had a breviary printed with Offices proper to the order.

She developed the *Ceremonial* and the *Directory* on the model of Solesmes and had inserted into the new books the deep bow which she instinctively made at the *Sanctus*. "I see in my mind's eye all the angels falling prostrate and adoring. We need to unite ourselves with them to adore, praise, love" (Testimony, Sister Saint-Louis of Gonzaga, May 2, 1956, p. 6, no. 213).

She had an eastern sense of the liturgy as an anticipation of glory.

The maxims which flowed from her pen or her lips go straight to the heart of the matter: "Every act against charity is a mortal blow to the Community," she would say. "Every act of charity, on the other hand, is a breath of life" (Notes of Sister Saint-René, November 29, 1932, no. 745).

And again: "Holiness does not consist of doing extraordinary things. It consists uniquely of letting yourself be consumed. Many do not know how to forget themselves. If they continue, that will end up stopping the flow of grace" (*Articles*, p. 135).

Her availability was total. "Free entry, like at the bazaar," she sometimes said. (Ibid., p. 132)

The obedience she expected was interior. She was, therefore, wide and generous in granting permissions requested because of tiredness or reasons of health.

She was innovative in assuring a better welcome for the families of the sisters. She participated "as if she had been waiting just for us," said visitors.

She had a strong concern for equity. She asked advice about the just salary of the hospital employees. (Letter to Bishop Picaud, October 8, 1941, no. 546)

In fact, her activity, dispersed in a kaleidoscope of expressions and varied tasks, was the radiation of the one love and mercy of God.

After an interview with her a visitor converted. People were astounded. She replied simply, "I spoke to her about Jesus's love, about his mercy. She broke down in tears" (*Articles*, p. 123).

17
Birth of the Federation of Augustinian Hospitallers

1937–1939

FOLLOWING THE TRICENTENARY CELE-
brations at Malestroit, the idea of a Federation of
Augustinian Hospitallers of the Mercy of Jesus (orig-
inating from Dieppe), with a view to providing a better service, advanced. All the convents looked naturally to Mother
Yvonne-Aimée, who Father Sauvage supported in Rome.

At the beginning of 1937 she suggested to the Augustinian
superiors that they all make a retreat together: "It is in great
simplicity that I dare to make such a request, as I'm fully
aware that as one of the youngest superiors in the Order, I
am little qualified for such a step.... Please consider it then,
in complete freedom, reverend and dear mothers" (Circular
to superiors of the Order, January 18, 1937, no. 37).

It was welcomed eagerly. The retreat preached by Monsignor d'Herbigny in October 1937 was fruitful. The link, so
long sought, was taking shape. It would be, suggested Mother
Yvonne-Aimée, a federation along the lines of the Trappist
and Benedictine Federations, where each house would retain
its autonomy.

And so it was decided to form a general council of the order,
tasked with planning the federation and drawing up a plan for
statutes. (René Piacentini, *Origines*, April 14, 1957, p. 373, no. 110)

A missionary novitiate was founded to respond to requests
for Augustinians in the southern hemisphere. (Minutes of
chapter decisions, October 22, 1937, no. 532)

All of that necessitated a journey by Mother Yvonne-Aimée
to Natal (then a province of South Africa) to see at first hand

the needs and how to respond to them. She set off on February 3, 1938, leaving a statue of Our Lady in her place in the refectory. (Letter of Sister Saint-Paul, February 3, 1938, no. 102)

After twenty days at sea on the ship *Giulio Cesare*, she arrived at Durban on March 2, visited the five communities, peacefully resolved the outstanding problems, restored the practice of the Constitutions, met each sister individually and brought a breath of fresh spiritual life. She left South Africa on April 24 and arrived back at Malestroit on May 18, less than four months after she left. A trip too short, she noted: "and yet the Good Lord so simplified the task for me that everything worked out well. The proof?—oh, I have a lot!" (Letter to Bishop Picaud, May 21, 1938, no. 505)

On July 2, 1938 she was a second time unanimously elected superior of Malestroit, and on October 18, president of the council of the order which had just been formed.

At the beginning of January 1939, along with Father Sauvage, she finalized the statutes of the future federation and of the missionary novitiate. She went to Rome, from January 9 to 18, to have them accepted. But she came up against a different point of view. She would like a *federation*. But this new model appeared utopian and risky. The cardinal recommended a "general union." She pleaded the case for her plan, which was more respecting of freedoms:

> This Federation would have as its aim, while safeguarding autonomy, the maintenance of a greater unity of spirit and of action in our convents. Each superior would, therefore, remain major superior of her convent, with the same rights as before. The superiors would choose a Superior General who would be the link between our houses. She would take care to preserve the same spirit everywhere and, while ensuring the spiritual interests, she would deal with—in the name of everyone and assisted by a Council—mainly the intellectual and material interests in what they have in common. (Letter to Mother Saint-Marc, Quebec, February 25, 1939, no. 125)

In July the Congregation for Religious informed the Bishop of Vannes that the concept of a federation was accepted. A few weeks later the Augustinian superiors met at Malestroit. Bishop Picaud preached them a retreat. There followed a general chapter. The statutes of the future federation were finalized, in line with the instructions from Rome, which were somewhat vague, but open.

Mother Yvonne-Aimée was confirmed in her post of president of the council of the order.

The statutes sent to Rome on November 15, 1938 made a big impression. But Cardinal La Puma, the prefect, hesitated before the novelty of this formula. He asked a preliminary question which posed, to his mind, a major objection: "Is it in conformity with the law (and allowable) to authorize an organization of independent convents of women which has no basis in canon law, nor any historical precedent?" (Letter of Father Sauvage to Mother Yvonne-Aimée, February 20, 1940, no. 125)

He launched a consultation on this thorny problem.

Father Sauvage requested an authorization "for six years, on a trial basis." Rome refused. But Father Sauvage encouraged Mother Yvonne-Aimée to pursue the work begun, in the hope of one day obtaining canonical recognition.

It would be a long wait, for the world was ablaze; the Second World War had come. 🙢

18

The Trial, the Danger, and the Glory

1939–1946

RETURN FROM QUEBEC

On September 3, 1939, as France declared war on Germany, Mother Yvonne-Aimée was in Canada. The Augustinians in Quebec knew about her planned federation. They invited her to the tricentenary of their foundation. She set off on August 19 with Mother Saint-Vincent-de-Paul, superior of Dieppe, and Mother Marie-Anne.

On August 25 she gave a talk at Quebec's Laval University on the training of nursing religious sisters in France. They had put this engagement into her schedule without informing her.

She had no difficulty in expressing what she constantly lived and put into practice daily in the communities—that alliance too rarely accomplished between religious life and the "works of mercy," according to Matthew 25:36 which she quoted: "I was sick and you visited me," but also the alliance between love drawn from God, who is Love, and the technical and human quality of the service which she had constantly cultivated in modernizing the hospital and organizing the training of the nuns. It was between these two poles that she had been able to establish a coherent life, out of which flowed the spark: "A hospitaller nun who didn't put her heart into the work that God assigned her close to his suffering members couldn't be a good nurse. And also, a nursing nun who doesn't seek her own perfection in carrying out perfectly her hospitaller service cannot become a perfect nun.... In the measure that we put all our conscience, all our good will, all our intelligence and our strengths into our service of neighbor, in the same measure God will allow our work to be an extraordinarily powerful means of sanctification" (Talk at Laval University, August 25, 1939, no. 540).

Her lecture merely formulated that harmony between love based in God and the enlightened service of others, which is the very vocation of the Augustinian Hospitallers.

In France the "phony war" was underway, complacent and sleepy behind the "invincible Maginot Line."

On her return to Malestroit on October 16 Mother Yvonne-Aimée intensified the prayer there and throughout the budding federation. The trials that she had foreseen fifteen years previously in the mysterious fog of her premonitions were beginning to reveal their meaning. She had had a little fore-taste during her return journey when the ship was threatened: "Followed by a submarine for thirty-six hours, we disembarked in England safe and sound. The Good Lord guarded us, the Blessed Virgin protected us" (Letter to Father Labutte, December 8, 1939, no. 808).

Doctor Queinnec had put his clinic at the disposal of the army and so was himself mobilized on site. A general doctor came to do an inspection. The surgeon who accompanied him retained an unforgettable memory: "It's not exactly Lourdes but everything similarly makes you think that everything here is holy. Mother Yvonne-Aimée made such an impression on me that I have ... never forgotten a single word that she said. Her intelligence, the way she explained everything to us (while showing us around her hospital), her great simplicity, her manner, everything has stayed with me.... She created an atmosphere around her which was not of this world" (Testimony of Doctor Serge Oberlin, former president of the Order of Doctors, 1956, no. 340).

In May 1940 the Germans invaded France. There was a mass exodus. On June 9, half an hour before midnight, some wounded officers who had left Lisieux at four in the morning arrived "black with smoke." They'd had nothing to eat. One of them would be baptized in the hospital. On July 16 they

signed an Address of Thanksgiving to Mother Yvonne-Aimée.
Two of them, who had been made prisoners on August 13,
managed to return for the procession of August 15. Several of
them, including Sub-lieutenant Thiery and Captain Perrette,
kept in touch for the rest of their lives.

Around June 18 the exodus brought sisters from Rennes,
Bayeux, Harcourt, and Dieppe.

On June 22 the Germans occupied Malestroit. A colonel
commandeered the hospital buildings. Mother Yvonne-Aimée
appealed to his honor. She had commitments. And she must
keep them: "We will make up beds to receive your military
patients but we shall not evict our civilian patients."

At first the cause seemed lost. But, in fact, it was won!

"You, woman who tugs at my heartstrings...!" concluded the
German colonel as he modified his requisition. (Testimony of
Sister Marie of the Trinity, 1972, Labutte 4, p. 81)

Taking in refugees was a heavy burden. Food shortages
began. The convent benefited from people's generosity but
also increased the aid it gave out. At a time when these problems were causing anxiety, Mother Yvonne-Aimée retained a
surprisingly broad view. She allowed the sisters "to personally
prepare food parcels for their families in need" (Articles, p. 83).

But the concern for equity never left her: "Scruples...gnaw
at me regarding poverty, charity, justice.... What I want above
all is to be in the will of God, to do everything with the
mindset that he wishes," she wrote to Bishop Picaud on
November 12, 1940 (no. 533).

BOUNDLESS AID FOR EVERY NEED

The requests for prayers—and for help—flowed in more
than ever. Mother Yvonne-Aimée multiplied herself, with the
gifts the Lord mysteriously granted her. The secret part of
her activity has largely escaped the scrutiny of history and
is still the subject of our critical investigation.[1]

In November 1940 she was informed of the arrest of

---

[1] Canon Laurentin later published studies of Mother Yvonne-Aimée's
bilocations.

two elderly English ladies in Rennes. They were going to be deported to Germany. (Letter of the Mother Superior of Gouarec, November 22, 1940)

She prayed for them, wrote to them, alerted her friends in Rennes, and predicted their liberation. Which is what happened on May 7, 1941 against all expectation. An emergency assistance among so many others. And more and more every day.

In March 1941, despite the war, she established a House of Studies in Paris, *The Oasis*, under the patronage of Our Lady of Consolation. She came to it often, for "missions" of those difficult times.

SPIRITUAL MARRIAGE

On July 5, 1941, after several months of no extraordinary graces and an assault that left her wounded by the prince of darkness (June 3, 1941, no. 293) Mother Yvonne-Aimée embarked on a new stage of total union with God, in a meaningful continuity of signs: "You said to me again, Lord Jesus, like nineteen years ago: 'Come!' You showed me a lily. It blossomed, this time in my hands. Here's how it all happened! The room had been prepared to receive you.... Like on the evening of July 5, 1922, I was sensing your arrival already since the afternoon. My heart was impatient to possess you more intimately, and looking at the bouquets of roses spread around for you... I thought you would not be able to resist the thoughtfulness of my daughters."

Mother Yvonne-Aimée, who attributed this grace to the community's prayer, continued:

> That evening, it was about 9:30 P. M. Suddenly your voice called me:
> "Yvonne!"
> Then you quickly added:
> "My Beloved, my Spouse, come."
> My Jesus, how sweet it was, and you wanted to cloak me with a veil of purity, a veil completely luminous, which seemed to be part of yourself.... And then I seemed to have come out of the darkness and I felt flooded by reflections of your brightness. The

light, your light, descended on me and I felt, in my whole being, like the freshness of a waterfall and at the same time (I was) as if plunged into an ocean of divine fire.

And then you said such beautiful things to me, so full of tenderness and full of love! You spoke to me about those whom I love.... You confided secrets to me and you also gave me some words of love and comfort to distribute. (Notebook, July 5–6, 1941, no. 318)

Then Jesus reassured her about her interior life and conduct, which she sometimes had doubts about:

You have served me well and your deficiencies have never offended me. You have been able to remain hidden and often not understood, living your poor life, attentive to my least desire, not allowing to enter into your mind, nor your heart, nor into your will, the least indocility. You have not asked why, nor expressed fear, nor excuses. You are the most loving and most docile of my creatures, you have allowed your flesh to be tortured, expiating the faults of my blind sons, taking their crimes upon yourself.... You are a tender and hidden spouse...your heart is like a candle that never burns out, and like incense rising constantly toward me.... You are a torch of fire burning in the night, you are like a dazzling sword fighting [for] the causes I charge you with.

Your role will expand more and more, but you will serve me yet a while in secret...you who go without hesitating where I tell you to go, who say what I want you to say, who keep quiet at a sign of my hand. (Ibid.)

The grace of July 5, 1941 recalled and replicated that of July 5, 1922, but Jesus called Yvonne "My spouse." Was it the Spiritual Marriage that Saint John of the Cross describes as "the total transformation of the soul in its Beloved"?

"The two parties give themselves entirely to each other, in total possession the one of the other in a union of love consummated as far as that is possible. The soul is here rendered divine. It becomes God by participation, as much as that can be done in this life" (*Spiritual Canticle*, stanza 27).

Nevertheless, this grace of July 5, 1941, the nineteenth anniversary of that of July 5, 1922, brought signs and sensible gifts that baffle us: a lily on those two dates, a ring in 1922, a veil in 1941. For John of the Cross "jewels and finery" would characterize the time of Spiritual Betrothal. (*Living Flame of Love*, stanza III, part 23)

The progress of union with God defies pre-established categories and routes too precisely signposted. The mystical advances of Mother Yvonne-Aimée will one day call for a fuller critical study. Let it suffice to point out this decisive step as Mother Yvonne-Aimée described it. This new step was marked by outward signs of solidarity with the Passion: the stigmata and scourgings, with the community knowing nothing about them. (Diary of Father Labutte, July 10, 1941, no. 339, and that of Sister Marie of the Cross, same day, no. 341)

During this same month of July 1941, she wrote on a loose sheet of paper: "Here you are, tenderness of God, appearing again today for me, out of the depths without looking. I see you and I merge into you.... See how you invade my heart, my blood, my flesh, my mind, my soul. I am no longer in this moment the poor small and fallen being that must die; I am she to whom God comes to tell a secret.... Here I am, free with the freedom of the angels.... I was small, weak, too small for big things, big sufferings, big joys. I got up. I walked for a long time, my heart breaking at the thought of all I was missing" (Sheet of paper no. 24, July 1941, no. 318).

She confided to a priest friend: "If I were to say to Jesus, 'Take me,' he would take me. But I don't want to say this word, because I'm too afraid of arriving in Paradise and seeing all the work that I've left [unfinished] on earth" (Diary of Father Labutte, July 3, 1941, no. 304).

After a rest at Brardière, at Father Labutte's place, she wrote to Bishop Picaud: "I thought, the night before last, during the night, that I was going to die. I had quite a long faint. An injection restarted my circulation. And then, openly,

I wept at not having died.... The Lord Jesus knows that I'm dying of the desire to see him again. Heaven has too much spoiled me recently, earth has become for me a terribly heavy exile.... However, my will remains attached to his...and he knows that I love him more than everything" (Letter to Bishop Picaud, October 8, 1941, no. 546).

DARK FOREBODINGS

After the luminous graces of July, it was a return to austere and nocturnal life, with her daily effort to identify her will with the Lord's will.

On December 3, 1941, she foresaw a hard trial: "Since yesterday evening she is in an abyss of physical and psychological suffering such as I haven't seen her suffer in many a long year" (Letter of Mother Marie-Anne to Bishop Picaud, December 4, 1941, no. 699).

On December 11, 1941, Mother Yvonne-Aimée wrote to her spiritual director: "The trial that I am going through right now is personal; it is the announcement of another one, also personal. If I have suffered so much at this revelation, it's because I'm not sufficiently abandoned. I couldn't immediately silence my *whys*, my human reasoning. Now, I seek no more. My mind is totally submitted. Jesus places no limits on his love for me. I, poor wretch, must place no limit on my gift of love" (Letter to Bishop Picaud, December 11, 1941, no. 720).

In April 1942 she was once again warned not to worry about the contradictions that her unusual paths were going to bring upon her. "The bitterness or the suffering of incomprehension of certain acts that I will ask of you and which in all humility, simplicity and docility you will do, will turn into joy, into sweetness. Don't worry about the inevitable demands stretching your reason and common sense. It has to be [that way], and I don't mean that you won't be marked and affected by certain painful things, but your heart will not be broken. You'll see. You'll come out of it more dazzling, you will radiate a clear light, radiant and beneficent" (Notes of Mother Yvonne-Aimée, April 8, 1942, no. 179).

For the moment, her daily worry was that she was not up to her task: "I'm fully aware that I can't manage to do everything and he only asks me to do well all that I am able to do. I couldn't reply to the 411 letters received, I can't satisfy everyone, read my letters...receive the visits...visit the patients...give permissions, listen attentively to work problems, etc." (Diary 1943, January 6, no. 21).

She overcame this daily difficulty: "Don't try to do everything. Possess myself in God, possess God, be possessed by him; everything is in that" (Diary 1943, January 7, no. 24).

But what cost her most was to be strict—"to reprimand, to correct" (Notes of April [8], 1942, no. 179).

PREDICTIONS FULFILLED

Mother Yvonne-Aimée's duties in the service of the trial federation obliged her to make numerous journeys, with more frequent stays in Paris. Thus was fulfilled the premonition of 1923, the strangeness of which she emphasized, to a date when her future remained uncertain.

> I saw myself as a nun and travelling. I was in Augustinian habit (and at that time Augustinians did not travel) and I saw airplanes dropping great cylinders onto the trains, onto the railway stations and destroying and burning down everything. I saw men dressed in green getting on and getting off the train, one would have said military uniforms but it didn't look at all to me like our soldiers.... A voice, deep and gentle...was saying:
> "It will be the trial, the great trial. Pray, pray much, especially for the priests, the prisoners." (Letter to Father Crété, September 29, 1923, no. 607)

In 1943 she acquired for the Augustinians the Home of the Daughters of Saint Francis de Sales, where she had received so many graces. She had forgotten the prediction of February 1, 1925: "In another scene, Jesus showed me Augustinian sisters in the garden of the Home and told me: 'This will be bought at the same time. Do you accept?' I said, 'Yes Jesus.' But I didn't understand" (no. 77).

ACTION OF THE GESTAPO

On January 24, 1943 she made a trip to Paris which she foresaw was going to be dangerous. She left drafts of letters to alert the sisters of Chateau-Gontier, where she was to go on Sunday, February 21, in case she didn't turn up. She feared she might disappear, and disappear she did on the morning of February 16. Arrested by the Gestapo, she made the fact known to Sister Saint-Vincent Ferrier and to Father Labutte who was at the time at Flers, in the Orne. She asked him to come to Paris urgently. His worries were justified. He spent a hectic day, culminating in a time of intense prayer in the chapel of rue du Bac, then at the Oasis, to which she had not come back since the evening before. Around 9:00 P.M. he asked permission to go upstairs to Mother Yvonne-Aimée's office. Once there, he suddenly heard "a thud" behind him. He turned around. And there she was, standing beside her desk, visibly traumatized and disheveled. There were bloody traces visible through the clothing on her back. Sister Saint-Vincent Ferrier would have to dress the wounds. Mother Yvonne-Aimée didn't realize yet where she was. It took a moment for her to recognize Father Labutte. It has never been explained how she got there. There were flowers in the room.

The discretion called for by the circumstances leaves areas of shadow over this incident. But on February 18 Sister Saint-Vincent Ferrier left this somewhat laconic account, which the other two witnesses confirm:

"So, our mother came back yesterday evening around 9:00 P.M., in the outfit that you know [lay clothing], minus head-gear and coat, and directly to the first floor [second floor American]. Father had just arrived in the office, reciting his chaplet and it was he who saw her" (Letter to Mother Marie-Anne, February 18, 1943, no. 130).

The precise memories of the other two witnesses (still alive at the time this book was written), whom I have questioned several times, are perfectly in agreement and overlap the above correspondence. The incident enacted what one of the premonitory dreams of 1922 foresaw, when she had to write them down every day, as instructed by Father Crété: "I saw myself in prison and an angel came and freed me, I was in civil dress" (Letter of August 18, 1922, no. 206).

"I got out of there miraculously," she confirmed in a confidential letter to Mother Saint-Jeanne, in Quebec. (October 1, 1946, no. 625)

THE GREAT TRIAL OF FEBRUARY TO JUNE 1943

Here are just some incidents and miscellaneous facts from this time of war.

At the beginning of February 1943 came the great threat that Mother Yvonne-Aimée had foreseen twenty years earlier and the imminence of which had been signaled to her since December 5, 1941. Foreboding gripped her.

On February 5, 1943, while in Paris, she wrote: "This evening in the chapel of the Home (the Oasis) I understood that I am entering a new phase in my life; a painful, incomprehensible phase. Lord, give me your favor, that I shall not succumb. Have pity on my weakness" (Diary February 5, 1943, no. 88).

Father Crété, now almost seventy-five, showed up in a harsh and unexpected manner. Contact between him and Yvonne had been limited since Bishop Picaud had removed him as spiritual director. The faculty to hear her confession, though, had been restored in 1941.

He, who had been her principal support in the first difficulties, now suspected her. By letter, on March 15, he asked her to question herself radically.

"Have you always been upright, my daughter? Aren't you in fact deluded, and deceived by the Devil? Before, you were so humble. But now? Everything about you has always worked, been successful. The saints, the real ones, on the contrary, were subject to all sorts of trials" (Extracts from that letter, not preserved, quoted in a letter of Mother Yvonne-Aimée to Father Henri Monier-Vinard, May 11, 1943, no. 301).

How could he not know the extraordinary burdens borne by Mother Yvonne-Aimée—her two posts as superior, local and federal, and the war? How was he unaware of her great sufferings as a very ill patient when she was standing up (see below, p. 217) and the enormous courage she had to deploy every day to resolve the impossible? And at what cost she put on a brave face so as to share only the most positive things with her daughters?

So, what had happened?

A priest, a friend of Malestroit,[2] a founder in his turn, had been disturbed on his path by the success of Mother Yvonne-Aimée, who attracted so many vocations. After having lived in her aura and celebrated her merits more than she would have wished, he was assailed by doubts. A book by Maurice Garcon, the lawyer and soon-to-be Academician, *Madeleine of the Cross, Diabolical Abbess* (Paris: Sorlot, 1939), had been a ray of light for him ... or rather, of darkness. Born in 1487, this Poor Clare abbess was too successful. It was because she was vowed to Satan. She was exposed and a famous Church trial deposed her in 1546. So, was Mother Yvonne-Aimée's remarkable success of the same sort? With his vivid imagination, the priest friend-turned-opponent drew up along these lines a whole charge sheet of accusations. If Mother Yvonne-Aimée did not wish to resign, then he would denounce her before a Church tribunal.

And thus was fulfilled the prediction that she had heard, without understanding it, twenty years earlier: "You will be accused of lying by those who had believed in you. Someone will make you out to be a false mystic, a sinful person; under the guise of defending my glory, he will act against my will and pierce your heart with a sword. However, you will also have friendly hearts to defend you, but many doubts will cross minds. Accept this trial as of now. The time of calamities during which this trial will come to you, will help powerfully to save the world" (Prediction of the night of July 5 to 6, 1923, recounted in Father Crété's letter July 6, first Friday of the month and first anniversary of the Spiritual Betrothal, no. 401).

---

[2] (At the time of writing this book....) The events are still too recent for us to disclose the name of this priest, whose sincerity is not in question.

Yes, those who had believed in her now turned against her, even Father Crété: "My God, is it possible," wrote Mother Yvonne-Aimée in her notebook, dated that March 15. "Am I everything that my father tells me I am? Have I lacked uprightness, or am I deluded? That would be too awful. What's happened? What's going to happen? Oh, my God, make me see clearly, if you deem it good, but above all make it so that I don't offend you. I don't want it. No matter what they make of me, as long as I am what you want and live in the truth" (*Notebook*, March 15, 1943, no. 174).

Despite this total abandonment, the shock was terrible: "I feel broken, crushed, lost," she wrote on March 17. "I don't see clearly. Oh, I do so want to believe my father but that would be just too terrible: I would have offended you, I would have been deluded! Can one want only the truth and live in error? Oh my God, make me see clearly. I can't take it anymore" (*Notebook*, March 17, 1943, no. 183).

She looked for support in heaven: "Oh, Saint Joseph! Help me to live like you, in abandonment, never to seek the why of the trials, to quite simply accept them. If it pleases God to keep me thus crushed and in the dark, *Fiat*. Succor me, but like you I want to serve Jesus at my expense, to be unknown to men but the Beloved of Jesus, to be his tiny little Beloved" (Diary 1943, March 19, no. 185).

To Juliette Cannieux, a friend from Rennes, caught up in this business, she wrote on that same March 19: "If it pleases the Good Lord to leave me in the dark, on the other hand a peace, even a joy, has settled in me and the suffering that I am going through is mastered by this completely new feeling. You see, at first I didn't realize that such a suffering could come to me via my father. But the Lord has done well because it is what could be the most painful to me. Therefore I thank him. I beg him to make me ever more conformed to his divine will" (no. 187).

This thanksgiving for and despite everything didn't extinguish the confusion and the suffering. She wrote to the same friend ten days later: "Jesus really does know, all the same, that I love him above everything. But the letter from my father has so shaken my soul that I no longer know where I am, what I am and if I am in the truth. And to think that that is all I have ever sought" (March 29, 1943, no. 207).

FATHER CRÉTÉ'S INVESTIGATION

However, Father Crété was perplexed. The conviction solidly established in the years 1922–1927 could not be overturned so easily.

On April 1 he wrote an encouraging letter to Mother Yvonne-Aimée: "How are you? I fear that you are suffering a lot. Like your father! *Fiat!*... Have courage. Trust! He cannot not love 'his little darling' of 1922.... We'd better believe it. *Fiat!*" (April 1, 1943, no. 218).

On April 25 he wrote to the priest accuser: "You imagine that you are acting solely for the glory of God. Since January 31 I understand that you are not led by the Spirit of Jesus. Mother Yvonne-Aimée will defend herself, it is her duty and I have commanded her to. But in the manner of holy souls, without passion. She well knows, as I do, that she has never been capable of what you accuse her of" (Letter of April 25, 1943, Easter Sunday, no. 257).

During this period Father Crété increased his consultations with Juliette Cannieux and with Sister Marie-Emmanuel. To her (the future superior general) he wrote as if by chance: "For you, what is humility?"

Sister Marie, not yet knowing anything about the accusations that motivated the correspondence, replied:

"For me, humility is Sister Yvonne-Aimée" (Testimony of Sister Marie-Emmanuel, August 29, 1981).

Father Crété warmly thanked her. Without knowing it, she had answered exactly the question he was asking himself, and the doubts that were tormenting him.

Father Henri Monier-Vinard, SJ, a renowned spiritual director that Father Crété consulted as an "irrefutable expert" encouraged him to overcome his doubts.

"Give fatherly support at this time to Mother Yvonne-Aimée.

Such a trial is the mark of the divine in someone's life" (Letter of April 28, 1943, no. 267).

On May 1 Father Crété's conviction had taken on an unprecedented firmness: "For me personally, never have I been more sure than I am today that Mother Yvonne-Aimée is a soul who greatly loves Our Lord and who is loved by him. My conviction of her holiness of life has become such that no condemnation could take it away from me" (Letter to Father Monier-Vinard, May 1, 1943, no. 275).

Father Monier-Vinard confirmed his convictions: "In every age God has permitted trials for his saints.... They are the crucible wherein souls are purified and from which they emerge holy. If she keeps calm, humble and confident at Our Lord's feet, this trial will bring down new blessings upon her dear convent" (Father Monier-Vinard, May 8, 1943, no. 292).

RETURN TO MALESTROIT

Meanwhile, Father Crété had returned to the convent, on April 7, 1943, "unrecognizable, aged, thin, pale and lifeless" wrote Mother Yvonne-Aimée to Father Monier-Vinard. "In the evening he hardly spoke to me. I felt he was annoyed, but he saw Mother Assistant, and told her that someone had proof against me. This proof tended to show that I was a false mystic; that, accused before a Church tribunal, there would be no doubt about the verdict. He added: 'That's what's making me ill, and is killing me'" (Letter of May 11, 1943, no. 301).

Since January his temperature had been rising in the evening—37.5°C (99.5°F) instead of 36.6°C (97.8°F). Was that bringing back his doubts? He remained worried and upset.

THE ACCUSER IS UNMASKED

On Good Friday (April 23, 1943) at 2:30 P.M. the Lord revealed to Mother Yvonne-Aimée the name of the adversary who was denouncing her as an ally of Satan.[3] "I felt a blow

---

[3] The proximity of events does not allow this person and others to be named. The accuser had been a passionate admirer and benefactor.

to my heart. My judge was no longer a stranger to me, it was someone I valued and who I loved in God" (Letter to Father Monier-Vinard, May 11, 1943, no. 301).

Nothing on the part of this erstwhile friend had given Mother Yvonne-Aimée any cause to suspect such a change— neither his attitude nor his correspondence, she said. (Ibid.)

The accuser soon revealed himself: "Your convent is the Devil's house." Satan "is at home there," he claimed. He gave the thus-charged superior a deadline for a "friendly" resignation. Failing that, the file, prepared three years before, would be handed to the ecclesiastical authorities.

She tried to examine herself in conscience, humbly before the Lord himself:

> For his love, I bore so many pains, suffering, lack of understanding, judgments of all sorts. I amassed in my soul, my body, my heart, so many pains that only he knows. If I were a demonic person, would I have this courage, this grace, rather?
>
> I'm accused of being proud, and yet never have I voluntarily had a single thought of vanity or pride, never have I indulged in these favors, I haven't desired them, haven't sought them. I have always wanted to be upright, true, straightforward. I have never sought human praise—I've been wary of it. I have never wanted to act humanly nor form a circle of admirers around me in the Community. And they're saying that I live in an atmosphere of admiration and praise. It's not true. My life here is the simplest among my daughters, and the most natural. I do not like flattery—they know that. And we do not seek a single extraordinary thing. If I have been surprised in certain mystical states, I have not sought it, and it has happened without my consent.
>
> Your Excellency, I'm telling you simply all these things. But to him who will judge me, what will I be able to say? One doesn't easily defend oneself. And then, does the Lord Jesus want it? (Letter to Bishop Picaud, May 4, 1943, no. 281)

She no longer worried for herself, but for the others: "If I am to be chased out of Malestroit, I only ask the Good Lord that my departure not be an occasion of trouble or scandal for my little sisters," she confided to Juliette Cannieux. (Testimony of Juliette Cannieux, April 20, 1956, no. 161)

She referred everything to the Lord alone: "If at certain times I can suffer even to the point of agony, I don't feel unhappy. I want to unite myself with all my heart, with all my soul, to the Passion of my Lord Jesus, and suffer peacefully whatever it pleases him to make me bear. I rely on grace and on the prayers offered for me," she wrote to Father Monier-Vinard. (May 11, 1943, no. 301)

"REAL FOLLIES" REVEAL THEIR MEANING

One of the accuser's grievances against Mother Yvonne-Aimée was that "not one of her prophecies was fulfilled." Then Mother Marie-Anne remembered, sometime between May 6 and 12, 1943, that Father Crété had entrusted to her the letters and notebooks written by Yvonne from 1922 to 1925. This folder, apparently of no importance, was lying in a cupboard. And so she found in them the premonitions that Yvonne had scrupulously written down out of obedience. She wrote them with repugnance, for she didn't understand anything in them. It was a humiliation for her to put down in black and white such "ramblings" as she herself described them. And so, now these "real follies" actually made sense. Those obscure words became clear and pertinent.

Mother Marie-Anne communicated them to Father Crété. He was relieved. He wrote to Bishop Picaud on May 17, 1943: "What a treasure!... I'm jealously keeping ownership of them. I had entrusted them to Mother Assistant over ten years ago, for the future, not dreaming of their present usefulness. In 1922–1923 we understood nothing in these predictions and I never thought any more about them, any more than Mother Yvonne-Aimée did.... They were covered in dust. Fortunately, the envelope was there, which guaranteed the authenticity of these letters. Often I had written a word there, I had underlined a date. No honest man can doubt their authenticity" (no. 319).

Since then, the handwriting experts consulted have confirmed the evidence that comes across in so many ways. Yvonne's writing is very easy to date and her notes in pencil, improvised day to day, do date from the beginning of the 1920s.

In the small notebook Father Crété found, along with several others, a premonition of his doubt. And this: "Today I think that you will always remain my father because I saw you, quite old. You were at least seventy-five to eighty, perhaps a bit older."

The first figure is the right one. He had just turned 75 on April 7, but he looked older: "And you were in the midst of Augustinians, at Malestroit," she concluded on October 28, 1922 (no. 392).

The priest accuser summoned Mother Yvonne-Aimée insistently, but circumstances delayed their meeting in those troubled times. He was invited to preach at Malestroit, which he hadn't visited in three years. But he declined, not particularly wanting to meet Mother Yvonne-Aimée *on her territory*, and sent another preacher, Father Joseph Henry, SJ, less talented. It was this priest that had once given Mother Yvonne-Aimée the penance of daily recitation of the Litany of the Sacred Heart for a whole year. Meanwhile, the accuser continued to summon her on dates and to places that she couldn't attend. It was like he was playing hide-and-seek. By letters of May 20, 1943, then May 21, he maintained his point of view: *she had deceived and she had been deceived.* The Christ to whom she gave herself was the devil. The accuser saw himself in the role of innocent victim. On five occasions "the Other One" (the name he gave the devil) had threatened him with everworse revenges. That is what had caused the stomach ulcer he was suffering from. His letters were filled with allusions to that painful and diabolical affliction. This satanic retaliation had stiffened his resolve: he had to bring about the resignation—either freely or judicially—of Mother Yvonne-Aimée.

She was at a loss to understand this relentlessness, so long hidden in the shadows. "I don't want to inquire why (he) who has been doubting me for three years didn't want us to speak sooner. Why, whenever I did meet him he said nothing to me, why his letters (of the time) so little reflected his feelings. It would be wrong to inquire, to wonder why. The real reason I must seek in the will of God, isn't that so? I do feel that despite the deep pain I'm going through, I don't harbor the least animosity. I pray for him. I'd like him to be my friend again, as before, if God permits" (Letter to Father Monier-Vinard, May 11, 1943, no. 301).

This abandonment didn't prevent pain: "If you knew how much I suffer, how I hurt," she wrote to Miss Bato. "And yet, I believe that I am abandoning myself and trusting in the Lord Jesus. Pray for me and save your tenderness for me as I need it so much. The Devil has certainly gathered false proofs against me, but the Lord Jesus is stronger than he" (Letter of May 18, 1943, no. 322).

On June 5–6 she went to Quimper, where the priest-accuser had summoned her. He was there as a judge. Sister Marie-Anne, who accompanied Mother Yvonne-Aimée, wrote:

> The father himself read out the famous file, oh not the sixty pages; about thirty. We had had enough and we asked the father to stop there... and to submit his indictment to a tribunal as he had previously threatened.
>
> I assure you, reverend father, that during this abominable reading, so humiliating for our mother, I many times admired her virtue. Mine was less strong and I leapt at certain statements that were so distorted. It was our mother who called me to patience and gentleness.
>
> When the father expressed his wish to see our mother alone for a few moments, I went to the chapel. When I came back a few minutes later I sensed a relaxation in the father. (Letter of Sister Marie-Anne to Dom Demazure, Abbot of Kergonan, June 16, 1943, no. 422)

Impulsively but rightly, the accuser had curbed his excess. In private, Father Labutte learned, he had asked for forgiveness on his knees, without losing face in front of the assistant with the strong reactions. On returning, she observed his calmer demeanor:

> It was then that I told him about the letters that you also know of [the prophecies of Sister Yvonne-Aimée, recently rediscovered]. The reading of these impressed him and bit by bit he changed his tone and his attitude. And the change was such that when we were taking our leave we had returned to how we used to be with each other before. Never have we felt so much the power of prayer.... The next day we saw the father again ... for quite a long time. He was completely transformed. He had burned his famous file the evening before. (Ibid.)

In her letter to Bishop Picaud, Mother Yvonne-Aimée summarized the whole interview in one phrase: "It was very hard but it ended well" (Letter of June 6, 1943, no. 387).

And to Juliette Cannieux, on June 19, 1943: "I was happy but astonished at the sudden turnaround which put an end to the trial.... I am curious about the future, not for myself (but for Malestroit). If this trial were ever to flare up again, I have too much trust in the merciful goodness of the sweet Lord Jesus for me to worry about it and I abandon this whole business to him" (Letter of June 19, 1943, no. 430).

In the middle of these torments she remained available to everyone and didn't spare herself, on every front. "In June 1943," wrote Sister Marie-Genevieve, of Malestroit,

> ... around midday ... I was quietly picking strawberries ... near the statue of Saint Joseph ... when I heard a noise on the terrace. I wondered who could be there, at this time. How astonished I was to see our very reverend Mother Yvonne-Aimée of Jesus, armed with a big broom taken from the nearby cellar, and sweeping the terrace.... I went and asked our very reverend mother to give me her broom. But she just said to me: "It's done. We just need to put the benches back

in place." There were many little benches that you put
under your feet, and she had gone to the bother of
removing them one by one so as to sweep everywhere.
   I was quite moved at seeing our dear reverend
mother flushed and perspiring after such work. (Testimony of 1954, no. 255)

A few days later, Father Crété, who had been hospitalized
at Malestroit since the month of April, returned to the Jesuit
boarding school at Vannes that the Germans were occupying.
He was reassured about Mother Yvonne-Aimée, but he was
only a shadow of his former self. He needed to go to bed
when he got there. His bedroom had been commandeered
by the Germans. He was relocated to a classroom of the
junior school.

On July 6 Mother Yvonne-Aimée wrote to him: "I'm asking,
as from now, Our Lady of Mount Carmel[4] to spread over
you her 'queenly mantle, her virginal veil and her maternal
heart' and to give you on that day a joy from Heaven.... Dear
Father, bless your darling daughter for eternity" (Letter to
Father Crété, July 6, 1943, no. 475).

Was it a premonition? On the vigil of Our Lady of Mount
Carmel, July 15, Father Crété died at Vannes. The evening
before, he had asked for Mother Yvonne-Aimée. She only
reached his bedside after his last breath. That July 16 was
her forty-second birthday.

ON A WAR FOOTING

The trial which has just been related was joined by the
German occupation of the convent, and the dangerous har-
boring of members of the Resistance.

It was on the feast of the Annunciation, March 25, 1943,
ten days after receiving the doubting letter from Father Crété,
that the convent was commandeered: "March 25! What a gift,
sweet Virgin Mary, on this day of salvation to send us the
Germans for an occupation" (*Notebook*, March 25, 1943, no. 197).

---

[4] The feast of Our Lady of Mount Carmel would be celebrated ten
day later on July 16.

The Guesthouse building which the nuns were occupying had become the providential refuge of French freedom fighters and parachutists in difficulty. They had been given the right address. The sisters accepted the risk of bringing them into the hospital.

Since March 12 Mother Yvonne-Aimée had been sheltering an American parachutist brought to her by Mrs. Lapierre. His name was Robert Kylius and he didn't speak French. She put him up in Bishop Picaud's apartment—where the copious smoke of his cigarettes created a dangerous signal! On March 16 she handed him over to the care of an escape line which ensured his clandestine passage into Spain. "In doing this act of charity I had only one single aim, to do what seems to me my present duty," she wrote in her diary. (March 16, 1943, no. 180)

She added: "I got surprisingly attached to this nice person, who appeared to me to be loyal and straightforward" (Ibid.).

At the end of the hostilities she took steps to find his address, which she got from Major White on May 6, 1946. A correspondence ensued. Thirty years later he had not forgotten. He came back to France, to visit Malestroit, in 1973.

But it was not the niceness of any person that decided whom she helped. According to a popular anecdote, when employees of the House told her that such and such a freedom fighter was a scoundrel, she replied: "That's very possible, but we must help him just like the others."

The occupation multiplied tenfold the risks for her and her community. Her calmness remained above the hubbub. Her letter of April 1 to the German commandant who had just occupied her house rings strikingly true:

> Commandant,
>   As you are settled in here under my roof, I entrust my house to your honor and goodness. It sheltered a work that was dear to me. I do not know how you feel toward us. To me, you are an officer who has to do his duty, whatever your nationality. You are a man in exile in a foreign land and I sympathize with your

pain at being so distanced from your homeland, and
no doubt from loved ones, especially your mother if
you are fortunate enough still to have her.

I hope, Commandant, that our bells won't bother
you. They are necessary for me to call together our
sisters. Have the goodness to put up with them. Fur-
thermore, one doesn't make noise in a house like ours,
where we practice silence.

I was struck by the attention of the officers and
men around you. It shows you are a good boss. I
congratulate you, Commandant.

Please excuse the liberty of my writing these lines
and please be sure not to consider me, though I am
French one hundred percent, as an enemy. (no. 216)

That same day she had the door between the occupied
building and the community blocked up, and she wrote in
her personal notebook: "May this trial serve even for the
[good of the] souls of Germans, souls redeemed like me, my
God" (*Notebook*, April 1, 1943, no. 215).

Sister Marie of the Cross reported how one day she
brought some fruit to a thirsty sentryman. (1956, no. 398)

SEARCH

On February 7, 1944 the head of the French Secret Army in
the west, General Audibert, asked for asylum. He was a hero
of the First World War and was now almost seventy years
old. He was integrated among the patients in room twelve
on the second floor under the name of Monsieur Chevalier.
But his numerous messengers and dispatch riders coming
and going were spotted by the occupier. At the beginning of
March Mother Yvonne-Aimée warned the general that he was
no longer safe. A line could see him through to Paris with a
false identity card. But the general seemed to believe in the
invincibility of the House and contented himself with just
a change of name. As of March 5, "Monsieur Chevalier" was
dead. He became "Monsieur Le Bihan." The outlook seemed
pretty foggy to him. But Mother Yvonne-Aimée's forecasts
were only too correct. Things were tightening up.

On March 14, 1944 the general's secretary, Agnes de la Barre de Nanteuil, returned home from Mass to find the Gestapo waiting for her. She was tortured in the prisons of Vannes and Rennes but gave away nothing. On August 6 she was with many others in the cattle truck of a train being deported to Germany when it was struck by a British bomb. She was injured. It was later reported that a German guard had shot her to prevent her escape. In this state she was transported, with practically no care or medical attention. She died of gangrene on August 13 at the railway station of Paray-le-Monial. She was twenty-one years old.

On March 17 the Gestapo arrived at Malestroit. Around 7:30 P.M. two officers at the door asked for Monsieur Chevalier.

"There is no one of that name in this establishment."

They insisted. Their anger rose. A sister went to tell the general to make his escape. He stayed where he was, playing a much too subtle game. But the search, which even removed the mirror from the bathroom cabinet, ended up finding—in the bottom of his suitcase—a yearbook of the French military academy Saint Cyr. The game was up.

As he was leaving the premises between his two captors, he stopped in the doorway. Turning to Mother Yvonne-Aimée, he stood to attention. (He used sometimes to call her "My General.") Looking her straight in the eyes, he gave her a military salute. Then they took him away.

He was sent to Buchenwald concentration camp, near Weimar in Germany. His wife Clare and their daughter were arrested and imprisoned in Nantes. Clare was deported to Ravensbruck concentration camp. She died there in the gas chamber, having taken the place of an eighteen-year-old girl. Of the nine French Generals interned at Buchenwald, Audibert was the only one to survive. He believed he owed his survival to a German *Schwester*, a nun, who secretly gave him a bar of chocolate. He managed to live on that until the last day of his captivity when the camp was liberated by the American troops under General Patton on April 11, 1945.

Of all those sheltered at Malestroit, only he and two

parachutists were caught. And these three had not heeded Mother Yvonne-Aimée's warnings to flee.

In this intolerable situation the prayer-life at Malestroit intensified. It produced an alert prudence and a calmness under every test or trial.

From April 16, 1944 the wounded of the Breton Resistance were clandestinely sheltered in the hospital.

On June 13 several parachutists who were wounded on their landing in the Saint-Marcel campaign were also taken in and treated.

On June 17, eleven days after the Normandy landings by the Allies, she had a very strong sense of an imminent danger. In a solemn act she consecrated the convent to Our Lady and decided that "from here on out all the sisters shall bear the name Mary" in thanksgiving to the Immaculate Virgin, Queen and Mistress of this convent. (Prayer of June 17, 1944, no. 275)

THE BATTLE OF SAINT-MARCEL

On the next day, June 18, the Germans attacked the Saint-Marcel unit of freedom fighters (*maquis*) consisting of more than 3,000 men. But the convent (which had served as a landmark for the landing parachutists) was spared. Eleven injured Germans were brought to the hospital and operated upon urgently.

"Every injured person, whoever he might be, is sacred, isn't he? We were aware that day of having somewhat appeased the wrath of the Germans, and having escaped their fury," said Doctor Queinnec in his talk to the community of Malestroit in June 1945. (no. 305)

NEW SEARCH

On June 23 the hospital of Malestroit was housing ten French freedom fighters (*masquiards*) as well as some parachutists directed there by Britain's Royal Air Force (RAF). Mother Yvonne-Aimée would recall this difficult moment in her annual circular of 1944: "The Gestapo, alerted two hours later, surrounded the whole house and conducted a thorough search. Armed soldiers on every floor, the stairs guarded at every level while others went into every room, inspecting even the cots and cradles. It was not easy to hide ten hunted men. But they did it. It lasted two hours. The whole house was praying" (February 15, 1945, no. 103).

It was on that day that she smuggled two parachutists into the enclosure: "Roger Bertheloot and Philippe Reinhart...still drowsy from their anesthetics. In two times and three movements, Bertheloot and Reinhart were transformed into 'Sister Roger' and 'Sister Philippe.' Monastic habit, rochet, wimple, veil, there was nothing missing. We sat them in the tribune of the chapel (normally reserved for sisters who are elderly—and which is part of the enclosure!). But there remained their beds—which the enemy might be surprised to find still warm" (*Jours de France*,[5] June 9, 1956, no. 246).

Mother Yvonne-Aimée wrote a note about the search of June 23, 1944:

> The two parachutists were quickly moved... I said to Sister Saint-Gérard:
>   "Put the maid or somebody in one of those beds."
>   Then, going down to the first floor, I saw Mrs. d'Antin, who was eating:
>   "Go, quickly—go to bed in number 27, third floor medical."
>   "What?" she said, her eyes wide.
>   "Quick. Go," I said to her. "You'll understand up there." (1944, no. 579)

Jours de France assures us that the traumatized young domestic was shivering so much, with her teeth clacking, that it looked like she was in the midst of a fever, in the bed abandoned by Philippe Reinhart.

Mother Yvonne-Aimée halted the search:
"There—that is the enclosure. No one goes any further."
"Ah!" exclaimed the German.

---

[5] A French news magazine

RECOURSE TO MARY

Mother Yvonne-Aimée had experienced a similar protection in Paris during an air raid on September 15, 1943 that destroyed the Avenue de Versailles. Seven-storey buildings were wiped out. Four bombs had exploded less than fifty meters from the Oasis and not one of its windows was broken. "She was praying at the time in front of a statue of Our Lady" (several letters of September 15 and 16, 1943).

On October 31, 1942 when Pope Pius XII pronounced a consecration inspired by Lucia, the seer of Fatima, Mother Yvonne-Aimée and all the sisters joined in. "We love the Blessed Virgin very much in this house, and we must love her ever more," she said at the time to Father Guillon, SJ. (Letter of Father Guillon to Father Labutte, 1968, no. 32)

LIBERATION

In mid-August 1944 the region of Lower Brittany was liberated.

The bridges over the Nantes-Brest Canal at the entry to Malestroit were mined, one of them very close to the community. But the Germans' departure was rushed, on August 5, 1944, and the explosive devices damaged but did not destroy them.

On August 21 the parish of Malestroit held a ceremony to celebrate the "Great Return." The statue of Our Lady made a stop in the hospital garden. This whole liberation seemed to have unfolded under the banner of the Blessed Virgin.

THE GLORY

At the end of the war, recognition came in from all over. On June 24, 1945 Mother Yvonne-Aimée's presence was deemed necessary to celebrate the town's liberation, which had been accomplished without damage, as she had predicted.

On that day the Minister for War (Monsieur Diethelm) presented the *Croix de guerre avec palm* (the War Cross, with palm frond) to Mother Yvonne-Aimée and to Sister Marie of the Trinity who had helped her to disguise the two parachutists.

A month later (July 22) General de Gaulle came to Vannes, where he presented Mother Yvonne-Aimée with the *Legion of Honor*. The leader of free France removed his hat and said to her: "Reverend Mother, I am aware of your conduct. In the name of France, I thank you."

The citation specified: "Heroine of a modesty and devotion pushed to the limit. Saved from certain death many wounded. Stood up to the Germans with a courage that won the admiration of everyone."

The next day (July 23) an English officer came to inform Mother Yvonne-Aimée that she was to be awarded the *King's Medal for Courage in the Cause of Freedom*. This medal would be presented to her by the Consul General of Great Britain four years later, during the presentation of arms of August 7, 1949.[6]

On January 3, 1946 it was the Medal of the Resistance, which Mother Marie-Anne would also receive in July 1947, and the Medal of French Gratitude. And during a trip to Paris on March 24, 1947 an American decoration, the *Medal of Freedom*, along with a certificate sizably initialed by General Eisenhower.

Finally, on August 7, 1949, during a presentation of arms performed on site, General Audibert presented the hospital with the *Croix de Guerre*. Immediately afterward the British Consul General presented Mother Yvonne-Aimée with the King's Medal, her final decoration.

That ceremony of August 7, 1949 fulfilled the prediction that Sister Yvonne-Aimée had written down without understanding what it meant. She committed it to paper on March 25, 1929 when she was "writing out of obedience" to Father Crété all this "nonsense" that came to her mind:

> I saw myself in front of the hospital with many nuns around me. It seemed to be a day of celebration, the weather was nice.
> On my breast I had four or five medals pinned, including the Legion of Honor.

---

[6] This British award, mainly for foreign heroes, was formally instituted on August 23, 1945 and distribution of the medal began in 1947.

I was in the middle of religious sisters and I
seemed to be their mother. A grand officer came
toward me to salute me. Another sister also wore
a medal. And a young voice behind me was saying:
"Listen carefully Yvonne-Aimée for later on you will
remember that and it will be your strength." (*Notebook*,
March 25, 1929)

It was now that this "nonsense" became clear: five decora-
tions pinned on her breast—the Croix de guerre, the Legion
of Honor, Medals of the Resistance and of French Gratitude,
and of Freedom, to which now was added the King's Medal.
It was now that she found herself "in the middle of nuns"
assembled in front of the hospital and she was indeed "their
mother" as superior general.

And to take an overall view of several events, perhaps
the "grand general" of this day was not in fact General de
Gaulle. It was more modestly General Audibert, the head of
the Secret Army in the west of France, who had established
his base at her place.

Mother Yvonne-Aimée was in no way over-awed by all this
national and international glory. She had carried out the
duties of her state. When they praised her "participation in
the Resistance," despite the supreme prestige of this term she
would smile and say simply: "The Resistance? Don't know it.
We practiced charity."

She wrote even more specifically in her first annual circular:

While we may have done all that we could, without
getting into politics but out of charity, others, more
than us, risked their lives and do not have any reward
here below. I know of heroic actions which will always
remain hidden from men. All of you, you who held
out under the bombs, who remained so as to simply
carry out your duty, in sometimes dire conditions,
you who without complaint, as if without fear, bore
deprivation and exhaustion, and who gave of yourself
without counting the cost—you all deserve a Cross of
Honor. This reward you will have one day and it will
be more beautiful than all the crosses here on earth,

because God never allows himself to be outdone in generosity. (1945 Annual, February 28, 1946, no. 135)

"The day of August 7 came to a close with the departure for Africa of Mother Marie-Dominique and her four little sisters of the missionary novitiate" (Annual of Mother Marie-Anne, February 8, 1950, no. 34).

Despite these appearances of glory, which is what the press noticed, the inspiration came from a deep interior life.

The hard years of 1943–1944 were a time of interior deprivation and spiritual night. Mother Yvonne-Aimée had written to Bishop Picaud on December 3, 1943: "Speak to you about my soul, yes I would like to. I feel so isolated on earth, so desperate and anxious at certain times, always being afraid that I'm not sufficiently doing the will of God—and it's a torment for me! I have times of great peace, but not mystical favors. I don't count on them, while I feel the void.

"I apply myself above all to putting real love into all the actions of my life. I don't know if I succeed, but the Lord sees my goodwill" (Letter to Bishop Picaud, December 3, 1943, no. 790).

The same, at the start of 1944: "My spiritual life is really simple, even difficult at the moment. I have absolutely no consolation or favor," she wrote to him again on January 26, 1944 (no. 31).

Her night was, in large part, the fact of physical suffering and an increasing deterioration of her health: "It's so hard to feel without strength, to have a body to drag around, to make a constant effort to walk, to work...even to think. In fact, it is he who orders everything for our good and it is thus that he treats his friends. And as we are, after all, only on this earth to earn Heaven, it is logical enough that we should pay a big price for it" (Ibid.).

The same difficulty the following year: "I've suffered a lot in my morale and with my physical deficiency, I need a grace from the Good Lord to keep me in equilibrium, in peace and in joy.... I don't even know if the Lord Jesus is happy with my poor efforts" (Letter to Bishop Picaud, January 25, 1945, no. 59).

Yvonne with the convent cat, Malikoko (c. 1928)

With Mother Marie-Anne (1931)

August 5, 1935. Open-air Mass for the Tricentenary
of the presence of Augustinian Sisters in Brittany

In Canada, with Mother Marie-Anne and
the Lieutenant Governor of Quebec, Esioff-Léon Patenaude (1938)

As Novice Mistress with one of her charges

The painful lymph oedema is
evident in Yvonne's left arm

With Mother Mary-Michael, Superior of
the community in north-west England.
Yvonne-Aimee enjoyed several stays at their
convent and nursing home Boarbank Hall

In South Africa (1938)

Two paintings by Mother Yvonne-Aimée

1941

*General De Gaulle greeting Mother Yvonne-Aimée (top)
and awarding her the medal of the Legion of Honor (bottom) (1945)*

As Superior General (ca. 1946)

In the cloister, near the end of her life

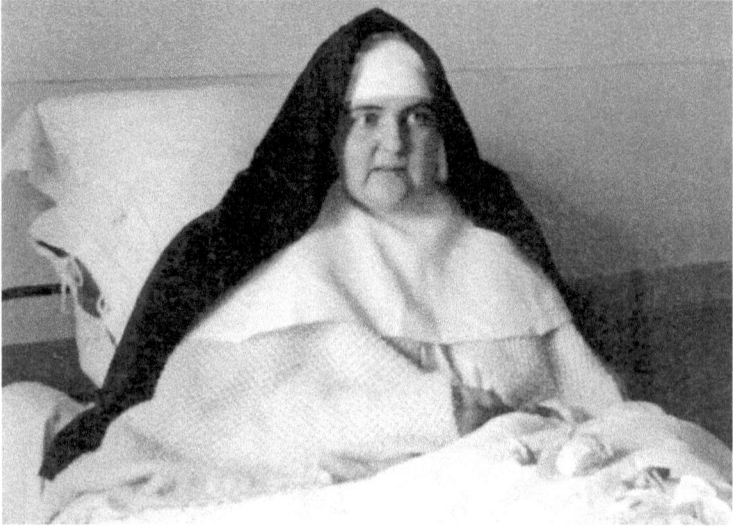

Bedridden with illness

Returned to the Father (1951)

IV

ॐ

Superior General

19

Superior General of the First Federation of Religious Sisters

1946

T HE WAR WAS OVER. NORMAL LIFE WAS resuming. Communications were being re-established. Mother Yvonne-Aimée renewed contact, which had become difficult, with the convents of the federation. She travelled throughout France and England, all the while retaining her heavy responsibility as superior of Malestroit.

INSOLUBLE PROBLEMS

The burden and the fragmentation were enormous. There were inextricable problems; many of the Houses of the order were worn out, and even Malestroit's numerous vocations were not sufficient to revive them. The war effort had worn down people's health: seventeen nuns, worn out by the deprivations and overworked, had fallen sick, and Mother Yvonne-Aimée had already had to "lend" fifteen professed sisters to other convents. (Letter to Bishop Picaud, January 25, 1945, no. 59)

Malestroit's abundance of vocations, which had seemed inexhaustible around Mother Yvonne-Aimée, became a dearth. She had to turn down an insistent request from the Bishop of Laval, the future Cardinal Richaud, who never forgave her. "I would like to have greater means to come to the aid of our unfortunate Houses," wrote Mother Yvonne-Aimée to Bishop Picaud. (Ibid., no. 59)

"I let myself cry many tears the other day. It wasn't, however, from discouragement. I'm sure that the Good Lord sees things better than I do, it was above all because of the weakness and the impossibility of resolving new problems that arise for me. I'm receiving requests for help from all over" (Letter to Mother Thérèse of the Child Jesus, Superior of Douarnenez, March 13, 1945, no. 145).

What's more, vocations were becoming rarer. Catholic Action, then at its height, was casting a shadow.

Don't become a nun, you'll be more useful in the world, seemed to be the advice all around: "This shortage is due in large part to priests who don't know how to encourage vocations, nor direct them," observed Mother Yvonne-Aimée, "not to mention those who prevent them from reaching, and turn them away from, the convent door, so as to keep the elite in the Catholic movements. Forgive me for laying out so boldly my thought but it is the divine thought and it is why I go there with so much assurance...with you" (Letter to Bishop Picaud, January 28, 1946, no. 83).

The missionary novitiate had trained sisters ready to leave for Natal, South Africa, but there were problems with their visas. Mother Yvonne-Aimée eventually obtained them.

Her state of health continued to undermine her apparently intact energy. At the end of 1945 she wrote to Bishop Picaud: "What to tell you about me Monsignor, my father? It is night in an almost continual fashion.... Some lightened moments from time to time, thanks to which I take heart again. My physical health is defective but in that there is a richness that I appreciate all the same. I rely on your prayers. I want so much, always and everywhere, to be and to do everything that God wants" (Letter to Bishop Picaud, December 13, 1945, no. 666).

Her health became poorer and poorer. And yet, she had to travel incessantly. The railways at the time were in a sad state. Her damaged spine felt the consequences.

On March 11, 1946, Mother Marie-Anne wrote to a superior who was calling upon her to help: "Our dearest mother cannot rest completely and always sets off on journeys with really painful sufferings. Until just now our mother was in too much pain to travel. Feeling a little better, she has decided on the journey Pont-l'Abbe—Dournanez. We leave tomorrow" (March 11, 1946, no. 162).

To the international burden of the order of Augustinians was added that of a convent which had to support so many others. Mother Yvonne-Aimée remained available to her ninety sisters, who she still managed to see individually in the days prior to a foreign trip. This superior, so efficient and indefatigable, whose successes delighted the sisters but seemed suspect to adversaries, was no longer able to muster her strength. "This time I feel at my limit, and I'm no longer capable of effort.... I leave everything pending and incomplete. I am content to do what the Lord wants, content to be so worn out. But it must not be at the cost of others having to suffer from my inability to fulfil my duties as I should" (Letter to Bishop Picaud, May 29, 1946, no. 323).

THE IMPOSSIBLE FEDERATION

The judicious help and assistance that she had brought throughout the war, as president of the hoped-for federation, increased the trust in her. The unanimous wish was to attain the desired goal with her. But Yvonne knew the opposition of Cardinal La Puma. This plan of a federation was contrary to canon law for convents of women. She was the president, without letters patent, of an informal project of which Rome contested the very principle. What Rome wished was a stricter "union," the only thing envisioned in canon law, but contrary to the traditions of the order.

She wrote to Father Sauvage, in April 1946. The letter remained unanswered.

And yet, it was urgent to prepare a meeting which would ordinarily be a foundational meeting. After the Congress of Hospitaller Works in Paris, she devoted herself to this during a "rest" at a convent in England. It was in prayer that she nurtured the project: "I have time to pray, and to think, without interruptions," she wrote to the community on July 1, 1946. (no. 386)

"My room overlooks the countryside and the sea...away from all main roads. It is good to be able to pray without being disturbed and almost without distractions," she added on July 17. (no. 431)

On July 25, with still no reply from Father Sauvage, she wrote to him again, urgently: "The meeting of superiors takes place from August 18 to 26 at Malestroit. We will vote for members of the Council. There will also be the election of the president or superior-general. Not having your responses, we'll go ahead with the elections. I will submit them [the results] to you. Rome will ratify or not, and we will submit to whatever is decided" (no. 448).

On August 4, Father Sauvage replied from Rome: "What troubles me in your situation is that you have never obtained permission to create a Federation, even on a trial basis. Cardinal La Puma was against it.

"The Sacred Congregation will judge. Will it accept your explanations and will it approve what you will have done? Please God!" (no. 477)

This confirmation of unresolved objections would normally have meant adjourning the chapter. But the letter did not arrive in time.

Mother Yvonne-Aimée proceeded, therefore, on tenterhooks.

On the feast of the Assumption (August 15, 1946) she felt very strongly the presence of the Blessed Virgin. (Letter to Bishop Picaud, August 16, 1946, no. 498)

But next the powers of darkness besieged her. She wrote to Bishop Picaud:

> Around three o'clock in the morning, I was suddenly gripped by a terrible anguish. I felt the Devil right next to me. He threw himself at me. My mind was darkened and in my head all sorts of ideas were swirling around, plunging my soul into an indescribable anguish.
>
> It is about the meeting of superiors and the elections that I am troubled now.... If I continue to proceed in the direction of a Federation, it is because I felt, or thought I felt the divine will and that alone. And also so as not to remove myself from a duty of help and charity toward Houses in need. (Ibid.)

In proceeding according to the needs and the interior logic of the whole order, wasn't she engaging in something unlawful?

A new objection assailed her: on the most realistic basis, her state of health ruled out her reelection. She was no more than a standing corpse. She thought of resigning, of avoiding these elections where all the votes would fall upon her with no alternative, because nobody else was willing to take on this task. Wasn't the solution to send out telegrams cancelling the chapter? "The only thought that would stop me ... is to create a type of unease among the superiors. It seems to me that I remember that the Lord Jesus encouraged me, on the contrary, to go forward but right now I remember nothing, and I'm suffering ... yes, terribly. It's because I am so incapable of thinking clearly at the moment and because I feel pulled between the desire to do the will of God and the fear of being mistaken as to this will, that I turn to you," she wrote to Bishop Picaud. (Ibid.)

Using the diplomatic channel of the nunciature to write to Bishop Picaud, she asked him to put an end to the uncertainty over "this burden that weighs on me more than ever" (Ibid.). Thus she paid for every step she took in the Lord, and for him alone.

THE FOUNDING CHAPTER OF AUGUST 1946

Two days later the chapter participants arrived at Malestroit. They represented thirty-two convents: twenty-two in France, three in England and seven in South Africa. Bishop Le Bellec of Vannes presided over the chapter.

On August 21 Mother Yvonne-Aimée was unanimously elected superior general of the federation. The same day a telegram sent from Rome approved the federation. It arrived the next day, August 22, 1946. (no. 526 and Letter of September 5, no. 559)

On August 26 and 27 the superiors departed. And it was on the next day, August 28, that at last arrived the negative letter from Father Sauvage which would have cancelled everything if the postal service had been more efficient.

WHAT WAS ROME GOING TO THINK?

At the start of the chapter (August 20) Mother Yvonne-Aimée had written to Rome to submit honestly the inevitable growth of the project during the wartime emergencies.

> Not being able to communicate...during the War, in order not to leave our Houses and our works which were in need of aid, help and assistance, I had to assume the role of a superior general, in accordance with the wish and the unanimous vote of the superiors in 1939. Having at hand the Statutes drawn up by the Sacred Congregation for a trial period of a Federation which awaited only an approval to function normally, I was guided by these directives, encouraged in the rest by the competent ecclesiastical authorities....
>
> I believe that thanks to that, an extremely close union between our convents and our works has been demonstrated between 1939 and 1945. (Report of Mother Yvonne-Aimée to the Congregation for Religious, August 21, 1946, no. 522)

Rome was not in the least bit offended. The impossible federation now had wind in its sails. On September 12, 1946 the Congregation for Religious sent the official document of approval. It arrived at Malestroit on September 24, the feast of Our Lady of Mercy. The approval of the statutes arrived on October 7, feast of Our Lady of the Rosary. It was granted for twelve years. Mother Yvonne-Aimée's doubts about her election to the generalate were resolved. "I'll only accept it definitively if Rome sanctions everything fully," she had written to Bishop Picaud on August 16, 1946. (no. 498)

She gave up her office of prioress of Malestroit. Mother Marie-Anne of Jesus, her right-hand, was unanimously elected to succeed her and at the same time became her assistant general. From then on Mother Yvonne-Aimée could devote herself completely to the federation, which she had assumed charge of along with so many local, painstaking, and tiresome tasks.

AUDIENCE OF PIUS XII

On December 4 Mother Yvonne-Aimée left for Rome, with Mother Michael of the English convent of Grange-over-Sands. In ten days they accomplished a considerable amount of work for the last finalizations.

On December 13 Pope Pius XII received them in private audience. He attached importance to this new model of federation, which he would consecrate by the apostolic constitution *Sponsa Christi* (November 21, 1950, completed by the Instruction of the Congregation for Religious, *Inter praeclara.*)

These documents took up the thoughts and expressions slowly matured by Mother Yvonne-Aimée with the assistance of Father Sauvage between 1936 and 1946, including union in the autonomy of the convents and the establishment of a general novitiate, of which the missionary novitiate established by Mother Yvonne-Aimée was already the prototype. The advantages were innumerable—economy of strengths, mutual aid, communication, renovation, et cetera. These federations are "highly recommended by the Apostolic See," states Article 7 of the General Statutes. (*Documentation Catholique*, 1950, col 1678–96; 1951, col 993–1202)

The supposedly anti-canonical project became the Pope's solution. It was one of the successes of his pontificate.

It would spread widely. Mother Yvonne-Aimée had served not only the cause of the Augustinians but the universal Church.

"Yes, Mother Yvonne-Aimée of Jesus had entered into our thought," Pius XII would say to Mother Marie-Anne when she returned to Rome shortly after the death of the foundress of the first feminine federation. ❧

20

Ubiquity of a Superior General

1946–1950

THE LAST PREMONITION

The new situation fulfilled to the letter a premonition that Yvonne had written down with repugnance because at the time it made no sense. It was the very last one that she had written, at the request of Father Crété, on June 4, 1929. "In the year that Sister Saint-Paul dies there will be a change of life for me. A few months beforehand there will have been an election" (*Notebook*, June 4, 1929, no. 200).

ROOM NUMBER THREE

Well, Sister Saint-Paul died on January 8, 1947. Less than five months previously, on August 21, 1946, Mother Yvonne-Aimée had been elected superior general.

She moved into the apartment with the Breton furniture which she had prophetically described back in 1929, even though neither the room nor the furniture were part of the convent in 1929! "I saw a room that I didn't know, with Breton furniture—but inside the Community—I couldn't place it. I was writing at a table." (Ibid.).

At the time of the premonition, two rooms still occupied the location of Mother Yvonne-Aimée's large office. It was in 1948, during a convalescence, that the assistant had another room built, jutting out from the building, a sunroom, "the green room" (which Mother Yvonne-Aimée used little but Mother Marie-Anne would adopt during her own generalate.) This modest suite comprised a dining room, a small kitchen, a little sitting room at the end of the corridor, and two bedrooms for visiting superiors.

Mother Yvonne-Aimée was back in room number three, which had hosted her as a young woman in March 1922. It was there that the grace of God had launched her on such an extraordinary path on July 5. It was there where she would soon draw her last breath.

NEW TASKS

Now she was the head of thirty-two Houses, totaling 1,500 sisters. All the Augustinians of France, England, and South Africa joined the federation. Only far-off Canada remained outside. Mother Yvonne-Aimée had visited the convents there from the end of August to mid-October 1939 at the outbreak of the Second World War. The difficulty of setting up a provincialate for that other continent (Letter of Mother Yvonne-Aimée, October 4, 1939, no. 646), the reluctance of Father Sauvage to bring into the federation sisters who were so different (reply of November 29, 1939), the wartime rupture of communications, and the distaste of the transatlantic bishops for such far-off journeys all made them decide against it.

In giving up her post of prioress, Mother Yvonne-Aimée was freed from a great dispersal of herself between sisters and novices, patients and doctors. She rediscovered a solitude that she had been thirsting for, but also a heavy workload of administration and writing, less gratifying than community life. "Parlors" were particularly hard for her: "How these visits cost me! It's not my fault but I find nothing to say to them. I no longer know how to talk. Oh, how I would like to speak only with God!" (Testimony of Sister Marie of the Trinity, 1956, no. 181)

She made a habit of being accompanied by her assistant in order to make the conversation somewhat easier. (*Articles*, p. 160) Mother Marie-Anne's exceptional memory and her complete availability were a constant help to her.

THE STYLE AND THE SPIRIT

Mother Yvonne-Aimée was respectful of each person, stimulating and nondirective. Mother Marie of Jesus, superior of

Rennes, described thus her conduct at the order's council meetings:

> Whether we were dealing with an important question or something trivial, she had her own way of presenting it, kindly, getting straight to the point, laying things out with precision and clarity, not clinging at all to her way of seeing things but full of common sense.
>
> "What do you think about it?" she would say.
>
> What we thought was that there wasn't much more to say; she had foreseen everything with an openness of mind and with the sole aim of seeking and wanting the good. And yet, the least suggestion from us got her attention and she would stop there. (Testimony, May 22, 1953, no. 19)

"She did not impose her way of looking at things, and she didn't cling to it either. And when she made a mistake, she didn't make a fuss or make excuses. In honesty and simplicity she acknowledged it" (Testimony of Sister Marie of Mercy, 1956, no. 178).

She inspired agreement and harmony. She remained stimulating despite her exhaustion. Her difficulty in bearing the weight of the day made her persuasive to the sisters and priests who asked her advice in periods of weariness.

> What merit would you have if you always had the joy of having worked well? It's not at those times that you give the most. You're satisfied—and it's good that you have this joy in order to continue a task that is not at all pleasant for you. But believe me, it's when you carry on without the taste for it, when you speak without knowing the result, when you confess without knowing a soul, it's when you simply do your duty conscientiously and solely for the love of God that you give, you gain, you purchase!
>
> And everyone—more or less obviously—but every one of us, must know these feelings of weariness.... And in no way must we ever let them sadden us.... I am not reassured when I hear someone boast that he is successful in everything he does. That can't be, or can only be for a time. It is not

the ordinary path by which God leads souls. (January
20, 1946, no. 64)

She spoke from experience, in the tone that she used to
encourage herself when faced with the impossible. How illu-
sory and laughable was the accusation which interpreted her
brilliant successes as a magical and diabolical ease. She went
from obstacles to setbacks, uncertainties to opposition, all of
which she kept to herself while spreading joy and generosity.
Her apparent triumphant successes she paid dearly for, in
the night, by trail and error, without easy proofs or personal
satisfaction, in the service of God alone.

Her successes were assuredly due to that power of God
that Saint Paul got to know in his greatest apostolic failures,
during the organized opposition of the synagogues (Acts 17:5–
8, 13–15) and his failure before the Areopagus reduced him
to taking up his old job of tentmaking and evangelizing the
dockworkers at the port of Corinth (Acts 18:3; 1 Cor 1). In
a similar way Mother Yvonne-Aimée attained a rare wisdom,
an unprecedented fruitfulness and an exceptional respect for
others. We see this in her response regarding a young nun
that a priest has forbidden from leaving her congregation
"under pain of damnation":

> It is neither the spirit of the Lord nor the spirit of
> the Church that could speak such a serious word. The
> Church in her Canon Law is so respectful of human
> liberty! There is here something rather upsetting, and
> I can understand that after that word the young
> woman wouldn't dare to leave. It's almost forcing her
> to stay and to despair. Judge the case I cannot do: I
> would need to know more about the circumstances
> and the persons involved. But even in the midst of
> the divine, the Devil can intervene and human beings
> are not infallible. I deem the word said to be in any
> case very imprudent and it cannot come from God,
> who is all gentleness, all mercy and seeks to save
> souls. The very fact that the young woman cannot
> settle in is a sign of non-vocation. It would seem
> logical to me to leave her free to give herself to the

Lord in another fashion. (Letter to Father Lebrault, November 10, 1950, no. 417)

She warned against activism, encouraged prayer: "After the hour of prayer you say your Mass so much better.... In every free moment that thought returns."

The presence of the Blessed Virgin Mary, so strong and blessed during the troubles of wartime, took root in the federation.

Her first annual circular for the year 1947 insisted on it. We don't love Our Lady enough. What it involves is not "adding extra prayers" but

> to imitate more and more the virtues of her who is the great chosen one of God, our model, our Queen, the rainbow in the midst of dark clouds. There are so many Christians, even nuns, who keep her on the margins of their lives and seem to say to her:
> "Now you've given us Jesus, that's fine!"
> They forget that God gave her a pre-eminent place in the work of the Redemption.... To go to Jesus, the surest path will always be Mary, for how can one dis-unite that which God himself has indissolubly united? However, to obtain the effect of these graces we have to be very small. Mary will be more a mother with us the more we are children with her. (January 25, 1948, no. 57)

In November 1947 the convent fervently welcomed the relics of Saint Thérèse of the Child Jesus which were being taken around Brittany. On that occasion Mother Yvonne-Aimée recovered the spirit of her First Holy Communion and herself led the preparatory *triduum* organized in the community: "Saint Thérèse is blind to the faults of her neighbor and enthusiastic about the qualities of her sisters. She renders every possible service with the greatest discretion," she commented. (Preparatory Triduum for the visit of Saint Thérèse, November 6, 1947, no. 553)

For the last day, Mother Yvonne-Aimée suggested to the sisters to "ask especially for an apostolic spirit."

She had now visited every one of the convents of the federation. She had witnessed and experienced the warm adhesion of each convent to the federation. She recalled it in the annual circular of January 25, 1948:

> Dearest Reverend Mothers,
> Now that I have met each of you, now that I feel even more yours, I would like to express to you here, before all your daughters, the esteem and deep affection in which I hold you.
> To everyone, I repeat: Love your superiors, they bear a heavy responsibility. Ease their task by your total obedience and docility.... At a time when in the world everyone's life is difficult, and often tragic, we sisters, despite some sacrifices, we live so much better than most people in the world! The material worries that the superiors bear spare the sisters the hassles of every day. We are supported spiritually by retreats, talks, spiritual exercises.... What gratitude you owe to God, to your community and to your superiors! (January 25, 1948, no. 57)

THE BURDEN AND THE CARES

The burden was heavy, for many convents were asking for help and Malestroit's vocations were no longer enough to provide for them. Mother Yvonne-Aimée could not respond to everything. It was her daily pain. She often had to exhort patience:

> I saw, I felt, my dear sisters, how much you suffer by not always being able to fulfil the obligations of your prayer life, because of being overloaded by work. As long as it is not you who are prolonging the time in activities, as much as you really do suffer this disequilibrium in your religious life, be at peace. It's only what we don't do when it would be possible to do it that God will reproach us for. In that case, God might show himself to be severe for, after all, we are religious, and the first service is his service. Also, we must keep ourselves well united to him to benefit from his graces and remain supernatural in a very active and even agitated life. (Ibid.)

In a letter to a superior she stated: "If there are no more postulants in our communities, it's because overwhelmed by the hospitaller service, we are unable to guarantee them the religious life that they have a right to. Obviously we cannot do the impossible, but we need to know how to do the possible."

And to another:

> Oh yes, I felt your distress, I know your urgent needs, the whole overload upon your poor valiant sisters. It pains me and I often think about it during the night, turning over these problems but finding no solution.
>
> And I who am the loving mother of all our houses, I suffer infinitely from not being able to do more for them. Poor mother, we can only abandon ourselves and be confident because it is that which God, on the day willed by him, will reward. But I do understand that the wait appears so long to you. (Letter of March 23, 1950, no. 81)

They all continued to be pleased with her encouraging, stimulating and efficient presence.

In a letter of June 29, 1948, she defined to Bishop Picaud what the nuns needed to hear in quite varied senses:

"The necessity to adapt ... to change the old way of doing things.... Justice ... so necessary to a superior, the spirit of discretion ... the spirit of truth" (no. 292).

She questioned herself on the importance of rest, the art of keeping a good balance. She seemed to benefit from what had been promised to her at the time of the mystical marriage: "You will possess the supreme meaning of all things, you will appreciate things in the truth, from a detached viewpoint, you will receive communications of the judgments of God" (Notebook, July 6, 1941, no. 318).

A NEW SPIRITUAL STEP AND TRANSFIGURATION

It was at this time that Mother Yvonne-Aimée seemed to reach the grace of Transforming Union, as described by the mystics. It's like a third great step, after the Spiritual Betrothal and the Spiritual Marriage.

On July 5, 1946, the anniversary of the great mystical call, she felt happy, completely so, far beyond any human expression.

At Pentecost 1948, May 16, at about 4:00 P.M. she was overcome by an experience of infinite love.

Sister Marie of the Cross experienced a sense of a transfiguration. "Having come back up from Compline, I was preparing tea. Mother General was in the north office, drawing. She came to look for something in Room Three.... I stood stock still with an 'Oh!'... Her heart was luminous, and what a light!... Mother Prioress arrived, I left" (*Notebook* of Sister Marie of the Cross, May 16, 1948, no. 218).

It was the last luminous moment of Yvonne's life, the last ecstasy reported. It was a reflection of her profound identification with God, in Christ. The love that she radiated so strongly transfigured for a moment her body on the threshold of the final trials. The radiating light that the two nuns observed in a sensible way ordinarily showed itself in a more discreet fashion.

"One day," recounted a sister, "she took my two hands in hers, looked deeply into my eyes and repeated to me three times:

'Oh my little daughter, love!...love...love...love!'

"I was really struck and she seemed to be as if in a fire that was burning her. My quarter-hour direction passed without me even realizing it. Then she dismissed me and stopped the visits [receiving the sisters individually, for that day]" (*Articles*, p. 131).

PAINFUL MARTYRDOM

She remained up and about and active. But her body's breakdown was accelerating and intensifying. She was going to need two serious operations. The promoter of all the successes was fighting in the shadows: "I have heavy and painful times to pass, psychologically and spiritually. For the physical, it's the same thing. But I try to go on, to do my work, to please the Lord Jesus, to keep myself in peace.

It's not always easy. I try not to get upset over my miseries and my numerous imperfections, my inabilities, and I count on the merciful Goodness, out of which he sometimes gives me some positive signs," she wrote to Bishop Picaud, June 13, 1948 (no. 268).

"In this painful martyrdom," noted Mother Marie-Anne, "she didn't change anything about her habitual activities but did everything at the cost of an infinite fatigue. Travel, especially, became more and more inconvenient. This caused her a double suffering because she couldn't respond as she would wish to the invitations from all the convents that wanted her to visit" (*Obituary Notice*, p. 30).

She was no longer fit to provide the many "relaxations" that she used to grant so as to give pleasure to others—improvising a "surprise supper" to give sister cook a break and fun for the sisters, inviting Mother Marie-Anne to dine with her, arranging flowers and, if a sister admired them, making a quick painting of them to give to the admirer.

In December 1948 she had to be confined to bed.

"I'm soon going to undergo a serious operation," she wrote to Yvonne Bato on February 5, 1949. "I have a very large fibroid. What worries those around me is my poor general state (liver, heart). Thanks be to God. He is powerful enough to heal me, and if he wants to take me it's a great opportunity. I'm really at peace as I have abandoned myself. Pray for me please, that I'll be a good patient" (Letter to Yvonne Bato, February 5, 1949, no. 69).

She refused all pain-relief medication. Doctor Queinnec performed a hysterectomy on February 16. "It was a success, against all expectations," wrote Mother Marie-Anne, "everything went well. The pains soon subsided, and three weeks after the operation (Mother Yvonne-Aimée) could make her first outing into the garden" (Annual of Mother Marie-Anne, February 8, 1959, no. 34).

They thought they saw her reviving, even if "she gets tired very quickly," observed Mother Marie-Anne. (Letter of March 25, 1949, no. 134)

Mother Yvonne-Aimée kept up appearances and her work, but for her it was "complete suffering with no consolation whatsoever," she confided to a friend. (Testimony of Juliette Cannieux, March 1955, no. 48)

1949 was a Marian Year in France. She wrote this oblation to the Blessed Virgin: "We salute you Blessed Virgin...Queen of the universe, today we solemnly proclaim you...Queen of our Institute" (Consecration to the Blessed Virgin Mary, March 25, 1949, no. 131).

ACTIVE CONVALESCENCE

The doctors ordered "a long and real convalescence, far from all the cares and worries inherent in her office" (Letter of Mother Marie-Anne to the superiors, March 25, 1949, no. 134).

She went to England, where she would remain until the middle of July, at the convent of Grange-over-Sands. She set about speaking English again. "I want to be just as at ease speaking with my English daughters as with the others" (Letter to Bishop Picaud, June 27, 1949, no. 343).

NEW OPERATION

On her return she looked good but the cancer was now consuming her. Doctor Queinnec had to remove her left breast, on September 6, 1949. "The illness is worse than we first thought," noted Mother Marie-Anne. (*Obituary Notice*, p. 96)

Her left arm was struck by phlebitis, a painful inflammation of the veins. "It has doubled in size" (Mother Marie-Anne, circular to the superiors, September 18, 1949, no. 516).

During the week violent pains spread across her back, and reached the right arm:

> Painkillers often produced in her the opposite effect than normal, to the point that the doctors feared that one day even the morphine would no longer work on her. Her patience, without complaint, and her smile amazed Doctor Queinnec.

> He had noted, apart from the illnesses, the traces
> of other mysterious sufferings: those she had had
> since 1922, when the Prince of Darkness harmed her.
> He didn't know about the more private suffering:
> the dark night that she felt like an environment of
> "opaque darkness" and "like a long corridor with walls
> made of ice that nothing can get a grip on." (Father
> Barral, *Au Service*, 1955, p. 188)

"I am in the winepress, for soul and for body," she confided
again. (Testimony of Juliette Cannieux, March 1955, no. 48)

In February 1950 her writing became shaky, exhausted,
painful: "It's not going well, dear Yvonne. I have some good
days from time to time. So I set off again from the back of
the train, and then—wham! Afterward, I pay for it with the
fever and days confined to bed. My arm still really hurts at
times. It's still heavy. It's difficult to write because of pain in
my right shoulder" (To Yvonne Bato, February 8, 1950, no. 32).

To Sister Marie of the Cross she made this unique admission of unprecedented suffering: "I have suffered a lot in
my life but never like this now. Sufferings [extraordinary as
they were, before] I knew that they could disappear, perhaps
even cease suddenly. But cancer, it is inexorable, it is a never-
ending night, the absence of hope. In a sense it is harder"
(Testimony February 1951, no. 122).

And yet she retained her sense of humor: "How lovely it
will be to take a walk in the heavenly gardens...without
having mail to answer!" (To Father Labutte, March 10, 1950,
no. 72)

LAST JOURNEYS

She went to Paris to chair a meeting of the general council
of the federation, on May 9 and 10, 1951. The doctors prescribed three months rest in the south of France. She took
just one month, at a priory of Camillian fathers at Théoule
in the Var region. In July two sisters were leaving for Natal
and she accompanied them to their ship in England. Then
she took a few days of rest at Grange-over-Sands.

She wrote to her friend Suzanne Loth, who was a research oncologist, giving her a more detailed health update but, keen to avoid worrying her, she stressed the positive aspects, as Bernadette of Lourdes used to do:

> It's difficult to speak to you about my health. I look well enough, I'm eating well, I'm less tired in the morning. My nights would be good enough if I didn't have this unfortunate swollen arm that I don't know how to place during the night. I have to change position often. For the moment this arm gives me a lot of pain right up to the shoulder and scapula. It might just be rheumatism setting in there. But it tires me out as much physically as emotionally. It's difficult and painful...when you have a post of responsibility not to be able to carry it out comfortably. I get tired very quickly and yet I think that I bring to everything as much energy and goodwill as I can. Effort, which in general used to be a joy for me, now causes me a real fatigue. All that might just be a normal consequence of the successive operations which, despite everything, have tired my body. Indeed, you know that I've already suffered a lot in many different ways. If the Good Lord wants me to suffer more then I want it too, but to be Superior General with all that is not at all practical. They claim that I'm still useful, that currently nobody else could take my place.... The Lord will show for sure, but if he wants more suffering for me and death in a short while, I will not be at all bothered. I want that rather than a long life.... My thoughts are not gloomy.... They are a normal result of what I feel. In every life the essential is to accomplish what God wants and to accomplish it as well as possible. I tell you, too, that I believe it better to wear myself out working in his service than to live long and take too much care of myself. I don't have, as you do, a home, children.... Another will replace me. (August 14, 1950, no. 280)

So she continued to "wear herself out" without sparing herself. At the end of November she was back in Paris to organize the annual charity sale for the student residence.

Despite her condition and her weight, to enliven this joyful event she even demonstrated a dance that she had learned in her youth in England.

On November 21, Pope Pius XII recommended the model of federation that she had set up through and despite everything. She hadn't wasted her time.

At Malestroit she worked until five o'clock in the morning preparing the Christmas gifts—a little package for each sister. She "really thought about what to include" that "would best please" each one. (Testimony of Sister Marie of the Cross, February 1951, p. 5, no. 119)

On New Year's Eve, December 31, 1950, she received the good wishes of the community: "The coming year must be the year of the Resurrection," she said. (*Articles*, p. 196) ❧

21

The Great Departure

1951

T HE 1950 YEAR OF JUBILEE—THE LAST
before the Council—had just ended. On January 3,
1951 Mother Yvonne-Aimée completed her annual
circular. Let us intensify "our spiritual life," she recommended, "not by innumerable prayers that would risk us
neglecting other aspects of our Constitutions in an already
heavily laden use of our time, but by a greater union of
our will to the will of God. Everything is there" (January
3, 1951, no. 4).

She commented on the proclamation of the dogma of
the Assumption of the Blessed Virgin Mary by Pope Pius
XII "which only reveals more the divine splendor" (Ibid.).

Finally she announced her departure for South Africa "in
the first half of February, probably the 15th."

On January 20, 1951 there were sixty letters piled up on
her desk, unopened. She couldn't keep up the pace. On
January 21 she confided to Yvonne Bato: "Excuse my silence.
I chase after my time but never catch up with it. At the
moment it is a case of being snowed under even more than
usual. And as I'm often stopped...flu, tiredness, etc., I never
have the satisfaction of seeing my work get ahead and feeling
'up-to-date.' You must know the feeling!...

"Please pray for me, the big trip to South Africa is
approaching. I'm right in the middle of all the preparations"
(Letter of January 22, 1951, no. 40).

To an Augustinian superior, she wrote: "Pray for me, I
don't know if I'd have the heart to go if my place hadn't
been booked for so long. But I shall do everything for the
success of this trip, which I'm undertaking for God and for

the souls over there" (Letter to Mother Marie-Madeleine, of Lannion, January 15, 1951, no. 22).

Her heart remained the same. It was overworked. Visibly, she looked her usual self. But she couldn't muster her usual enthusiasm for preparing trunks and suitcases. She used to have them brought down a month ahead and would begin to put in souvenirs and gifts adapted to each person as she thought of ideas for them. To her nurse who reminded her of this habit, she replied: "Oh, never mind! Don't speak to me about this departure."

Around January 25, however, a couple of weeks before her planned departure, she asked for her suitcases, but she wrapped and unwrapped her parcels several times, contrary to all her usual habits.

She put her affairs in order as she had never done before. She sorted and tore up, during several nights, many letters and other documents. She seemed relieved when she was finished; the novice mistress was struck by the fact. (*Articles*, p. 195)

On February 1, baggage completed, she went outside to record film of herself, the convent, the hospital, and the gardens. The next day she would take the photos of three missionary postulants that she wanted to show to various communities in order to strengthen the links of the federation.

On February 2, feast of the Presentation, when Simeon sings his *Nunc Dimittis*:

Now at last, Oh Lord, you let your servant depart in peace . . .

Mother Yvonne-Aimée spoke brightly during lunch about this trip which was going to last until July 8. She marked the stages of the journey on a map which would let the sisters pray better for each step.

The last photo they took of her shows an expression of peace and even a relaxed joy. She is seated and conceals her swollen left arm which rests on the table.

On Saturday, February 3, the first Saturday of the month, a day dedicated to Mary, Yvonne continued her preparations. The departure was set for Thursday. She appeared "completely cheery, joyful, and alert. No apparent indication, no observable warning signs or symptoms would lead one to suspect that in a short time she was going to be brutally struck down" (Sermon of Bishop Le Bellec, February 8, 1951, no. 89).

She was preparing herself for the Profession which she was going to preside over on Tuesday, February 6, two days before her scheduled departure. She went to Confession. Two hours later, around 6:30 P.M., her nurse, Sister Marie of the Cross, came to see if the superior general needed anything before she herself went to the refectory. She found Mother Yvonne-Aimée seated at her desk, her head in her hands.

"Oh my head, my head!" she groaned.

As the pain didn't lessen, the sister nurse informed the superior. (Ibid.) The chaplain and the two house doctors ran to her. Mother Marie-Anne was there:

> Our very reverend mother recognized me and said to me, pointing to her poor head:
> "It hurts.... Oh, how it hurts!"
> Faced with the seriousness of the event, the thought of the trip to Africa came to my mind and I was telling her that she mustn't think of going now. After a moment's hesitation, she answered me,
> "Yes, if I can go, I'll go. It's my duty" [underlined in the text].
> They were her last words. Already...the paralysis was setting in. Her vision had become clouded and our doctors...who had now arrived, could only observe the terrible reality.... Nothing more could be done for her. She must have had a massive cerebral hemorrhage. Bleeding her or other interventions would give no result. Father chaplain just had time to anoint her.
> Carried to her bed, a few moment later it was barely perceptible, the last breath. (Obituary Notice, p. 33)

During her first years at Malestroit, she was asked one day how she would like to die. She replied: "It's all the same to me, provided that it is in the manner that may bring him the most glory and, as far as is possible, cause the least bother to those who love me" (*Articles*, p. 121).

It all happened in less than half an hour.

During her prior illnesses, the sisters had already feared losing her. And she would reply: "But no, but no.... I shan't die this time. I will leave between an evening and a morning, when you are least expecting it, and I will be long gone while you are still unable to believe it" (*Obituary Notice*, p. 33).

And that was indeed the state of mind of the sisters and of Bishop Picaud. One couldn't become accustomed to this empty space, so long filled against all the odds. And it was indeed the sudden and ordinary death that she had foreseen: "At my death, my body will be in humiliation," she said at Dieppe on September 16, 1947. (Letter of Mother Marguerite-Marie, superior of Dieppe to Mother Marie-Anne of Jesus, July 2, 1955, no. 105)

In fact, "from the next day...the body began to swell, and they had to hasten to put it into the coffin" (Henri Monier-Vinard, *Le monastere de Malestroit et la mére Yvonne-Aimée*, 1958, p. 21, no. 210).

The funeral took place four days after her death, on Thursday February 8, 1951, the day planned for her departure to South Africa. It was the meeting with Our Lord that Yvonne had so wanted and had delayed as much as possible, willingly, in order to serve more.

She was struck down at her desk, in the midst of her work, about to leave on a long journey to the other hemisphere.

Her death had nothing of the extraordinary, no ecstasy, no signs, only a very great suffering, in a lucidity that allowed her to communicate right up to the last. She finished her life in this complete poverty and simplicity that she had wished for.

The final journey that she had desired for so long came to replace the one she was preparing.

Mother Marie-Anne, elected unanimously to succeed her, would write in the death notice circular: "Rarely is it granted to meet a personality as complete as that of our very reverend mother Yvonne-Aimée of Jesus, and to find within such a beautiful equilibrium such an array of virtues. It is sometimes said of certain persons that they have the faults of their virtues. That was not the case with her, in the sense that her qualities of intelligence, mind and heart, like her natural gifts, were accompanied by a humility so deep that she lived always in the truth" (*Obituary Notice*, p. 34).

In the funeral discourse, prudent and measured, Bishop Le Bellec of Vannes could only observe: "The grace of God breathed on the house where we are, in a manner really out of the ordinary, ever since Yvonne Beauvais entered it.... In this fervent home, which she has marked with her imprint ... her name will be held in benediction to the furthest future generations of Augustinians" (February 8, 1951, no. 89).

An Extraordinary Love

W AS MOTHER YVONNE-AIMÉE'S LIFE "extraordinary"? This label was too quickly given to her, and in a narrow and deforming sense. Some people will be surprised that this book gives it such a discreet place. Truth itself was inviting us to put it back in its secondary and functional place, so as to reveal the essential, which had been momentarily obscured. It was to avoid this real risk that the Congregation for the Doctrine of the Faith prescribed silence, since 1960.

THE SUPERNATURAL: A LIMITED DOSSIER

In the life of Mother Yvonne-Aimée the marvels that were spoken about were in no way the essential. They were only an extra. She knew how to keep them in their discreet place.

She in no way desired them, she never asked for them, she underwent or received them with surprise. She lived these phenomena as a simple highlighting of the wonders that God works secretly "in all souls" (1957, no. 125, p. 32, quoted above, p. 111).

Seeing the worry and the difficulties that these unusual facts aroused, even for a long time blocking her entry into the convent, she fervently asked to be freed from them. For this intention she performed austere penitential acts. She obtained it, momentarily, in 1928 during a part of her novitiate. And these exceptional phenomena were limited in time. They began for her in July 1922—a few days before her twenty-first birthday—after a somewhat austere childhood and youth. It was not one long string of miracles as some have suggested by their over-emphasis of the extraordinary. The marvels that flourished at the time of the Spiritual Betrothal (leading to the breaking-off of the reasonable human betrothal) only had a limited duration. Her predictions and premonitions practically ceased from June 4, 1929. The calendar of other exceptional phenomena is a bit more prolonged, but the final years of her life, even her death, bring her back to the basic simplicity of her childhood.

When the marvelous is of negative origin, and sometimes even when it is of the good (as at Lourdes where an epidemic of fifty visionaries followed on from Bernadette between April 11 and July 11, 1858), it normally incites "illuminated" imitators or bitter opposition and dissension in the environment where it occurs. We see nothing of the sort at Malestroit. The marvels of Mother Yvonne-Aimée were never contagious. And they were absorbed with neither tensions nor reactions within her community. Those who were in on the secret, if only to help Mother Yvonne-Aimée in the related difficulties, accepted it simply, with the candor of children who receive a gift from heaven, without dwelling on it. Many others were unaware of it, as our investigations have verified.

What is very remarkable is the discretion that Mother Yvonne-Aimée was able to maintain, both inside the community and without. How many sober and strong letters she wrote to silence the indiscreet, with the same aim that would later motivate the silence imposed by the Congregation for the Doctrine of the Faith. She based everything solely on the Faith.

PROVEN FACTS

We have in no way camouflaged the reporting of the marvelous, for history must record the facts. We have presented fully everything that played a functional role in the life and work of Mother Yvonne-Aimée, while pruning that which was peripheral or uncertain.

The completion of further study, which is in progress, will take more time and more work.

At this point, where the adversaries of Mother Yvonne-Aimée formerly suspected fraud, certain facts are now scientifically established—notably the predictions which we report quite widely, because they have been verified beyond all objection.

PROBLEMATIC FACTS

But other facts can never be proven or established, due to lack of documentation proportionate to what the observation of the extraordinary would demand.

We mustn't anticipate the multidisciplinary long-term studies that we have begun on these unusual aspects.

To properly situate the person of Mother Yvonne-Aimée, and to put in their right place the conclusions on these particular points, it will be necessary to enter into the doctrine, the teaching, of Mother Yvonne-Aimée. It is traditional, and it is the key to everything else. But that teaching is inseparable from the life lived, which this book has adhered to.

THE ORDINARY FRAMEWORK OF HER LIFE AND HER WORK

One cannot stress this point enough: to focus this biography on the exceptional would be to condemn oneself to missing the essential. Yvonne's great interior and exterior successes are not the effect of a *deus ex machina*.

They have a meaning and a coherence independent of the extraordinary. They are the result of a tireless patience, an unflinching courage, an unwavering attention, and the art of being able to bring together diverse wills in a loving symphony performed for God alone. If around Mother Yvonne-Aimée there was never either incoherence nor an outbreak of illuminism, it is because her daily life was the model of an activity that was intelligent, regular, persevering, God-focused, and rising above every trial. It was a modest holiness, with its feet on the ground, attentive to the most material details and the most mundane, and to the humility of the human: cooking, flowers, good order, a smile, being present to each, and also maintaining the correct distance. In fact, an availability without limits toward everyone—novices and elderly sisters, hunted Resistance members and German occupiers in forced military service. She could shelter the first at the risk of her own life, and bring something to drink to the guardsman thirsting under the hot sun, cunningly hide and tend hunted parachutists and treat the German Commandant with a clear dignity in her esteem for persons and her care for souls. In all this everyday life and activity, notably during the Second World War, which made her a national heroine, there was no miracle properly so-called, but an exceptional dose of balance, of wisdom, and of ingenuity bordering on inspiration. The occasional marvel occurred as an inspiring or helpful extra.

Extraordinary, therefore, in a sense were her human qualities, without her being great or gifted. She had been an ordinary child and her scholarly failings had irritated her mother. The extraordinariness of her normal activity flowed from this perfect synergy that the love of God produces when it is integrally lived.

Such is the essential. Such is the key to the enigma.

WHAT WAS EXTRAORDINARY WAS HER LOVE

Her life was nothing but a determined drive to live the love of God alone.

The supernatural phenomena, which fascinate human curiosity, in no way detract from this profound truth.

These sensible and transitory graces are less extraordinary than they appear. They fit into a long Christian tradition that certainly did not die out with the Middle Ages. The remarkable phenomena which she lived are frequent, even classic, in the annals of sainthood, collated by Herbert Thurston, SJ, in his book *The Physical Phenomena of Mysticism*.

These phenomena are the accessory to, and only make sense based on, what is essential. If Mother Yvonne-Aimée's life was extraordinary it was not because of this sometimes disconcerting out-of-the-ordinary; it was only because of love. In her it was total gift and, more radically, abandonment. And it is how she found the strength to accept everything, to take on everything, by so many paths alien to her desires and requests.

The surface foam that captured imaginations must not hide the depths. And the vivid colors of the fabric must not hide from us the regular and impeccable weave.

THE SECRET OF THE CROSS

What amazes us in this life is a love pushed beyond known limits—the pure love, freely given to God alone, under the inspiration of God alone, from Yvonne's earliest childhood. At her First Holy Communion, in the act that she wrote with her own blood, this love expressed itself without limits. Like Christ, she knew that there is no deeper and unquestionable proof of love than the acceptance of suffering. She not only accepted this intolerable test, she asked for it. It was not masochism—for she loved life and everything good, being a talented cook, and a daughter of a father who was a gourmet and a connoisseur of fine wines—but by deep union to Christ and his Passion.

Her life was not at all rooted in the marvelous but, like the lives of the saints (Ignatius of Antioch, Francis of Assisi, Louis-Marie de Montfort, and so many others), in the Cross of Christ. That was the root of her fruitfulness.

Some readers to whom I submitted this book to test it found it harsh and austere. They were expecting a gilded legend, and they found intolerable trials. But it was indeed out of concern for the truth that the unknown essentials must be mined, however steep the path.

"Greater love has no man than this, that a man lay down his life for his friends," said Christ (Jn 15:13). Yvonne passionately desired this, like the little Teresa of Avila who, in her childhood, went off to find martyrdom among the Moors.

But for her, as for Saint Paul, the desire "to depart and be with Christ" (Phil 1:23) was an irresistible impulse.

At the request of the Lord, in whom she lived, she passed from there to the desire to survive in order to serve. And this sacrifice cost her dearly. She several times expressed a nostalgia about it, without regrets.

EXCESS IN LOVE?

Did Mother Yvonne-Aimée sin by excess of love?

As a little child, learning of the Desert Fathers, she did violence to herself by eating maggot-infested or rotting fruit. Her grandmother scolded her. Father Grizard likewise reproached her for kissing the purulent and repugnant wounds of the sick person she was tending as she regretted not loving her more wholeheartedly.

Her desire to love Jesus more than he had ever been loved before (except, of course, by Our Lady) might appear an outrageous ambition, but in fact it was not a personal desire. She had *received* this desire—and God sometimes inspires those he loves to ideals that life doesn't stop testing.

If Yvonne pushed the radicalism of love right to the point of folly, in this she is not far from the Scriptures (1 Cor 1:18–25; 3:19) or Christian Tradition. The natural virtues, including the cardinal ones, are a happy medium, said Thomas Aquinas, according to Greek wisdom. And it is true also for the theological virtues of faith and hope. They are subject to contrary errors, not only by lack but by excess—credulity for faith, presumption for hope. But for charity there is only error in the lack of it. There can be deviation of charity but not an excess.

The love that pushed Mother Yvonne-Aimée to suffering was never complacent about suffering. She was overwhelmed with it, from on high and from below, in body and in mind, for God alone.

SUPER-EFFICIENCY OF AN INVALID

Yvonne-Aimée's medical file amounts to a sort of world-record. Before she had reached thirty years of age, problematic levels of albumin, which would plague her for the rest of her life, enlarged her body and disfigured her natural beauty. Her influence owed nothing to her appearance. To that would be added, among other things, tuberculosis, frequent and exceptionally high fevers, often over 40°C (104°F), or even 42°C (107.6°F), heart conditions, every possible hemorrhage, such that one wonders how she survived. A uterine fibroid required a hysterectomy in February of 1949. Cancer necessitated a mastectomy of her left breast the following September. Finally, her hypertension caused the cerebral hemorrhage from which she died, in the midst of her activities.[1]

To the ongoing burden of chronic illnesses there was added strangely, by a sort of transfer, those that she took on when she was praying for ill people, as if taking onto herself their illnesses, with their obvious symptoms. The sisters of the hospital no longer dared to confide their intentions to her, for fear of causing such illnesses in her. The illnesses thus taken on, often presenting violent symptoms, ended in a surprisingly rapid manner, with neither transition nor convalescence. Thus she bounced back from a fever of 42°C (107.6°F) to resume an immediate and overflowing activity.

HOW SUFFERING WAS GIVEN HER

While as a child Yvonne sometimes asked for or provoked suffering, later on she did not have to seek the Cross. The Cross came to her in all sorts of ways in this world of sin.

It came to her in the errors and suspicions of others, including her mother and friends.

It came to her in the onerous tasks piled upon her shoulders.

It came to her, in a strangely contrasting manner, in the horrible attacks of the devil and the sharing in the Passion of Jesus Christ, even to the stigmata.

Her total availability was consumed to the maximum. She never flinched. She didn't shout "time out." She never retracted the desire to give everything, to suffer everything, that she expressed ever since her First Holy Communion.

THE PRICE PAID FOR SUCCESS

Mother Yvonne-Aimée's many apparent privileges were often turned against her. The faults of others were more than once pinned on her, even during the happy phase of her schooling in England. Loyalty—her most obvious quality—was taken

---

[1] A medical file, prepared by Sister Marie of Christ, examined by Doctor Mahéo (and then submitted to Doctor T. Mangiapan, President of the Lourdes Medical Office) was established. We summarize it here.

for concealment or falsehood. She found herself sitting—by force—"at the table of sinners" for whom she was praying. The excess of her gifts and graces were counted against her, as an adult, even to confused admirers ready to burn that which they had acclaimed. Her completely pure gifts for friendship had her suspected of "particular friendships," we have seen, at Le Mans and even at Malestroit where Father Crété himself reproached her for using the informal form of address with Mother Madeleine of the Sacred Heart, her nurse, or for simply expressing her affection. She obeyed and took a step back while purifying everything human in her existence.

She was not at all focused on nor attracted to suffering. She underwent it. She benefited from it in order to go forward without looking back or carrying useless burdens.

She was certainly not fascinated by the devil, who she forgot the moment his attacks ceased. She survived thanks to that remarkable facility to forget and to rise again immediately. The diabolical attacks on Mother Yvonne-Aimée (which she underwent like Marie of Jesus Crucified, recently beatified) call for a multidisciplinary study based in depth on exceptionally well-established bases, for several doctors have studied them without finding any plausible natural explanations for them. Witnesses saw the bleeding wounds form before their eyes. Automutilation, which would be foreign to the psychological profile of Yvonne, has been excluded by qualified eyewitnesses.

Mother Yvonne-Aimée underwent more than what would destroy physically or psychologically any ordinary human being. And yet she achieved such a fullness of life and activity that her prodigious diligence was suspected of being diabolical (see above, pp. 174ff.). Those who accused her thus did not know the martyrdom she was undergoing, the price she was paying, and so many failures kept to herself.

This extremely active person was a seriously ill person. This patient remained aloof from any retreat into herself and from any absorption by the suffering.

In the interior and exterior burden, one is amazed to see her remain intact, radiating only love of God and of others in all the daily small things as well as the great.

Her love was able to feed constantly on the best and on the worst with an indifference marked by a preference for suffering, through which she strengthened the bonds of her earthly life with Jesus himself. She well illustrates the words of Saint Paul, "We know that in everything God works for good with those who love him" (Rom 8:28).

Injustices suffered never pushed her to the revolt that the power of her temperament would have rendered formidable.

What would Mother Yvonne-Aimée have been if she had succumbed to evil, of which God allowed her to know the invading and abysmal temptation?

We cannot adequately grasp the inconceivable energy that she had to mobilize in order to survive and to fight on. When Yvonne was twenty-two an evil spirit threw her from a third floor. She was not carried by angels' hands (Mt 4:6)! She suffered her entire life from the resulting injury to her spine, which she could only maintain upright by a constant effort—one detail among many.

One is amazed that she stood straight until the end, under a burden of which her daily thoughts give us an idea:

If I fall, they'll pick me up; if I die, they'll replace me.

It's when things are going really badly that one needs to have recourse to such maxims.

She had so habituated others—and herself—to the impossible that she died while finalizing the preparations for an exhausting journey to South Africa by an improbable relay of trains and ships. The impossible not having been excluded thus far, she continued to say, even during her short final agony:

If I can, I'll go. It's my duty.

And thus was accomplished that word that she used to say to encourage herself when reaching every limit:

If I die, they'll replace me.

THE SECRET

The extraordinary in Mother Yvonne-Aimée—was it ascetic practice? No. That was only the surplus of a love that was able to desire, ask for, assume, bear, and make fruitful all gifts and burdens for the love of God and men, in the forgetting of self. Her extraordinary activity sprang from the depths of the passive virtues which made her subject to the Holy Spirit.

This overburdened woman was never overburdening and depressing to others. She served all, right to the end. She radiated joy and life right up to the last journey, when the terrestrial itinerary was replaced by heaven's shortcut.

This paradoxical contrast is a revealing touchstone of sanctity. It is found with Bernadette and Thérèse of Lisieux. Yvonne took burdens upon herself without appearing laden. Her obesity, due to an excess of water not fat, remained amazingly light as film footage still shows. It's like a symbol. Life handed her increasing burdens to lighten those of others.

In the worst of her trials, she remained encouraging, positive, and stimulating, always and for everyone, simply and without grand phrases. She woke the sleeping, and restored savor to life.

With her adversaries she never responded with retaliation, even less with bitterness, but tried to bring them around to better feelings.

Yes, all that testifies to an extraordinary love, and an extraordinarily effective love.

What astonishes, when one analyzes this life constantly subjected to so many contradictory shocks, is its internal coherence. This coherence, humanly speaking, came from further away: from Love Itself.

God is Love. Mother Yvonne-Aimée's life was founded on Love alone. Her authority was free from authoritarianism, because it flowed from a deep source and brought about contact with God.

What was extraordinary in Yvonne was the love of Jesus Christ and her response to it. This very response was a gift from God. But with what freedom she engaged in it! The unity of this multifaceted life well illustrates an experience which every Christian worthy of the name will recognize: in the work of grace, everything is first from God, but everything is also and at the same time the free choice and response of man. And God gives to these souls that he arouses a coherence and an authority which surpasses all human plans and calculations. In this world of broken and deviant loves, God's love reveals its transcendence.

Mother Yvonne-Aimée witnessed to it, or rather God witnessed to it in her. It is possible to live for God alone and Love alone. The Cross is mysteriously at the heart of Christianity. It is not destructive. It is the source of life in Jesus Christ. Everything is grace and Love is the victor. ◉

ABOUT THE AUTHOR

MONSIGNOR RENÉ LAURENTIN was a French priest and theologian who authored over 150 books. Born in Paris in 1917, he began university studies in 1934 simultaneously at the Catholic University of Paris and at the Sorbonne. He graduated with degrees from each in 1938. In 1940, serving as an officer in the French army, he was captured by the Germans in Belgium. After liberation and his return to France he was ordained to the sacred priesthood on December 8th, 1946. As an expert in Mariology he was a member of the Preparatory Commission of Vatican II's constitution on the Church. He became well known to French readers, as he authored several in-depth biographies and studies of modern-day saints, such as Bernadette of Lourdes, Catherine Labouré, and Thérèse of Lisieux. In 1981 the Vatican authorized him to carry out a study of French mystic and war heroine Yvonne-Aimée of Malestroit, whose Cause had been introduced after her death in 1951. Earlier, in 1960, after exaggerated and speculative articles in the French tabloid press, the Vatican had placed a moratorium on all publishing regarding Yvonne-Aimee. The lifting of that ban in 1981 was specifically and solely for the research and eventual biography by Laurentin, who went on to author several studies of Yvonne-Aimée: her untiring and lifelong charitable works, her stigmata, her recorded cases of bilocation. Pope Benedict XVI created Laurentin a Prelate of Honor of His Holiness in 2007. He died in 2017, a month short of his 100th birthday.

www.ingramcontent.com/pod-product-compliance
Lightning Source LLC
Chambersburg PA
CBHW021221090426
42740CB00006B/318